The U... Bobby Fischer

IM John Donaldson

IM Eric Tangborn

International Chess Enterprises

Seattle, Washington

M000283880

Copyright © 1999 by International Chess Enterprises

All rights reserved. No part of this book may be reproduced or transmitted in any form or by any means, electronic or mechanical, including photocopying,recording, or by any information storage and retrieval system, without permission in writing from the publisher.

International Chess Enterprises, P.O.Box 19457, Seattle, WA 98109
1-800-26CHESS   http://www.insidechess.com

Editor: Frederick Kleist
Proofreaders: Holly Lee, Duane Polich
Diagrams: Jonathan Berry's YesWeDoDiagrams program
Typeset by Frederick Kleist using Ventura Publisher

Donaldson, John
Tangborn, Eric
The Unknown Bobby Fischer

First Printing: November 1999
204 pages

ISBN 1-879479-85-0

Cover Photo: Courtesy of Ruth York

E.T.   *To my parents*

J.D.   *To John Watson and Val Zemitis,*
         two of the great gentlemen of the chess world

Table of Contents

Fischer's 1964 Transcontinental Tour   81

Articles, 70s Simuls, Blitz, and Last Game   133

Table of Illustrations

Preface

The idea for this book came shortly after the publication of *Legend on the Road* (International Chess Enterprises, 1994), which took an indepth look at Bobby's 1964 transcontinental simul tour. The many readers who wrote in afterward offered a wealth of new material with games and anecdotes. Sometimes gold would appear in the most unexpected places.

Playing in the 1997 McLaughlin Memorial in Wichita I was delighted to meet former Kansas Champion Robert Hart, who had kept his copy of the mimeographed bulletin of Bobby's 1964 visit to Wichita. I had heard rumors of this bulletin, but until Mr. Hart generously sent me the games, I feared that all existing copies had disappeared. My co-author Eric Tangborn and I, with the help of Erik Osbun, were able, using a little detective work, to convert 18 of the games (2 scores were unplayable) from sometimes questionable descriptive notation into playable algebraic. Only D Ballard's win, Fischer's sole loss in the exhibition, was previously known. The games from this exhbition offer a rare look at a typical Fischer simul — usually only a few wins and, more typically, his losses and draws surface.

As work progressed on the sequel to *A Legend on the Road*, Eric and I decided to expand the scope of the book. Pouring through old magazines and books, we were struck by how little attention had been focused on Bobby's early career. We decided we would make a dedicated effort to tracking down some of his lost games from the 1950s and early 1960s. This proved easier said than done. In many cases, like his match with Dr. Daniel Beninson from 1957, we succeeded only in discovering that the games have been lost forever. Hope remains that the missing three games of the Fischer–Matulovic 1958 training match will surface, but chances are slim. That this match was undocumented remains a great mystery, for Fischer was already U.S. Champion and Yugoslavia has a great chess tradition.

While researching Bobby's early career, Eric and I were struck by how rich American chess life was in the 1950s. This decade didn't have the large U.S. Chess Federation membership (less than 5,000 in the 50s) or the huge Swiss system tournaments that are the norm today, but it was a time when many bright stars were developing. Some, like Grandmasters Bill Lombardy, Robert Byrne, Larry Evans and Arthur Bisguier are still active and well-remembered, but many others have been forgotten. We decided to offer the reader a glimpse at some of the lesser-known stars that Bobby crossed swords with on his way to becoming World Champion, players such as Max Pavey, Abe Turner, Charles Kalme and Larry Remlinger.

The final chapters offer a potpouri of Fischer material, including an annotated bibliography of books by and about Bobby. We have included excerpts of little-known Fischer writing from his *Boys Life* column and *The Leaves of Chess*.

We have not limited ourselves to just Bobby's games and writings. Through the generous assistance of Ruta York we are able to offer several new or little known photographs of Bobby. Ruta, whose father Alexander Liepnieks organized the 1955 U.S. Junior Championship, well remembers Bobby's visit to Lincoln and how he kept in touch with her family.

A project to preserve Bobby's creative legacy can never be considered finished. Inevitably new material will come forth. Some of the players Bobby faced, Arthur Feuerstein, for instance, think they still have some of the missing games scores tucked away — have you ever tried to find something from over 40 years ago! One would think someone would have the games from the Matulovic match or a copy of the *Louisiana Chess News Letter* from 1964 edited by Woodrew Crew.

Whenever I get too optimistic that things will turn up, I recall the words of chess historian and book dealer Dale Brandreth who describes items like state and club publications as among the rarest of rare items in chess literature. Such publications were typically printed in small quantity and often not on the best paper. They didn't have any commercial worth and people usually didn't realize their important content until the last copies had long since disappeared. Today it is easier to preserve and pass along information with the Internet, but this was not always so. We can only be thankful that people like Robert Hart and Ruta York have done such a good job of preserving the past.

The authors would like to thank Rudy Aden, Dennis Allan, Carlos Almarza-Mato, D Pierre Ballard, Dr. Daniel Beninson, Frank (Kim) Berry, Jonathan Berry, Neil Brennan, Ross Carbonell, John Collins, Charles (Kit) Crittenden, George Flynn, Steve Gordon, Michael Greengard, Gordon Gribble, Ron Gross, William Haines, Jerry Hanken, Robert Hart, Eliot Hearst, Allan Jensen, Allen Kaufman, Harlan Lee, Holly Lee, David Luban, David Kerman, Richard Lunenfeld, Jerry Markley, Spencer Matthews, Robert Moore, The Mechanics' Institute (San Francisco) Library, Erik Osbun, Jack

O'Keefe, Duane Polich, Viktors Pupols, Nick Pope, Richard Reich, Donald P. Reithel, Larry Remlinger, Thomas Richardson, Hanon Russell, Andy Sacks, Leon Schorr, Macon Shibut, Jorge Szmetan, Art Wang, Fred Wilson, Alex Yermolinsky, Ruta York and Val Zemitis for their help with this project. We regret leaving anyone's name out. This book would not have been able possible without all the generous support we received. It goes without saying that any errors or mistakes are the sole responsibility of the authors.

JD, October 1999

Readers who have new material, corrections, etc., may contact the authors at:

Inside Chess
PO Box 19457
Seattle, WA 98109
or
imwjd@aol.com

The Early Years

The introduction to *Bobby Fischer's Games of Chess*, a book that Bobby wrote in 1958 with assistance from John W. Collins, tells the story of Fischer's early years.

I was born in Chicago, Illinois, on March 9, 1943, and learned the chess moves early in 1949 from my sister Joan, who was eleven. She often bought different games at a local candy store and one day happened to buy a chess set. We figured out the moves from the directions that came with the set. For the next year or so I played chess occasionally with the boys I taught or by myself.

On November 14, 1950, my mother sent a postcard to the chess column of the old Brooklyn *Eagle* (we were now living in Brooklyn) asking if they knew any boys my age I could play chess with. A reply came from Mr. Hermann Helms, dean of American chess. He suggested I go to a chess exhibition at the Grand Army Plaza Library on January 17, 1951. There I played against Senior Master Max Pavey and managed to last about fifteen minutes. Watching in the crowd was Mr. Carmine Nigro, President of the Brooklyn Chess Club. After the game he came up and invited me to join his club.

Mr. Nigro was possibly not the best player in the world, but he was a very good teacher [Nigro was rated 2028 on the May 5, 1957, USCF rating list]. I went to the Brooklyn Chess Club practically every Friday night. Later I started playing chess at Mr. Nigro's home on weekends and often went with him to play chess at Washington Square Park.

A genius doesn't appear from nowhere. Bobby came from a very well-educated family and couldn't have found a better place to develop as a chess player than New York City. Had his family stayed in Mobile, Arizona, it's almost inconceivable that Bobby would have developed into a World Champion. Today, with the Internet, databases, computer programs and tons of chess literature, a player from an isolated area can go far. This was not the case when Bobby was growing up. It was pretty much New York or forget it.

Few games are preserved from the beginning of Bobby's career. He started playing tournament chess in 1953, but his earliest recorded games in standard Fischer anthologies (Wade and O'Connell plus Hays) date back only to the summer of 1955 and the U.S. Junior Open in Lincoln, Nebraska.

The following three casual games, played at the Brooklyn Chess Club, take us back a little further. The first is provided by Dan Mayers, a former English Senior Champion. The other two, which seem to be from the end of

1954 or the beginning of 1955, appear courtesy of the Russell Collection.

How good was Fischer at the time? It's difficult to say, but he may have been around 1700-1800 by the beginning of 1955, though he didn't yet have a rating. The following May he scored 3.5-2.5 at the U.S. Amateur Championship at Lake Mohegan and his post-tournament USCF rating was 1830.

---

[1] *King's Gambit*   *C33*
Dan Mayers–RJF
                    Brooklyn (blitz) 1953

1.e4 e5 2.f4 exf4 3.♗c4

The Bishop's Gambit is a line that Bobby was to make his own in the future. He played it twice in tournament games (beating GMs Evans and Minic) and countless times during his 1964 simul tour. His interest in 3.♗c4 didn't wane with the years. When he faced the Greenblatt computer in 1977, he trotted out the Bishop's Gambit to win a miniature.

Bobby wrote his famous article "A Bust to the King's Gambit" (*American Chess Quarterly* 1961), advocating 3.♘f3 d6!, a year after his tough loss to Boris Spassky (Buenos Aires 1960) in the 3.♘f3 g5 line. Interestingly enough, while Fischer consistently played 3.♗c4 throughout his career, he varied at least once with 3.♘f3 and his opponent chose Bobby's Bust! Fischer–K. Mott-Smith, Chicago (simul) 1964, saw *1.e4 e5 2.f4 exf4 3.♘f3 d6 4.d4 h6 5.♗c4 g5 6.0-0 ♗g7 7.c3 ♘e7 8.g3* (all according to Bobby's analysis), but now Black varied from 8...d5! with *8...♘g6 9.♕b3*

0-0 10.gxf4 gxf4 11. ♔h1 ♘c6 12.♕c2 ♘ce7 13.♘bd2 ♗e6 14.♖g1 ♗xc4 15.♘xc4 d5 and unclear play.
3...♘f6

Evans tried 3...♕h4+ and Minic 3...♘e7. Fischer faced 3...d5 on several occasions in simuls and against the Greenblatt computer.

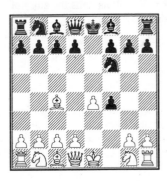

4.♘c3 c6 5.d4 ♗b4 6.e5 ♘e4 7.♕h5 0-0 8.♘ge2 d5 9.♗b3 g6 10.♕h6 ♗g4 11.♗d2 ♘xd2 12.♔xd2 g5 13. h4 gxh4 14.♖xh4 ♗f5 15.♖ah1 ♗e7 16.♖g4+ ♗g6 17.♕xh7 mate

---

[2] *King's Indian*   *E70*
RJF–Jacob Altusky
Brooklyn (offhand), Dec. 1954 or Jan. 1955

1.d4

No 1.e4! Several years were to pass before Bobby started to consistently open with 1.P-K4. Six months after this game, at the U.S. Junior in Lincoln, Nebraska, Fischer was opening with 1.e4, but hadn't progressed to his later standard Ruy Lopez.

1...g6 2.c4 ♘f6 3.♘c3 ♗g7 4.e4 0-0 5.♗g5 d6 6.♘f3 ♘bd7

Here 6...c5 and 6...h6 are seen more often.

7.e5 dxe5 8.dxe5 ♘g4 9.♘d5 ♘gxe5?? 10.♘xe7+ ♔h8 11.♘xg6+ hxg6 12.♗xd8 1-0

---

[3] *Ruy Lopez Steinitz Deferred   C71*
Jacob Altusky–RJF
Brooklyn (offhand), Dec. 1954 or Jan. 1955

1.e4 e5 2.♘f3 ♘c6 3.♗b5 a6 4.♗a4 d6 5.d4 b5 6.♗b3 ♗g4?

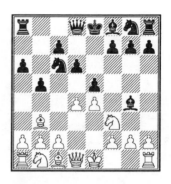

7.♗xf7+??

Overlooking Black's eighth move. The correct way to take advantage of 6...♗g4? is by 7.dxe5 ♘xe5 8.♘xe5! ♗xd1 9. ♗xf7+ ♔e7 10.♘c6+. Of course, 7...dxe5 fails to 8.♕d5! and 7...♗xf3 is answered by 8.♗xf7+ ♔xf7 9. ♕d5+ ♔e7 10.♗g5+ ♘f6 11.exf6+ gxf6 12.♕xc6, winning.

7...♔xf7 8.♘g5+ ♕xg5 0-1

USA vs. USSR Match 1954

The United States was the reigning chess power in the 1930s, winning the Chess Olympiad on several occasions, but one important country was missing from the competitions — the Soviet Union.   Immediately after the Second World War, a radio match was held between the two rivals that was to have a significant impact on the chess world.

The United States was crushed in the match, and in several subsequent encounters, in no uncertain fashion. Except for Sammy Reshevsky, masters of the older generation were unable to cope with their Soviet counterparts. Even Reshevsky had difficulties, as the following chart shows. It incorporates the head-to-head battles between Americans and Soviets from 1945 through 1954: USA vs.

USA–USSR match 1954
June 16-24 at the Roosevelt Hotel in New York City

USSR Radio Match 1945, USA vs. USSR Match 1946, World Championship Tournament 1948, Helsinki Olympiad 1952, Saltsjobaden Interzonal 1952, Zurich Candidates Tournament 1953 and USA vs. USSR Match 1954.

Americans versus Soviets

Name	Score	Tnmts	Pct.
1. D. Byrne	3-1	(1)	.750
2. R. Byrne	3-3	(2)	.500
3. L. Evans	3-3	(2)	.500
4. A. Kevitz	1½-1½	(2)	.500
6. O. Ulvestad	1-1	(1)	.500
7. G. Koltanowski	½-½	(1)	.500
8. S. Reshevsky	18-23	(6)	.439
9. H. Steiner	3½-5½	(3)	.388
10. I. Horowitz	3-5	(3)	.375
11. A. Dake	1-2	(2)	.333
12. M. Pavey	1-2	(1)	.333
13. R. Fine	1-3	(2)	.250
14. A. Pinkus	1-3	(2)	.250
15. A. Kupchik	½-1½	(1)	.250
16. A. Bisguier	½-4½	(1)	.250
17. A. Denker	0-7	(3)	.000
18. A. Santasiere	0-2	(1)	.000
19. H. Seidman	0-2	(1)	.000

Source: *Chess Life* May 5, 1955

Fortunately for the United States, one of the most talented groups of juniors the country had ever seen was starting to blossom. The 1954 match between the two powers in New York City occurred a few years too early for future Grandmasters Bobby Fischer and William Lombardy to appear in the lineup, but young stars Larry Evans and the Byrne brothers, Robert and Donald, had outstanding debuts. The top scorer for the U.S. team was Donald who beat Yuri Averbakh 3-1. The only other plus score on the American team was by Larry Evans, who defeated Mark Taimanov 2.5-1.5.

Today, when one strong tournament follows another, it's hard to get too excited about any single event, but times were different in the mid-1950s. The match, which was held at the Roosevelt Hotel, had political as well as chessic significance. The *New York Times* gave the event front-page status and crowds of over 1,000 came to watch the action. Several future American stars were inspired by the event.

Anthony Saidy, who was to be a key member of the 1960 U.S. team that won the Student Olympiad, was a wall-boy for the event as was another future IM, Karl Burger. Frank Brady's *Profile of a Prodigy* mentions that Nigro brought Fischer and several other juniors to the 1954 USSR-USA match. There can be little doubt that the event had a big impact on the 11-year-old Fischer.

The Soviet Union won the match, held June 16-24, by the score of 20-12, but U.S. chess fans took heart in that, according to the report by Jack Staley Battell in the July 1954 issue of *Chess Review*, "we showed a rough equality on the last five boards." In addition, the Americans, facing a team beefed up by the presence of Vassily Smyslov, exceeded the score of the Argentines in their 1953 match against the Soviets by a half point.

Annotations to the next three games from the match are by **GM Igor Bondarevsky** *from his book* Soviet Chess Players in the USA, England and Sweden.

[4] *King's Indian Classical   E98*
GM Mark Taimanov
GM Larry Evans
USSR–USA, New York (4) 1954

1.c4 ♘f6 2.♘f3 g6 3.♘c3 ♗g7 4.e4 0-0 5.d4 d6 6.♗e2 e5 7.0-0 ♘c6 8.d5 ♘e7 9.♘e1 ♘d7 10.♘d3

It's interesting that this position was reached in the first round between the same two partners, but there Evans was White . . . Taimanov had previously used 10.♗e3 f5 11.f3 with success, but Black has succeeded in strengthening his kingside attack. So, in this game, Taimanov develops his pieces a little bit differently, but the general plan remains the same: White tries, as quickly as possible, to open the c-line for operations on the queenside.

10...f5 11.f3

Evans continued 11.exf5.

11...f4 12.♗d2 g5 13.♖c1 ♖f6

Black begins preparations for an attack on the kingside.

14.c5

Taimanov achieves his aim of opening the c-line by sacrificing a pawn.

14...♘xc5 15.♘xc5 dxc5 16.♘a4 b6 17.b4 cxb4 18.♗xb4

This is the position that Taimanov was aiming for when he sacrificed the pawn. Does he have enough positional compensation? To answer this question let us look at several variations. Black could play *18... c5*, trying to get rid of the weak pawn. After *19.dxc6 ♕xd1 20. ♖fxd1* (or *20.♗xd1 ♘xc6 21. ♗b3+ ♔h8 22.♗d5 ♗d7*) *20... ♘xc6 21.♗d6*, White has better development, but he can't gain anything concrete, for example, *21... ♗b7* (if *21...♘d4*, then *22.♗c4+* and *23.♗xe5* and in case of *21... ♗d7* the continuation may be 22. ♗c4+ ♔h8 23.♗b5 ♖c8 24. ♗xc6 ♖xc6 25.♖xc6 ♗xc6 26. ♗xe5*) *22.♗b5* (after *22.♗c4+ ♔h8 23.♗b5* Black has the answer *23...♘d4*) *22...♖d8! 23.♗xc6 ♗xc6 24.♖xc6 ♗f8*. Of course, the above-mentioned variations don't exhaust the possibilities, but they help us to "feel" the position better. So it seems White's compensation is not enough. By the way, the bad position of the Knight on a4 must be mentioned.

So Taimanov's "improvement" can hardly be recommended.

18...♗f8

This move is weaker than 18...c5. White could answer 19.♕b3 with strong pressure. Taimanov, overlooking an interesting counterblow by his opponent, makes a bad combination.

19.♖xc7?

On account of 19...♕xc7 20.d6 ♕b7 (20...♖xd6 21.♗xd6 and 22. ♗xe5) 21.dxe7 ♗xe7 22.♗xe7 ♕xe7 23.♕d5+.

USA vs. USSR 1954

Bd	USA	1	2	3	4		USSR	1	2	3	4	
1	Reshevsky	½	½	½	½	2.0	Smyslov	½	½	½	½	2.0
2	Dake	0				0.0	Bronstein	1	1	1	1	4.0
	Denker		0	0	0	0.0						
3	Pavey	0	0		1	1.0	Keres	1	1	1	0	3.0
	Kevitz			0		0.0						
4	D. Byrne	1	0	1	1	3.0	Averbakh	0	1	0	0	1.0
5	Horowitz	0	½	½	0	1.0	Geller	1	½	½	1	3.0
6	R. Byrne	0	½	½	½	1.5	Kotov	1	½	½	½	2.5
7	Bisguier	½	½	0	0	1.0	Petrosian	½	½	1	1	3.0
8	Evans	0	1	½	1	2.5	Taimanov	1	0	½	0	1.5
		2.0	3.0	3.0	4.0			6.0	5.0	5.0	4.0	

19...♘f5!

A beautiful in-between move that wasn't accounted for by White. Now the Rook and Bishop are under attack, and, moreover, we must take into account the move 20...♘e3. After 20.d6 there is no sense in Black's playing 20...♘e3 because of 21.♕a1, when it's not good to capture the Rook due to 22.♕xe5. So

it's better to answer 20...♗xd6, gaining an extra pawn. Taimanov prefers to give up the Exchange to preserve his Bishops.

20.♗xf8 ♕xc7 21.♗a3 ♘e3 22.♕c1 ♕g7

Black could win a second Exchange by 22...♕d7. White may have been counting on this. After 23.♘b2 ♘xf1 24.♗xf1, White has counterplay in connection with the e5-pawn by ♘d3 and ♗b2. So Evans decides not to lose time capturing the Rook and immediately initiates a kingside attack.

23.♖f2

On 23.♗b2, Black wouldn't take the Exchange, but would play 23...♖g6.

23...♗d7 24.♘c3 g4

Black's attack, combined with his extra material, quickly decides the game.

25.♗b2 g3 26.hxg3 ♕xg3 27.♗f1 ♖c8

On 27...♖h6, White would defend the mate by 28.♖d2. So Black brings up the reserves to make the decisive blow.

28.♕e1 b5 29.♘e2

The pawn, of course, mustn't be captured: 29.♗xb5 ♖h6 30.♖e2 ♕h2+.

29...♕h4 30.g3 fxg3 31.♘xg3 ♘xf1

Black goes around the trap. If 31...♕xg3+, then 32.♖g2.

32.♘f5 ♖g6+ 33.♔xf1 ♕h1+ 34. ♔e2 ♖c2+ 35.♔d1 ♕xe1+ 36.♔xe1 ♖g1+ 0-1

Except for Reshevsky, the United States was heavily outmanned on the top boards, especially on board two where World Championship challenger Bronstein scored 4-0 against Denker and Dake.

---

[5]   *QGD Tarrasch*   *D30*
GM Arnold Denker
GM David Bronstein

USA–USSR, New York (3) 1954

1.d4 e6

With the obvious intention of playing the French or Dutch Defense, but, after Denker's reply, Bronstein changes his plans.

2.g3 c5 3.dxc5

This exchange helps Black to develop. Better was 3.♘f3.

3...♗xc5

Who is playing White now?

4.♗g2 ♘f6 5.♘f3 ♘c6 6.c4 d5 7. cxd5 exd5 8.0-0 0-0

It's interesting to note that now the position is the same as the Tarrasch Defense of the Queen's Gambit, but with the difference that White's Knight is on b1 and not c3. White has lost an important tempo, the consequence of his third move.

9.♕c2

Before developing his pieces, White wants to find out where the Black Bishop will go, to b6 or to e7.

9...♗b6 10.♘c3 ♗e6

Stronger was 10...d4. Now unclear complications could appear.

11.♗g5 h6 12.♗xf6

Inconsequential! It's strange that Denker, who has a sharp style, didn't play 12.♗h4. On 12...g5 it's possible to play 13.♘xg5 hxg5 14.♗xg5 with a very double-edged position. If Black refuses to play 12..g5, then White could strengthen the pressure on the d5-pawn with ♖ad1.

12...♕xf6

Now Black has the better position.

13.♖fd1 ♖ac8

Before advancing the d-pawn, Black puts his Rooks on good squares. Of course, now 14.♘xd5 is impossible due to 14...♗xd5 15.♖xd5 ♘b4.

14.♖ac1 ♖fd8 15.♘a4 d4 15.♘xb6 axb6 16.b3?

White should defend with 17. ♘e1, for if 17...♗xa2, White has an answer in 18.b3, and 17...♘b4 gives nothing because of 18.♕d2. After the move in the game, Black begins an energetic attack.

17...d3!

This advance caught Denker by surprise. The pawn mustn't be taken, as White loses material after 18...♘d4.

18.♕d2 ♗g4!

Now Black threatens 19...dxe2 20.♕xe2 ♘d4. Denker finds a good answer.

19.♖c4! dxe2 20.♕xe2 ♖de8

Black chooses the most energetic continuation of the attack. In case of *20...♖xd1+ 21.♕xd1 ♖d8 22.♕e2* (only move) 22...♕a1+ (22...♘d4 23.♖xd4 ♖xd4 24. ♕e8+) *23.♗f1*, it's not possible to exploit the awkward position of the White forces, for example, *23... ♗xf3* 24.♕xf3 ♖d1 (24...♘e5 25.♕c3) 25.♕e2 and if 25... ♘d4, then 26.♕e8+ ♔h7 27.

♔g2 etc., or *23...♗h3* 24.♖e4 ♖d1? 25.♖e8+ ♔h7 26.♘g5+.

21.♖e4

If 21.♕d3, then 21...♖cd8 and 22...♗xf3, and 21.♕f1 is disproved by 21...♗xf3 22.♖f4 ♗xg2.

21...♘e5

After 21...♖xe4 22.♕xe4 ♘e5 23.♘xe5 ♗xd1 24.♕xb7, White has a pawn for the Exchange with the Queens still on the board. Bronstein wants more.

22.♖xe5

Denker gives up the Exchange at once, after which the endgame is hopeless for him. His last chance was the move *22.♖f4*, for example, *22...♕xf4* 23.gxf4 ♘xf3+ 24. ♗xf3 ♖xe2 25.♗xg4. Matters aren't changed by *22...♘xf3+* 23. ♗xf3 ♖xe2 24.♖xf6 gxf6 25. ♗xg4. Black must play *22...♕c6!* with the decisive threat of 23... ♘g6. In case of 23.♘xe5 ♗xe2 24.♗xc6 bxc6, White loses a piece.

22...♖xe5 23.♕xe5 ♕xe5 24.♘xe5 ♗xd1 25.♗xb7 ♖c7

The rest is a matter of technique.

26.♗e4 ♗c2

Black doesn't win a piece by 26...♖e7 because of 27.f4 f6 28. ♗d5+.

27.♗d5 ♔f8

Here 27...♖c5 leads to a winning ending after 28.♗xf7+ ♔f8 29.♗g6 ♖xe5 30.♗xc2 ♖e2.

28.♘c6 ♗b1 29.a3 ♗f5 30.♔f1 ♗e6 31.♗xe6 fxe6 32.♘d4 ♖c1+ 33.♔e2 ♔e7

Bronstein thinks that 33...e5 was simpler.

34.♔d3 ♖f1 35.f4

If 35.♔e2, then 35...♖b1 with the threat of 36...e5. At this point, there are many ways to win.

35...♖f2 36.♔c4

On 36.h4 the best is 36...♔d6.
**36...♖xh2 37.♔b5 ♖d2 38.♘c6+
♔d6 39.♔xb6 ♖d3 40.b4 ♖xa3 41.
g4 ♖f3 0-1**

Many know that Fischer played in
his first simul against Max Pavey, but
very little else is remembered about
one of the greatest gentleman of
American chess. Pavey, one of America's top players after the Second
World War, was also a key figure in
the U.S. Chess Federation. Montgom-
ery Major wrote this obituary in 1957.

Death claimed Max Pavey on
September 4, 1957 at the age of 39
after a long confinement in the Mt.
Sinai Hospital. Leukemia and coro-
nary complications "with a suspicion
of radium intoxication" were the
causes ascribed for his untimely
passing.

Ranked as a Senior U.S. Master,
Pavey had a very distinguished career in chess. While a student in Ed-
inburgh in 1939 he won the
championship of Scotland. In 1947
he won the U.S. Lightning Chess
Championship in New York and in
1949, the New York State Championship. He finished second to Donald Byrne in the 1953 U.S. Open at
Milwaukee, and was a member of
the U.S. team that traveled to Moscow in 1955. He was also a ranking
tournament bridge player.

Max Pavey was a chemist by
profession and for several years had
been manager of the Canadian Radium and Uranium Corp. Labora-
tory in Mt. Kisco, N.Y. It is suggested
that he might have been the victim
of radioactivity, according to a statement from the State Labor Department of New York which has
brought court action against the Ca-

SM Max Pavey (1918-1957)

nadian Radium and Uranium Corp.,
alleging laxity in reprocessing and
salvaging radium.

Chess players in the USA owe a
great debt of gratitude to Max
Pavey, not only for his distinguished
career which reflected glory on
American chess but for his faithful
and efficient labors as the chairman
of the USCF International Affairs
Committee. His zeal for chess was
such that he continued to conduct
important international chess nego-
tiations from his hospital bed at Mt.
Sinai — and the participation of an
American team in the first International Women's Team Tournament
at Emmen, Holland was his final
successful negotiation on behalf of
American Chess. Invariably soft-
spoken and affable in his relation-
ship with others, Max Pavey will be
long remembered and his premature
passing deeply regretted by all who

cherish the best in American chess. Our sympathy goes to his widow, parents and sister.

Chess Life September 20, 1957

Here is Pavey's greatest victory.

[6] *King's Indian Fianchetto E67*
SM Max Pavey
GM Paul Keres
USA–USSR, New York (4) 1954

1.d4 ♘f6 2.♘f3 g6

Keres seldom plays the King's Indian Defense.

3.c4 ♗g7 4.g3 O-O 5.♗g2 d6 6.O-O ♘bd7 7.♕c2 e5 8.♖d1 ♖e8 9.♘c3 c6 10.e4!

This move is better than the colorless exchange of center pawns with 10.dxe5 dxe5 as was played in Petrosian–Kotov and Euwe–Geller in Switzerland 1953.

If 10.b3, then Black advances 10...e4 with good play. See Stoltz–Kotov, Stockholm 1952, and Euwe–Boleslavsky, Switzerland 1953.

10...a6 11.h3 b5 12.dxe5 dxe5 13. ♗e3

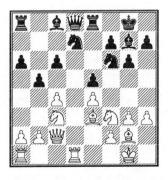

All of these moves are already known from the game Terpugov–Bronstein, 19th Soviet Championship [Moscow 1951]. GM Bronstein in his theoretical survey of the Championship came to the conclusion that White's position is better and that Black needs to find a more energetic plan of counterplay after 10.e4! ...

13...♕a5

Bronstein played 13...♕e7 in the afore-mentioned game. The move played by Keres is worse, as White transfers his Knight with tempi to a stronger square.

14.♘d2 b4

White gains an obvious positional advantage after this move. Better was 14...♗f8.

15.♘b3 ♕c7 16.♘a4 ♗f8 17.c5 a5

Otherwise, after White plays ♘b6, his second Knight could come to a5.

18.♗f1 ♘h5

Black's intention is to follow with ...♘h5-g7-e6 from where it will put extra pressure on the pawn on c5 and may be able to come to d4 in some cases.

19.♘d2

The White Knight starts traveling, but with more concrete goals — Black has weak points on b6 and d6.

19...♘g7 20.♘c4 ♘e6 21.♘cb6

Pavey loses track of the correct plan. Better was *21.♘d6*, for example, *21...♖d8* (if 21...♗xd6, then 22. cxd6 ♕b7 23.♖ac1, winning a pawn) *22.♗c4 ♘dxc5* (the threat was 23.♗xe6 fxe6 24.♕b3) *23.♘xf7 ♖xd1+ 24.♖xd1 ♘xa4 25.♘g5* with the advantage, as White regains the piece.

21...♖ab8

The Rook would stand worse on a7, but the a-pawn would be defended. This latter factor soon proves to be more significant.

22.♖ac1 ♗g7

Black couldn't take the pawn: 22...♘exc5 (if 22...♘dxc5, then 23.♘xc5 ♘xc5 24.♘xc8) 23.♘xd7! ♘xd7 24.♕xc6 with an obvious advantage.

23.♘xd7 ♗xd7 24.♘b6

Now Black has no defense to 25.♕a4, winning the a-pawn, but he seizes the d4-square, which is an achievement. Keres will soon try to introduce maximum complications.

24...♘d4 25.♕a4 ♗e6 26.♕xa5 b3 27.a3

White had the opportunity to play 27.♗xd4 exd4 28.axb3 ♗xb3 29.♖d3 with a pawn up in a relatively simplified position. Pavey decides to preserve his passed pawn, but why not 27.a4?

27...f5 28.♗xd4 exd4 29.exf5 ♗xf5 30.♗d3?

White gives up an important pawn for nothing. Better was 30.♕b4, if 30...♗c2, then 31.♖e1 and not 31...d3 because of 32.♗xd3.

30...♗xh3 31.♕b4 ♔h8 32.♕xb3

Pavey loses his ground rather quickly in the complications. He should have played 32.♔h2, but White's position is already difficult.

32...♗h6

The immediate 32...♖e3 would be met by 33.♔h2.

33.♖c2 ♖e3!

The White King is under a strong attack.

34.♔h2 ♗g4! 35.♖f1 ♕e5! 36.♔g1

The Rook can't be captured: 36.fxe3 ♕h5+ 37.♔g2 (37.♔g1 ♗xe3+ 38.♖cf2 ♗f3, mating) 37...♕h3+ 38.♔f2 ♗xe3+ 39.♔e1 ♕xg3+ 40.♖cf2 ♗xf2+ 41.♖xf2 ♖e8+, winning.

36...♗e6

Black could have won immediately with 36...♗f3. It should be mentioned that Keres was in time pressure.

37.♕b4 ♖xd3

It seems White can resign, but . . .

38.♖e1 ♕f6?

The blunders begin. Much simpler was 38...♖xg3+, winning. Keres would have been able to make the time control with two instantaneous moves.

39.♘d7 ♖xb4?

After 39...♗xd7 40.♕xb8+ ♗f8, Black has a material advantage. [Russians value the Rook at four and a half points and not five as in the United States.]

40.♘xf6 ♖c4 41.♖ce2 ♖c1?

Here the game was adjourned. Under the influence of his previous blunders, Keres sealed the wrong move, as he himself showed later. Necessary was 41...♗f7 42.♖e7 ♔g7 43.♘e8+ ♔g8! 44.♖xf7 ♖c1. If 43.♘d7, then 43...♖c1 44.♖xf7+ ♔xf7 45.♘e5+ (45.♖xc1 ♔e6) 45...♔e6. So, after 41...♗f7, Black could still save the game.

42.♖xe6 ♖xe1+ 43.♖xe1 ♔g7

Meeting the threat of 44.♖e7. Now White realizes his advantage step by step.

44.♘g4 ♖b3 45.♖d1 ♗g5 46.♖xd4 ♖xb2 47.♖d7+ ♔f8

Necessary, as 48.f4 was strong on other moves.

48.♖xh7 ♖c2 49.♘e5 ♔g8 50.♖c7 ♖xc5 51.♘xc6 ♔h8 52.a4 ♗d2 53.

♖d7 ♗e1 54.♘e7 ♔g7 55.♘d5+ ♔h6 56.♘e3 ♖c8 57.♔g2 ♖a8 58. f4

White creates a mating net.

58...g5 59.f5 ♖xa4 60.♔h3 g4+ 61. ♔h4 ♗xg3+ 62.♔xg3 ♖e4 63.♘d5 ♔g5 64.f6 ♖d4 65.f7 ♖d3+ 66.♔g2 ♖f3 67.♘e3 ♔h4 68.♘xg4 1-0

U.S. Amateur Championship 1955

Ukrainian Ruslan Ponomarov currently holds the world's record for becoming a Grandmaster at the youngest age. Ponomarov, who made his final norm only two weeks after his fourteenth birthday was almost a year and a half younger than Bobby Fischer when he got the title. Fischer held the record for 34 years, but what is really impressive is Bobby's fantastic leap of strength between ages 12 and 15. Judit Polgar, Peter Leko, Etienne Bacrot, Boris Spassky (at age 16 he finished equal fourth at Bucharest 1953 with a victory over world number two Smyslov), Garry Kasparov (at age 16 he finished first at Banja Luka 1979 a point and a half over the GM norm as a FIDE unrated) and Ponomarov all were master strength by their 12th birthday, if not much earlier. Bobby, on the other hand, was rated only 1830 when he went to Lincoln, Nebraska, to play in the U.S. Junior in the summer of 1955 at age 12 and a half. Roughly two years later, Fischer was 2231 on the USCF rating list which appeared

in the May 5, 1957, issue of *Chess Life*.

Until recently, the 1955 U.S. Junior was the first tournament of Bobby's from which we have game scores. Now we can go back a little farther, to Memorial Day weekend of 1955. Fischer sources document his playing in the 1955 U.S. Amateur, but little more. Thanks to New York City book dealer and chess teacher Fred Wilson, who picked up the score at an auction, we have a new example of Fischer juvenilia.

The following game was played at Lake Mohegan, located directly north of New York City about 40 miles. Albert B. Humphrey was an active amateur player from Barrington, Massachusetts. *Chess Life* (May 5, 1957) lists an A. Humphrey of Cleveland at 1850. We are not sure if this was Bobby's opponent. The event was held May 21-22, 1955.

[7]   *King's Indian Classical   E90*
A.B. Humphrey–RJF
Lake Mohegan 1955

1.d4 ♘f6 2.c4 g6 3.♘c3 ♗g7 4.♘f3 O-O 5.e4 d6 6.h3 ♘bd7 7.♗e3 e5 8. d5 a5 9.♗e2 b6 10.O-O ♘e8 11. ♕c2 ♘c5 12.♘h2 f5 13.f3 f4 14.♗f2 ♕g5 15.♔h1 ♗d7 16.♖g1 ♘f6 17. g4 fxg3 18.♖xg3 ♕h6 19.♘d1 ♘h5 20.♖g1 ♗xh3 21.♗e3 ♘f4 22.♘f2 ♗f6 23.♖g3 ♗d7 24.♘g4 ♗xg4 25. ♖xg4 ♕g7 26.♖ag1 ♗e7 27.♕d2 ♖f7 28.♖1g3 ♖af8 29.♗xf4 ♖xf4 30. ♖h3 ♕f7 31.♖4g3 ♗h4 32.♖g4 ♗f2 33.♗d1 **Draw**

The final position is a more than a bit puzzling. Bobby is a pawn up with a big positional advantage. Yes, there still is some work to be done, but White has no counterplay. So why did Bobby give the draw? Maybe he was in time pressure, or maybe the young Bobby wasn't feeling confident. The latter theory bears some credence. Consider Bobby's account of the tourney.

My first tournament out of New York City was the United States amateur, held May 1955 at Lake Mohegan in upstate New York. Mr. Nigro (Carmine Nigro, President of the Brooklyn Chess Club) had to persuade me to play in this tournament as just before the beginning of it I lost my nerve and only wanted to watch. I played, got a minus score, but found it interesting.

Bobby Fischer's Games of Chess.

Three years later this same player qualified for the Candidates Tournament at Portoroz, scoring 12-8 for equal fifth versus the world's best. That's a record for progress that may never be beaten.

U.S. Junior Open 1955

The 1955 U.S. Junior Open in Lincoln, Nebraska, was Bobby's first major tournament outside of New York state. The 12-year-old Fischer hooked up with Charles Kalme (born 11-15-39) in Philadelphia and the two traveled by train together to Lincoln, where they were met by the organizer, Alexander Liepnieks.

Today young players have so many big events to choose from — the National, New York, and World Opens to mention but three — that it is hard to remember a time when the pickings were few. Go back forty years and the

Participants and Officials of the 1955 U.S. Junior Open:

First Row (l-r) Bobby Fischer, Andy Staklis, organizer Alexander Liepnieks, Ken Opp, Ron Gross, and Larry Remlinger; **Second Row** N.N., Elliott Froomess, Charles Kalme, John Winkelman, John Rinaldo, Sandy Greene; **Third Row** Barton Lewis., Bob Cross, N.N., Bob Lorber, N.N.; **Fourth Row** N.N., N.N., N.N., John Briska, Jim Dick; **Last Row** N.N., N.N., N.N., Jim Thomason.

U.S. Junior Championship

Lincoln, Nebraska   July 1955

		Age	Rtg.	1	2	3	4	5	6	7	8	9	10	
1. Charles Kalme	Philadelphia, PA	15	2186	+23	+6	+2	+4	-3	+11	+5	+8	+9	+12	9.0
2. Larry Remlinger	Long Beach, CA	13	2114	+17	+15	-1	=5	+14	+6	=4	+3	+11	=8	7.5
3. Robert Cross	Santa Monica, CA	20	2068	=7	+16	=14	+12	+1	=4	=11	-2	+5	+6	7.0
4. Ronald Gross	Compton, CA	19	2123	+22	+10	+11	-1	+6	=3	=2	-5	=8	=9	6.0
5. Andris Staklis	Lincoln, NE	16	1823	+21	=12	+15	=2	-11	+13	-1	+4	-3	+18	6.0
6. John Rinaldo	Long Beach, CA	16	1847	+25	-1	+17	+7	-4	-2	+12	+11	=13	-3	5.5
7. Robert Lorber	Reseda, CA	16	1600	=3	=8	+9	-6	-12	+24	+14	=13	=15	=10	5.5
8. Sanford Greene	Mt. Vernon, NY	18	1950	=16	=7	+23	=14	=13	=12	+18	-1	=4	=2	5.5
9. Victor Pupols	Tacoma, WA	20	2027	+24	-11	-7	-13	+25	+16	+20	+17	-1	=4	5.5
10. Barton Lewis	Lincoln, NE	20	1785	+18	-4	-16	=17	-19	=22	bye	+24	+23	=7	5.5
11. Elliott Froomess	Palo Verdes, CA	19	unr	+13	+9	-4	+16	+5	-1	=3	-6	-2	=14	5.0
12. Kenneth Warner	Bakersfield, CA	17	1550	+20	=5	=13	-3	+7	=8	-6	+15	=14	-1	5.0
13. Ben Shaeffer	San Bernadino, CA	19	1700	-11	+24	=12	+9	=8	-5	=15	=7	=6	=16	5.0
14. William Whisler	Concord, CA	17	unr	bye	-20	=3	=8	-2	=18	-7	+19	+12	=11	5.0
15. Dale Ruth	Midwest City, OK	18	1785	+19	-2	-5	+23	=18	=17	+13	-12	=7	+22	5.0
16. Kenneth Stone	Los Angeles, CA	19	1600	=8	-3	+10	-11	=20	-9	=21	bye	+25	=13	5.0
17. Max Burkett	Carlsbad, CA	16	1600	-2	+22	-6	=10	+21	=15	+19	-9	-18	+23	5.0
18. David Ames	Quincy, MA	18	unr	-10	bye	+19	=20	=15	=14	-8	=21	+17	-5	5.0
19. John Briska	Albany, NY	17	unr	-15	=21	-18	+25	+10	=20	-17	-14	bye	+24	5.0
20. Robert Fischer	Brooklyn, NY	12	1830	-12	=14	+21	=18	=16	=19	-9	=23	=22	=25	5.0
21. James Thomason	Ft. Worth, TX	14	1600	-5	=19	-20	+22	-17	+25	=16	=18	=24	bye	5.0
22. John Winkelman	Lincoln, NE	14	1650	-4	-17	+24	-21	bye	=10	-23	+25	=20	-15	4.0
23. Robert Blair	Midwest City, OK	18	1650	-1	+25	-8	-15	-24	bye	+22	=20	-10	-17	3.5
24. Jim Dick	Lincoln, NE	15	160	-9	-13	-22	bye	+23	-7	+25	-10	=21	-19	3.5
25. Franklin Saksena	Fort Worth, TX	17	1600	-6	-23	bye	-19	-9	-21	-24	-22	-16	=20	1.0

situation was markedly different. American players in the 1950s didn't have the luxury of deciding which tournaments to play in — they played in what was available.

These days, the U.S. Junior Open is not an especially significant event, having been superseded by the U.S. Junior Closed which brings together the eight to ten best young players in the country. Things were different when Bobby went to Lincoln. Then the Junior really meant something and the best players traveled considerable distances to participate in a time when plane travel was not the norm. Lincoln, Nebraska, might seem seem a unlikely venue for a chess tournament. The hometown of the perennially high-ranked University of Nebraska

Cornhusker football team could pass for a typical Midwestern steak and potatoes kind of place, but for one unusual ingredient — Latvians.

Many people from this small Baltic nation, which was savaged during the Second World War, immigrated to the United States in the late 1940s and early 1950s. A small colony of them had settled in Lincoln, bringing with them a love for chess. Liepnieks, a Latvian of master strength who was to later bring the 1969 U.S. Open to Lincoln, was the driving force behind the 1955 U.S. Junior, taking command of every detail.

One of his first duties was to schedule the event for July 15-24, to enable 20-year-old Viktors Pupols, with a July 31 birthday, to meet the age requirement. Pupols was one of several Latvian-born players (Kalme, Staklis, Briska) competing in the event, and had ties to Lincoln, having first moved there with his family, before relocating to the Pacific Northwest.

Shortly after the second Fischer–Spassky match, the Seattle Chess Club held a special Bobby Fischer night with GM Yasser Seirawan, IM Nikolay Minev and NM Viktors Pupols as guest speakers. The event, which was videotaped and shown on local cable television, was a great hit. Pupols, whose skills as a raconteur were documented in *Viktors Pupols, American Master*, entertained the audience with his impressions of the young Bobby.

The first thing Pupols stressed was that Bobby was very much an unknown player. He was only 12 and hadn't yet begun the growth spurt that

brought him to 6'2". This was his first trip far from home and it's doubtful that Bobby would have been allowed to make the trip if his mother hadn't had the assurance that he would be spending the next two weeks in a domestic environment with the Liepnieks family.

Bobby is often portrayed in the media as a loner who forms few close personal relationships, but conversations with Bobby's friends and an examination of written records show no basis for this judgement. Fischer may initially be on his guard, but once he understands you respect chess, he can be very friendly.

Bobby and the Liepnieks family hit it off very well and maintained a friendship for many years. Alex and his wife had two daughters, Ruta and Sylvia, and a son, Andy, who befriended him. Fischer, subject to some teasing as the youngest player in the event, got a little homesick, but greatly enjoyed his stay.

In 1972, Alexander Liepnieks was a member of the Fischer camp at the World Championship match against Boris Spassky in Reykjavik, where his skills as a Russian translator proved invaluable for Fred Cramer and other high-ranking members of the American delegation. When Liepnieks passed away in 1973 the *Chess World/Sacha Pasaule* ran a letter of condolence from Bobby under the headline:

An Inspiring Example to Me

Thank you for your note informing me of your father's death. I was very sorry to hear this because I considered him to be a good friend. His enthusiasm, good will, dedication and love of chess was an inspiring example to me. And I am sure to many others.

I have certainly enjoyed *Chess World* very much over the years and especially the section on the Latvian Gambit, which was highly entertaining and instructive.

It is my sincere hope that someone will follow in your father's footsteps and continue the monthly publication of this fine magazine. Again please accept my condolences.

Sincerely,
Bobby Fischer

The 1955 U.S. Junior was easily won by top-rated (2186) Charles Kalme, who defeated two of his chief rivals, Larry Remlinger and Ron Gross, in the first four rounds. His sole loss, enroute to a 9-1 score which garnered him the title and a $75 suit of clothes, was to Robert Cross. Kalme, who was only 15 at the time of his victory in Lincoln — a record for the youngest U.S. Junior winner that Bobby would beat the next year — was a great talent and easily had the potential to become a strong GM.

The following piece, exerpted from the article "Young American Masters" by the late California master Charles Henin brings his career up to the early 1960s. Shortly thereafter, Kalme retired from chess to concentrate on a career in academia.

There is no doubt that the rise of the United States to the No. 2 spot in world chess has been due mainly to the emergence in recent years of some very talented young players. Along with the spectacular rises of

Fischer and Lombardy have been those, less spectacular but no less important, of several other young masters.

One among these is Charles Kalme of Philadelphia. That city's leading player for several years, Kalme is a former U.S. Junior and U.S. Intercollegiate titleholder, having won the former title in 1955 and the latter in 1957. He tied for 1st place in the strong North Central Open in 1957, in which he defeated Fischer, a feat which has not since been duplicated in an American chess tourney. Charley has competed twice on the U.S. student team, and his most outstanding success was in the recent student team tournament in Moscow, where his dazzling score of 12 1/2 - 1 1/2 on board 2 helped in no small way to bring the United States its first international team title in over 25 years. In the recent U.S. championship event Kalme scored a respectable 5:6, good for 7th prize in a powerful field. Only a loss in a rather wild last round game with Lombardy prevented a really fine result, for if Kalme had won that game he would have tied for 3rd place, so close was the finish.

Kalme was born in Riga, Latvia, home of many fine chessplayers, including the present world champion. Just after the war his family fled to Germany, where they lived for several years in Displaced Persons Camps in the Allied zone. It was here that Charley learned chess, though he didn't play seriously until his high school days in Philadelphia, where he and his family came to settle in 1951. His rapid development to master strength he attributes mainly to his association with the veteran master Attilio DiCamillo, who also schooled Lisa Lane to fame. Kalme is currently completing his B.S. in electrical engineering at the University of Pennsylvania, and plans to continue graduate work to obtain a Ph.D. in mathematics.

Tall, thin, and blond, Kalme presents a physical picture of ease and relaxation. He is, in fact, known for his nonchalance, and I am told that in a recent tourney, half an hour after the first round was scheduled to have begun, into the playing room leisurely strolled Kalme and asked "Where do I register?"

When it comes to chess though, Charley becomes very serious. He has a complex style which often leads him into difficult and complicated positions in which he fights intensely. With regard to his part in the student team victory he says, "For many reasons, some best understood only by me and my native country Latvia, this was the greatest thrill of my life. I do not think there has been anything in my life that I wanted more than for our team to win the title, and it was definitely the most determined effort ever put into chess by me. That is not to say that the quality of my play was so high, but that the effort was great. Generally, I seldom find the effort to sit through 40 or so moves and try to make every one of them to the best of my ability. In the Student's Team Tournament, however, I did so in 13 of the 14 games played. The one exception was in the 5th round against Yugoslavia. With the U.S. leading by some 4 or 5 points over the field (including Russia) I left a piece in take in an even position, af-

ter having played rather carelessly throughout. We lost the match by 1/2 - 3 1/2 and this enabled Russia later to catch up with us and even move ahead. After this disaster I walked around sulking till 5 A.M. next morning, only then feeling convinced that there was no reason for us still not to win the championship!"

Chess Life, 1961

In 1955, soon-to-be IM James Sherwin wrote about Kalme's style and personality in a *Chess Life* article entitled "Masters of the Future."

He has a solid positional style and prefers not to take too many chances (which accounts for his very few losses and many draws — he was undefeated in three recent tournaments). He is remarkably modest for a strong chess player and is always announcing that the best he can do is draw — only when a Rook

Charles Kalme

ahead does he admit there are some winning chances. And unfortunately, he is a good poker player. This deprives him of needed sleep during most tournaments in return for pocket money. It's hard to see what is more necessary. As soon as he begins to take his games more seriously he should become a master.

Kalme stayed away from the game for thirty years before returning to tournament play in the mid-1990s at the World Open. Despite the long layoff, his performance was quite impressive, 2450 USCF. This might not seem that remarkable for a player of such great talent, but as Philadelphia IM Richard Costigan points out, "He was getting absolutely nothing from the opening, even against experts. His strength was a strongly developed positional sense."

Bobby had yet to show his great strength, but was probably playing close to expert level (2000) in Lincoln, though only rated 1830 at the time. His score of 5-5, good for shared eleventh through twenty-first, included two wins, two losses and six draws.

Fischer was not the top young talent at the U.S. Junior. That distinction belonged to 13-year-old Larry Remlinger of Long Beach. Remlinger was considered a brilliant prospect at the time and was strongly supported by his parents. A regular at the Long Beach Chess Club, then a full-time facility, he was clearly stronger than Fischer in 1955. Here is Sherwin's description of Remlinger from "Masters of the Future."

Most New York players provincially determine the strength of "out of

Larry Remlinger at 1954 U.S. Junior

towners" by examining their records against the New York masters. That was how Larry Remlinger's play came to be respected in N.Y. Karl Burger attended the Kansas City Junior two years ago and returned to report that an eleven-year-old named Remlinger was going to be U.S. Champion in six years and that Karl was lucky to have drawn with him.

Larry learned to play chess from an uncle when he was ten and a year later joined the Lincoln Park Chess and Checker Club. Fortunately, Mr. John L. Looney, the club secretary, and Lionel Joyner recognized Larry's talent and helped him study the theory of the openings and endings — midgame theory must be learned more by experience. The members of the club and local merchants contributed to send Larry and his parents to the Kansas City tournament where he was coached by Herman Steiner.

Last year in Long Beach, Larry finished second in the U.S. Junior ahead of Kalme, Harrow, Cross, Shelby Lyman and Bob Cross, to mention only a few.

Chess Life, July 5, 1955.

---

[8] *Max Lange Attack   C55*
NM Charles Henin
Larry Remlinger
U.S. Junior Championship, Kansas City 1953

1.e4 e5 2.♗c4 ♘f6 3.d4 exd4 4.♘f3 ♘c6 5.0-0 ♗c5 6.e5 d5 7.exf6 dxc4 8.♖e1+ ♗e6 9.♘g5 ♕d5 10.♘c3 ♕f5 11.♘ce4 0-0-0 12.g4 ♕e5 13.♘xe6 fxe6 14.♘g5?

Correct is 14.fxg7 ♖hg8 15.♗h6

14...♕xf6 15.♖xe6 ♕f8 16.♕e1 h6 17.♘e4 ♗b6 18.♔g2 ♕f7 19.♘g3 d3 20.♖e4 ♘d4 21.♖f4 ♕d5+ 22.♕e4 ♘xc2 23.♖b1 d2 24.♗xd2 ♕xd2 25.♘f5 ♖he8 26.♕xc4 g6 0-1

Like Kalme, Remlinger soon stopped playing. He played in the occasional event till the 1990s, then he dedicated himself totally to chess. He achieved his first goal of becoming an International Master in his early fifties, and wrote extensively about the quest in *Chess Life*.

Bobby, Kalme and Remlinger were not the only players in Lincoln destined to become well-known names. Robert Cross, who finished third, would develop into a strong correspondence player. Max Burkett became a noted chess book seller and produced the Lone Pine tournament bulletins for many years.

Bobby's opponent in the following game, veteran Northwest master Vik-

tors Pupols, is one of the top senior players in the United States with a rating over 2300. He provided the background for the following game in the pages of *Chess World/Sacha Pasaule*, April 1972.

We had known all day what the pairings and the colors would be (Alex Liepnieks directed the tournament), and I tried to impress Bobby Fischer (he was only 12 years old) with the glories of the Latvian Gambit. Fischer refused to believe that this opening would indeed be played and analyzed other open games.

There was a continuing poker game at Alex Liepnieks' home, and throughout the day Charles Kalme, the eventual tournament winner, and I kept playing skittles games using the Latvian Gambit against Fischer whenever we folded at poker, but at the end of the day Fischer was still analyzing the Ruy Lopez and Giuoco Piano. Bobby took his loss very hard. I did, of course, announce in advance my intention of playing the Latvian Gambit.

---

[9] *Latvian Gambit   C40*
RJF–Viktors Pupols
U.S. Junior Open, Lincoln (7) 1955

1.e4 e5 2.♘f3

Bobby was greatly interested in double King-pawn openings. He not only played the standard Ruy Lopez, but also the King's Gambit and 3.♗c4 in tournament practice. During 1964 his repertoire was broadened, at least for simultaneous exhibitions, with the addition of the Vienna Game. Dr. Leroy Dubeck, whose term as USCF President (1969-1972) coincided with Bobby's World Championship run, had much unpublished Weaver Adams analysis on the Vienna which he and Fischer looked at a couple of times in the early 1960s.

2...f5

Bobby would probably have played 3.♗c4 against 2...♘c6.

3.♘xe5 ♕f6 4.d4 d6 5.♘c4 fxe4 6.♘c3

The opening sequence of this game is sometimes given as 6.♘e3 and 7. ♘c3, but, as Pupols points out, Black might be able to avoid ...♕g6 by answering 6.♘e3 with 6...♘c6.

6...♕g6 7.♘e3

This blockading move is often attributed to the "Great Blockader" Aron Nimzovich who was born in Riga, Latvia.

7...♘f6 8.♗c4

Grandmaster Tony Kosten, in his book on the Latvian Gambit, prefers 8.♗e2.

8...c6 9.d5

This stops ...d6-d5, but yields the e5-square. The more Nimzovichian strategy was to allow Black to play ...d5 and then attack the pawn chain with c2-c4.

9...♗e7

Here, 9...c5 yields the b5-square.

10.a4 ♘bd7 11.a5?

The plan of a2-a4-a5 loses valuable time.

11...♘e5 12.♗e2

12.♗a2 c5 and White doesn't control b5.

12...O-O 13.O-O ♗d7 14.♔h1 ♔h8 15.♘c4 ♘fg4 16.♕e1 ♖f7

This loses a tempo. Pupols suggests 16...♖f5 17.♗xg4 ♘xg4 18.♘xe4 cxd5. And 16...♗h4!? is another try.

17.h3

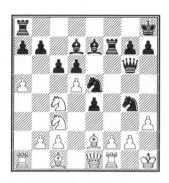

17...♘f6?!

Black could have played the very interesting piece sacrifice 17...♘f3!. The position after 18.♕d1 ♖af8 19. hxg4 ♕xg4 20.gxf3 exf3 21.♘e3 fxe2 22.♕xe2 ♕h3+ 23.♔g1 ♖f3 leaves Black with very strong threats of 24...♖8f4 and 24...♖8f6.

18.♘xe5 dxe5 19.♗c4 ♖ff8 20.♗e3 ♘h5 21.♔h2 ♗d6 22.♗b3 ♘f4

Necessary.

23.♗xf4?

This exchange brings Black's dark-squared Bishop to life and gives him strong mobile pawns on e4 and f4. A better try is 23.♖g1, meeting 23... ♕h5 with 24.♕f1.

23...exf4 24.♕xe4?

This should lose immediately. The ugly 24.f3 had to be played, but Black would, of course, have a large advantage.

24...f3+ 25.g3 ♗f5?

Here, 25...♕h6! or 25...♕h5! would have won immediately, as 26.h4 is met by 26...♖f4! with the threat of 27... ♖xh4+, mating.

26.♕h4 ♖ae8 27.♖ae1 ♗e5

Avoiding exchanges.

28.♕b4?

Black is only slightly better after 28.dxc6 bxc6 29.♖g1 ♗xc2 30.♕b4. The text should lose immediately.

28...♕h6 29.h4 g5?

Black had a forced win with 29...♗xg3+, as 30.fxg3 ♕d2+, 30.♔h1 ♗xh4, and 30.♔xg3 ♕g6+ all lead to mate.

30.♖h1?

Bobby misses a chance to put up strong resistance with 30.♖xe5! ♖xe5 31.♕d4 ♕g7 32.hxg5 cxd5 33.♘xd5.

Life master Viktors Pupols today

30...gxh4 31.♔g1

31...h3?

This mistake, which closes lines for the attack, overlooks two forced wins. Black had much better in 31...♗xg3! 32.♕d4+ ♗e5 33.♖xe5 ♕g7+ or if 33.♕xh4 ♗h2+! (Pupols) or 31...♕g7! 32.♖xe5 hxg3 33.♘e4 gxf2+ 34.♔xf2 ♕xe5 35.dxc6 ♗xe4.

32.dxc6?

Better is 32.♘e4, although Black would still have a large advantage after 32...♗xb2 33.♔h2 ♗e5.

32...bxc6?

Pupols overlooks 32...♗xg3! Black wins after 33.♕d4+ ♗e5 34.♖xe5 ♕g7+ 35.♔f1 ♖xe5.

33.♕c5?

This wastes valuable time with the Queen.

White should have brought his Knight to the defense with 33.♘e4.

33...♕g7?

The contestants have a blind spot for ...♗xg3. 33...♗xg3! is crushing, e.g., 34.♕d4+ ♗e5 35.♖xe5 ♕g7+ 36. ♔f1 ♖xe5 37.♘e4 c5.

34.♔h2 ♕f6 35.♕xa7 ♗d4 36.♕c7 ♗xf2

36...♗e5 allows White to resist with 36.♖xe5.

37.♖xe8 ♖xe8 38.♖f1 ♗d4

The time control was 45 moves in two hours. For the following phase, White had only two minutes on his clock; Black, but one.

39.♖xf3?

Bobby had to play 39.♕f4. After the text Black has a powerful shot.

39...♗xc3?

Pupols misses a chance to conclude the game in brilliant fashion. Black has a forced win with 39...♗g1+!! White loses whether he captures the Bishop or not: 40.♔h1 ♗e4 41.♕f4 ♗xf3+ 42.♔xg1 ♖e1+ 43.♔f2 ♕xf4 44.gxf4 h2 45.♔xe1 h1=♕+ or 40. ♔xg1 ♕d4+ 41.♔f1 h2 42.♔g2 h1=♕+ 43.♔xh1 ♖e1+, mating.

40.bxc3 ♖e2+ 41.♔h1 ♗e4 42.♕c8+ ♔g7 43.♕g4+?

White could have drawn with 43. ♕d7+ ♔h6 44.♕xh3+ ♔g7 45. ♕d7+ ♔h6 46.♕h3+. After the text, Black has a significant advantage.

43...♕g6 44.♕d7+?

Bobby misses the last chance to continue the fight. White had to play 44.♕f4, when Black has two choices, though neither one leads to a forced win. On 44...♗xf3+ White has 45. ♕xf3 ♖g2 46.♗e3 ♕xg3 47.♕e7+ ♔h6 48.♕f8+ ♕g7 49.♕f4+ ♖g5 50.♕h4+ ♔g6 51.♕e4+. The alternative is 44...h5 45.♕e5+ ♔h7 46. ♕e7+ ♕g7 47.♕xe4+ ♖xe4 48.♖f7.

44...♔h6 0-1 {time}

This may be the only time Fischer lost a game on time in his career.

The Lincoln event is one of the rare U.S. Juniors that had a bulletin, thanks to the efforts of Omaha chess enthusiast Jack Spence (1926-1978). Spence produced many limited edition bulletins of important events in the 1950s, 60s and 70s, and quite a few games from these events would have been completely lost if not for his tireless efforts.

The bulletin for Lincoln doesn't have all the games of the event, but it offers a pretty good selection. Bobby, who was not one of the top finishers, had his first four games selected for publication (Warner, Whisler, Thomason, and Ames), but then nothing more. This tallies with Wade and O'Connell's *The Games of Robert Fischer*, — the first systematic attempt to locate all of Bobby's games — which undoubtedly used Spence's bulletin as primary source material.

Viktors Pupols sent his game in, which brings the tally to five, but that still leaves Stone, Briska, Blair, Winkelman, and Saksena unaccounted for. In *My 60 Memorable Games*, in the notes to 3.♗c4 in a Two Knight's Defense game with Bisguier, Bobby writes, "The last time I played this move in a tournament was when I was 12, at the 1955 U.S. Junior Championship." As near as can be determined from the crosstable, Bobby is referring to his game with Briska or Winkelman.

---

[10] *Two Knights Wilkes-Barre C57*
RJF–(Briska!? or Winkelman!?)
U.S. Junior Open, Lincoln 1955

1.e4 e5 2.♘f3 ♘c6 3.♗c4 ♘f6 4. ♘g5

Here, 4.♘c3, as Bobby played against Ames in this tournament, has the widely held reputation of being a beginner's mistake. The fork trick after 4...♘xe4 is supposed to easily equalize for Black, if not lead to a better game, but rarely are things one hundred percent clear in chess. Check out Morovic–Sagalchik, North Bay 1996, (*Chess Informant, 67/406*) where the GM-duel saw White quickly emerge with a big advantage after *5. ♘xe4 d5 6.♗d3 f5 7.♘c3 e4 (7...d4 8.♘e4) 8.♗b5 exf3 9.♕xf3 ♗e6 10. O-O ♕d7 11.♘e2! ♗d6 12.d4! O-O 13.♗f4 ♗xf4 14.♕xf4 ♖ae8 15.♕d2 a6 16.♗xc6 ♕xc6 17.♘f4 ♗d7 18. f3 ♕b6 19.b3 ♕h6 20.♖f2! c6 21. ♘d3 f4 22.♖e1 g5 23.♖xe8 ♖xe8 24. ♖e2 ♖xe2 25.♕xe2 ♕e6 26.♘e5.*

Queen and Knight work much better together than Queen and Bishop, as they can both cover all the squares.
4...♗c5

Fischer, annotating his game with Bisguier from the 1963 N.Y. State Open in *My 60 Memorable Games*, remarks after 4...d5:

> On that last occasion in Nebraska, referred to above, my opponent played 4...♗c5, alias the Wilkes-Barre line of the Two Knights. At that time, I was unfamiliar with this variation and nearly laughed out loud at the thought of my opponent making such a blunder in a tournament of this importance. I was just about to let him have it, when I noticed that he had brought along a friend who was watching the game very intently. This aroused my suspicion — maybe this was a trap, straight from Horowitz's *Traps and Pitfalls*. But a Rook is a Rook — so I continued with . . .

5.♘xf7 ♗xf2+ 6.♔xf2 ♘xe4+ 7. ♔e3? ♕h4

> And somehow I got out of this mess. Afterwards I showed him a forced win that he had missed. The game was actually drawn on my request. I had no chance for first place and my trophy for the best scoring player under 13 was assured already, since I was the only one under 13!

The trophy that Bobby won was the Dittman trophy for the top scoring player under 13. Herman A. Dittmann of Salt Lake City, who died in 1954, was internationally known for his artistic creations in wood, particularly beautiful chess trophies as well as wood sets and inlaid boards. Some of his sets sold for over $500 in the

1950s! Among his masterpieces was a trophy for the World Championship which Botvinnik possessed. Dittman was a tireless promoter in the inter-mountain states and for many years a key figure at the Salt Lake City Chess Club. His collection of over 200 bound chess magazines and books was donated to the Salt Lake City Public Library as the Hermann A. Dittmann Memorial Chess Library.

In addition to the main event, the U.S. Junior Blitz Championship was held on July 17, 1955. The eighteen players were divided among three preliminary sections. Southern California expert Ron Gross beat Bobby in the last round to advance to the final, which he won ahead of Kalme and Remlinger.

Preliminary Section B

1. R. Cross	4.5
2. R. Gross	4.0
3. R. Fischer	3.0
4. B. Lewis	2.0
5. D. Ruth	1.0
6. D. Ames	0.5

Final

1. R. Gross	4.0
2. C. Kalme	3.5
3. L. Remlinger	3.0
4. R. Cross	2.5
5. A. Staklis	2.0
6. R. Hervert	0.0

Typical of the era, the time control was ten seconds per move, with a buzzer acting as a prompter. Today we think of five-minute chess as the only game that has ever been in town, but the switch from ten-second chesss to five-minute chess took place at the U.S Open in Aspen in 1968. Gross, who became good friends with Fischer during the event, gained his master's title not long after the U.S. Junior and played a match with Robert Sobel (he lost) for the final position on the 1957 U.S. entry to the World Team Championship. He was one of the top players in Southern California for several decades before retiring to Las Vegas in the 1990s.

The First Fischer Simul

Bobby's first simul was well publicized. The *New York Times* for December 11, 1955, has a montage of photos captioned "Chess War on 12 Fronts." The largest photograph has Bobby playing twelve of the eighty-six members of the youth group (ages 7-12) of the Yorktown Chess Club on November 26. Bobby took two hours and twenty minutes to score 12-0.

Twelve-year-old Stuart Siepser lasted the longest.

The January 1956 issue of *Chess Review* adds that Bobby opened 1.e4 in every game, and that most of them continued 1...e5 2.♘f3 ♘c6 3.♗c4 ♘f6. Unfortunately, the young Yorktowners weren't acquainted with all the finesses in the Two Knight's Defense. After 4.♘g5 they allowed Bobby to follow up with ♘xf7.

Bobby received an inscribed watch from the Manhattan Chess Club and a check from the Yorktown Chess Club for his efforts.

Bobby as a Correspondence Player

Bobby's career as a correspondence player is a bit of a mystery. His mentor, John W. Collins, who was a strong postal master and wrote a correspondence chess column for *Chess Review*, writes in *My Seven Chess Prodigies*:

Bobby never played correspondence chess. Probably the pace was too slow and the dramatic personal confrontation, which is such a large part of the excitement of the game, was lacking. Consulting books while the game was in progress would not be his idea of legitimate chess either. In fact, very few grandmasters, and potential grandmasters, with the no-

table exception of Paul Keres in his formative years, have cottoned to correspondence chess. This is in contrast to its popularity with experts and lower-rated players who delight in it. Possibly the difference of appeal is due to the reasons just mentioned, to preference for public or private competition, or to causes which are psychological in nature.

Actually, Bobby did play in at least one correspondence tournament. The reason Collins didn't know about it is because he first met Bobby on Memorial Day Weekend in 1956. By then Bobby's short-lived postal career appears to have either finished or been winding down.

The first indication that Bobby played correspondence chess appears in *Legend on the Road*. There, on page 12, Donald P. Reithel, who played Bobby during his 1964 simul tour, writes:

In 1955 I played Bobby in postal chess — a prize tourney in *Chess Review*. I remember him as a typical American kid: Brooklyn Dodger fan, somewhat opinionated about school and somewhat desirous to exchange ideas and thoughts. He printed his name in lower case letters, "bobby fischer." He didn't finish the event because he was starting to play over-the-board tournaments."

In a later communication, Reithal added:

A. W. Conger was one of my opponents in [a] *Chess Review* Prize Tourney . . . [*a player named Fisher played in 54-P 38-100*] . . . That is the event Bobby Fischer competed in . . . For myself, I discarded many of my early tournament results and no longer have my scorepads covering that period of time.

I did have several of Bobby's cards, but they too were tossed out in Spring cleanups. What was interesting about them was that Bobby had notes on all of them covering various subjects.

Our individual game was a King's Indian Defense (I was White) and the game lasted 12-15 moves when he wrote me that he was withdrawing from the tourney to pursue a lengthy cross-country trip and series of over-the-board tournaments, which, he said, was his entry toward capturing the

world chess title — build skills, gain exposure, make results and earn a reputation. A year or two later he won the U.S. Championship for the first time and he was true to his word.

I did not find his comments to be egotistic, but rather showing youthful optimism and self confidence as to his talent and ability.

We shared considerable note exchanges, as I was only a teen myself and I think he related to that, as we had similar interests outside of just chess. I recall responding to his direct statement that he intended to win the world championship and return it to the USA, advising him to complete his education which he would need to handle his affairs during his adulthood. His response was that I sounded just like his sisters and teachers. His follow-up card listed only the moves. But then he responded in a more friendly way to my comments about his note . . .

In all, I found him to be a rather lonesome kid who was trying to find himself and purpose. He no doubt caught the chessbug early and it was a burning fire inside him. Who exactly contributed toward his maturity, I cannot say. He told me he studying the Bible and I wrote that he might find Rev. Rice and Herbert W. Armstrong and Garner Ted Armstrong's religious broadcasts informative, which he apparently checked out, as he later became interested in the latter's Worldwide Church of God.

. . . I found him to be a nice, normal kid with a lot of dedication to chess, but also having interests that all kids seem to share. He was a Dodger fan and I a Yankee fan. Maybe that it is why we hit it off. Anyway, I followed his career and was most pleased that his youthful dream was fulfilled.

Al Horowitz's *Chess Review* was one of the major organizers of correspondence tournaments in the 1950s. The record is spotty, but it appears Bobby played in a Prize Tourney section during 1955 and 1956. The May 1955 issue of *Chess Review*, on page 159, lists an R. Fischer under new postalites, assigning him a Class B (1200) rating. The piece mentions that newcomers to postal chess are "rated" on their estimated ability with Class A running from 1300 on up. Class B was from 1000-1298. Note that the postal ratings were about 500-600 points lower than over-the-board USCF ratings at the time.

Postal ratings appeared in *Chess Review* approximately twice a year. The August 1955 issue (p. 252) lists a B. Fischer at 1198. Later he drops to 1082 in March 1956. The August 1956 issue again lists him at 1082, which suggests that he was no longer active.

The following game is the only correspondence effort of Bobby's that we have discovered. A.W. Conger of Pennsylvania was rated 1274 in the August 1955 issue of Chess Review. It first appeared in *Zugzwang*, the newsletter of the King of Prussia Chess Club which is located in King of Prussia, Pennsylvania, just west of Philadelphia.

---

[11] *King's Indian E70*
A.W. Conger–RJF
corre. (54-P 38-100?)

1.d4 ♘f6 2.c4 g6 3.♘c3 ♗g7 4.e4 d6 5.♗g5

This line, sort of a hybrid between the Averbakh (5.♗e2 and 6.♗g5) and the Four Pawns Attack (5.f4), is a long-time favorite of American Grandmaster Arthur Bisguier. White aims for an aggressive formation combining ♗g5, f4 and ♗d3.

5...h6 6.♗h4 O-O

Spassky–Fischer, Belgrade (m-16) 1992, saw 6...c5 7.d5 g5 8.♗g3 ♕a5! 9.♗d3?? (9.♕d2 is correct, though 9...♘h5 gives Black an easy game) 9...♘xe4! 10.♗xe4 ♗xc3+ 11.bxc3 ♕xc3+ 12.♔f1 f5 and Black regained his piece with a superior position and went on to win in 34 moves. This game is deeply annotated in *No Regrets* by GM Yasser Seirawan and George Stefanovic, the classic book on the 1992 Revenge Match.

7.f4 c5 8.d5 ♕a5 9.♕d2 ♕c7??

An incomprehesible move. Black not only loses time with his Queen, but puts it on an unfortunate square to boot. Correct is 9...e6. One example from GM praxis is 9...e6 10.dxe6 ♗xe6 11.♗d3 ♖e8 12.♘f3 ♘c6 13.O-O ♗g4 with equal chances in Ermenkov–Martinovic, Groningen 1988.

10.♗d3 e6 11.♘b5 ♕b6 12.♘xd6 1-0

If 12...♕xd6, then 13.e5 ♕e7 14.d6 ♕d7 15.exf6 ♗h8 16.f5 g5 17.♗xg5 hxg5 18.♕xg5+ ♔h7 19.fxe6 mate (Conger). Of course, this isn't all forced, but Black's position is indeed quite miserable.

Source: *Zugzwang*, Spring 1976

Note that *Zugzwang* gives the date of the game as 6/27/55. We are not sure if this is the starting or ending date. Bobby was around 1800 at that time, which might suggest the game started earlier, as his play vs. Conger suggests a less-experienced player conducting the Black pieces.

**Bobby playing a board game (not chess!)
with Ruta and Andy Liepnieks.**

"The Year 1956 turned out to be a Big One for me in Chess"

Bobby started to appear regularly in the U.S. Chess Federation organ *Chess Life* in 1956. Today we know *Chess Life* as a monthly glossy, but in the 1950s it appeared twice a month as a newspaper. One of the first issues of 1956 had a mention of Bobby:

USCF master William Lombardy of the Bronx won the first Greater New York Open with a score of 6-1, nosing out Dr. Ariel Mengarini, also 6-1, by one-half a median point. Arthur Feuerstein of the Bronx and Edgar McCormick of East Orange, N.J., scored 5.5-1.5 each, but third prize went to the former on tiebreaking points. The Class A Trophy was captured by McCormick, while the Class B trophy went to twelve-year-old Bobby Fischer of Brooklyn. Fischer tied for fourth at 5-2 with Anthony Saidy and E. S. Jackson in the event held January 21-26 at the Churchill Chess Club in Manhattan.

A year after his first out-of-town event (Lake Mohegan), Bobby played again in the U.S. Amateur over Memorial Day weekend. This time the venue was Asbury Park, New Jersey, and Fischer acquitted himself much more ably, tying for twelfth with a score of 4-2. A picture of Bobby playing veteran Philadelphia amateur Samuel Sklaroff was printed in *Chess Life* in the July 20, 1956, issue after he won the U.S. Junior.

"Let's schusse!"

One of Bobby's most unusual adventures had to be his trip with the Log Cabin Chess Club of New Jersey down to Cuba in February of 1956. The 12-year-old Fischer was accompanied by his mother who doubled as a *Chess Review* photographer. Bobby needed a chaperon, as the Log Cabin crew included several larger than life characters including convicted felon IM Norman Whitaker and Log Cabin founder E. Forry Laucks.

The Marshall and Manhattan CCs have reigned supreme as the New York area's top clubs for much of this century, but, for awhile, the Log Cabin CC gave them a run for their money. Located in West Orange, New Jersey, just across the river from New York City, the Log Cabin CC was a true original. T. A. Dunst's article in the

January 1958 issue of *Chess Review* gives ample testimony to this.

First Here, First There, First Everywhere

The year is 1980. The first American space-liner has just landed on Mars. Who are those passengers briskly climbing out ahead of all the other people in the ship? There can only be one answer: the space-traveling chapter of the Log Cabin Chess Club of West Orange, New Jersey, led by that intrepid pioneer, E. Forry Laucks. They are seeking Martian chess players for the purpose of engaging in the first interplanetary chess match, the greatest and grandest "first" in the interminable history of "firsts" piled up by the Cabineers.

Do you think, tough-minded reader, that we are jesting? Nothing of the kind. This is as sure a prophecy as that the Irish will celebrate next St. Patrick's Day. In order to extrapolate, we merely need to take a look at some of the actual "firsts" on the log of these ubiquitous wanderers: They were first in the Western Hemisphere to travel by yacht and plane to other clubs, first to be televised while en route to Fairbanks and first to play matches in forty states. Whimsically, they were first to play a tournament by gas light in modern times and first in the Western Hemisphere to hold a blindfold tournament. As for their heavy guns, they have won the championship of the country's strongest chess league (beating out the powerful Marshall Chess Club in New York City to do so) and have had on their membership list all classifications of U.S. champions, including the national,

open, amateur, women's, correspondence and junior. Even the bright face of danger has been stared down by the Cabineers, as on the occasion when they went on a hazardous trip of exploration to snow-capped mountains near Mexico City, almost losing one of their two motor cars during the journey.

Who is this almost legendary figure, Log Cabin chieftain E. Forry Laucks, the man with the vast enthusiasms, untrammeled imagination and passionate devotion to the cause of chess? Born back in 1898 [*sic*], he looks like a man in his forties, darkish, intense, ready at a moment's notice to laugh at himself and at any of life's ludicrous situations. Neatly balancing his social and business interests is his gift for art, as evidenced by the paintings which hang upon the walls of his home and which have been exhibited at the Montclair Art Museum, the Trenton Academy of Art, and the Art Center of the Oranges.

He was reared in York, Pennsylvania, as the son of a prominent industrialist and attended [Governor] Dummer Academy, Mercersburg Academy and Philips Exeter. He first took notice of chess when he was about nine years old and at eleven visited the Manhattan and Marshall Chess Clubs in New York City. During his boyhood, however, the game did not mean much to him, so that it was not until many years later that he began his checkered career (harmless pun intended) as player and impresario.

In 1933, four years after his marriage to Josephine Frances Lehmann, Laucks joined the West Orange YMCA Chess Club. As far as he was personally concerned, he immediately discovered a fatal flaw in the set-up — the relatively early closing time. To a born "night person" such as Forry, who is at his best at three or four in the morning, midnight is the signal for coming awake, not going to bed. Surely, reasoned Forry, there must be nocturnal chess players like himself.

Inspiration: Why not establish a haven for these kindred souls, irked as they are by regulations which absurdly put the need for slumber above the lure of Caissa? With Laucks, to get an idea is to act; so he went to work at once to create the world's liveliest chess club.

In a way, the Log Cabin's "club personality," if one may use this term, was just a happy mushroom growth; in another sense, it was the natural result of effort, planning and devotion. When the idea for a chess club first took root in Laucks' mind, the spacious basement of his residence at 30 Collamore Terrace in West Orange, New Jersey (he has another home at Old Lyme, Connecticut, where he lives with his wife and two children), seemed just the thing for his purpose. He wanted a comfortable, relaxing, "different" atmosphere; the answer was to transform his basement into a "log cabin" with furnishings to match. Here, in his own words, is what he sought to accomplish:

"[The clubhouse was to be] a log cabin that would be neither too palatial, as some wealthy clubmen's are, nor so poor and roughshod that it would lack comfort or a certain degree of refinement . . .

". . . I realized that everything, even to the wall decorations, furniture and utensils, had to be in keeping with the surroundings, or else just one piece out of place could spoil the effect of the whole . . . Therefore I made and designed all furniture just as if I were in the backwoods where there can be no machined, finished pieces."

When this labor of love was done, Laucks' chess-playing friends descended with a cry of joy upon the new chess club. Where else, indeed, could they find rooms whose main house rule came close to avoiding all rules and whose perfect playing conditions were not marred by orders of "lights out" and other intolerable interruptions of chess genius in the throes of creation? The first session, held on January 31, 1934, did not break up until 4 a.m. Subsequent meetings lasted till 5 a.m. or dawn or such time as Morpheus claimed his own.

Formal organization of the Log Cabin Chess Club took place on July 28, 1934, and resulted in the election of E. Forry Laucks as president. No constitution was drawn up at that time and none is in existence now; the club simply does not need this kind of machinery.

It did not take the Log Cabin long to become a rendezvous of champions, deep in tournaments and league matches. The greatest victory of all, duly celebrated at the Waldorf-Astoria Hotel in New York City, occurred when the Cabineers won the championship of the Metropolitan chess League of New York ahead of the famous Marshall Chess Club. Although the perennial champions of the Manhattan Chess Club were not competing that year (1948), many of the nation's strongest players took part in these matches, and the triumph of the Cabineers therefore took on epic proportions.

Not to be outdone in any sphere of operations, the Log Cabin claims to publish, and to be the subject of, more reading matter than any other chess club. In addition to a stream of letters, circulars, advertisements, and so forth, literature includes *Log Cabin Chess Divertises*, issued irregularly as a news bulletin, the book of the Log Cabin Chess Club Championship tournament of 1951, edited by A. N. Towsen, and *Selected Games from the Log Cabin Chess Club Spring Tournaments, 1957*, edited by Jack Spence. Titleholder of 1951 was Weaver W. Adams, while joint winners of the 1957 Log Cabin Independent Open were A. Feuerstein, G. Fuster, M. Green, A. E. Santasiere, and S. Wanetick. Among titles of the future books will be *Log Cabin Firsts* and *Tournament Games and Barnstorming Trips of the Log Cabin*. Spence is also preparing a book of Log Cabin games which will include scores taken from its first 1957 Morphy Centennial Tournament (played in Alabama!), on the occasion of which the Log Cabin donated a monument and plaque in honor of Morphy.

It is safe to predict that any little thing that Laucks and his merry men have not yet attended to will be taken care of in due time. Laucks himself, the center of all this ferment, is determinedly unobtrusive and unassuming, as player, as host and as pro-

moter. Thus, although strong enough to have defeated E. S. Jackson, Jr., in a New Jersey championship tournament, he grades himself as Class B and shrinks from having any of his winning scores included in Log Cabin publications "so people won't think this fellow Laucks is such hot stuff as a player." His hospitality has been likened to that of the Great Gatsby in Scott Fitzgerald's novel of the 1920s, except that Laucks entertains on a more modest scale and without benefit of a staff of servants. Chess players, after all, cannot be bothered with folderol when they are intent upon the serious business of stalking the opponent's King.

E. Forry Laucks (1897-1965)

The membership card of the Log Cabin Chess club, as might be expected, is a unique item. On the front are listed no less than three telephone numbers — standard, loudspeaker and mobile car. Underneath the name, "Log Cabin Chess Club," we read, "The most diversified, animated chess club in the Western Hemisphere." On the other side of the card is printed the club's motto:

"We are the Pioneers For the most animation. First here, first there, First most everywhere, We are ready, up and forward! Let's schusse! Log Cabineers!!!"

"Let's schusse," an expression of the Pennsylvania Dutch, is roughly translated as "Let's be up and doing." That just about sums up the club spirit. To return to our opening theme: if there is ever an interplanetary chess match, we know who will be first to face the extraterrestrials over the chessboard.

An ad for the club in *Chess Review* in August 1960 had the following capsule description of the Log Cabin's activities.

Champions of the N.Y. "Met" League 1948. Organized and founded the North Jersey Chess League and Inter-chess League. First to help in large scale inter-state matches. First to fly by air to Deep River Chess Club. First to promote largest international matches of 18 and 19 boards. First to make transcontinental and international barnstorming tours. Played interclub matches in 5 Mexican states, 5 Canadian provinces and all 49 United States but 5, to 1958. Visited 11 countries and flew by plane to 3 — all in 1958.

Fischer fans will remember that Bobby played in the 1965 Capablanca Memorial via phone and attended the Havana Olympiad the following year in person. However, that wasn't his first trip to Cuba. A decade earlier, he visited the Caribbean island as a member of the colorful E. Forry Lauck's Log Cabin Chess Club.

The name might suggest the club was formed in the 1800s in a rural town, but as we have just learned it was started back in 1934, a stone's throw from New York City in West Orange, New Jersey. Laucks (1897-1965) was an enthusiastic promoter. Besides running strong events at the club, which was located in his large basement, he also took to the road. The Log Cabin irregulars made trips to all corners of the United States, even making it to Alaska! This was more of an accomplishment than it might seem, as Laucks, who typically did much of the driving, had the disconcerting habit of taking his eye off the road and talking face to face with riders in the backseat — for minutes at a time!

Palo Alto master Art Wang remembers Laucks as a good-natured eccentric who was a real patron of the game. Wang, who played in a U.S. Junior organized by the Log Cabin, stayed as a guest at Laucks' home for a few weeks with fellow Northern California juniors.

Wang recalls that the Log Cabin was located in a very exclusive neighborhood in West Orange. Laucks' father, a very successful safe maker, passed on much of his wealth to his son while leaving his son's wild streak intact.

Laucks often took the California juniors out to dinner, but, when they dined at home, he had certain specific rules that had to be obeyed. For example, bananas were to be eaten only at breakfast with cereal which was to be consumed only with a soup spoon. Failure to comply with the rules wasn't tolerated.

Wang was witness to E. Forry's penchant for excessive speeding. Laucks loved to race his cars and would often try to outspeed pursuing police cars, a practice that kept his lawyer busy. During major cross-country trips it was not uncommon for Laucks to abandon a troubled car on the highway and buy a new vehicle in the next town.

One of the Log Cabin Club's bigger trips was a February 1956, 3500-mile junket that took in matches in Philadelphia; Miami, Tampa, St. Petersburg and Hollywood, Florida; Havana; and Clinton, North Carolina. Playing for the club besides Laucks and Fischer, were the infamous IM Norman T. Whitaker—then the director of the Washington Chess Divan, team captain Ted Miller of the Fool's Mate C.C. in Newark, Robert Houghton of the Public Service C.C. in Newark and E. R. Glover, President of the Franklin Mercantile Chess Club in Philadelphia.

Incidentally, the Franklin Mercantile holds an annual tournament to honor Glover's memory. Thanks to his generosity, it is one of two clubs in the United States (the Mechanics' Institute in San Francisco is the other) that are open seven days a week with nominal dues ($60 a year).

Ed Tassinari, writing in *Chessnotes* (Nº 1306), gives the most comprehensive coverage to the highlight of the Log Cabin Chess Club's 3,500-mile road trip, the visit to Cuba.

C.N. 1267 concerning Fischer's previously unpublished games, including one from his twelve-board simultaneous exhibition at the Capablanca Chess Club in Havana, shed a little light on an aspect of his career that remains fairly obscure. Several years ago I made a modest attempt to survey several Cuban publications for news and/or game scores of Fischer in Havana, with meager success. What I did find was basically this:

In his column in *El Mundo* (Havana), Carlos Palacio mentioned the presence of the U.S. visitors from the Log Cabin (N.J.) Chess Club (column of 26th February 1956). He noted that E. Forry Laucks had extended an invitation to Cuban players while they were in New York the previous November (participating in a match with the Marshall Chess Club). A reception was held on the afternoon of 25th February for the visitors, and during this the pairings were made for a team match which was held that night. He gave the results in his column, but with no game scores.

Log Cabin CC		Capablanca CC
1. Whitaker	1-0	Gonzalez
2. Fischer	1-0	Florido
3. Glover	0-1	Calero
4. Walbrecht	0-1	Cobo
5. Miller	0-1	Ortega
6. Houghton	0-1	Aleman
7. Laucks	0-1	Romero

The 28th February issue of *El Mundo* had a picture of Fischer giving the si-

Bobby giving a simul at the Capablanca CC in Havana

multaneous exhibition and in Palacio's chess column of the same date there is a picture of Fischer playing Jose A. Gelabert in a skittles encounter, together with a reference to an article that appeared in *Chess Review* for January 1956 (which was actually a reprint of a *New York Times* piece describing a Fischer simultaneous exhibition against twelve members of the Yorktown Chess Club (N.Y.) given at the Manhattan Chess Club in November 1955). A list of Fischer's opponents and the result of the 26th February simultaneous display are also given: Raimundo Plasencia, Sergey Pavol, Rogelio Ferrer, E. Houghton, E. Forry Laucks, Dr. Luis F. de Almagro, Antonio Higuera, Dr. Armando Bermudez, Alberto Reyes and Raul Martin all lost; Jose Arango Casado and Ramon Merendez Bermudez drew.

Unfortunately, no game scores were given by Palacio, nor in any of his columns for the following weeks. Mention of the Log Cabin aggregation was made by the then Cuban champion Dr.

Juan Gonzalez in his column (26th February 1956) which occasionally appeared in the *Diario de la Marina* (Havana). He gave the line-up for the team match, but nothing beyond what appeared in Palacio's column.

I also scanned several weeks of the *New York Times* for February and March 1956 in the hopes of locating something about the Log Cabin tour and/or Fischer's game scores; the only mention apparently was on 5th March 1956, p.26, which noted that the three-week Log Cabin Chess Club tour had ended; the team had played matches with Miami, Tampa, St. Petersburg and Hollywood, Florida, Clinton, North Carolina and Havana, with a result of twenty-three and a half to twenty-six and a half. It was noted that Norman Whitaker played first board for Log Cabin and won five, lost one and drew one. Fischer made exactly the same result on second board."

Here is the sole surviving example of Fischer's first trip to Cuba.

---

[12] *Sicilian   B32*
RJF–J. Casado
Havana (simul), February 26, 1956

1.e4 c5 2.♘f3 ♘c6 3.d4 cxd4 4.♘xd4
♘xd4 5.♕xd4 d6 6.c4 e5 7.♕d3 ♘f6
8.♘c3 ♗e6 9.♗g5 ♗e7 10.♗e2 a6
11.b3 O-O 12.O-O ♖e8 13.♖ad1 ♕a5
14.♖d2 ♖ac8 15.♗xf6 ♗xf6 16.
♖fd1 ♖ed8 17.♘d5?!

White throws away most of his advantage with the text.

17...♗xd5 18.♕xd5 ♕xd5 19.♖xd5
♗e7

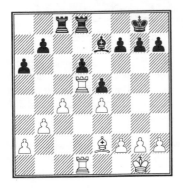

20.f3?!

This just blocks in the Bishop.

20...g6 21.c5?

Blundering a pawn.

21...♖c6?

Blundering right back. The position is still a draw after 21...♖xc5 (Bobby's idea must have been 21...dxc5 22. ♖xe5) 22.♖xc5 dxc5 23.♖xd8+ ♗xd8. Black's extra pawn gives him encouragement to play on, but White should be able to hold on without difficulty.

The primary source for this game, David Levy's *How Fischer Wins*, gives

the score as 21...♔g7 22.♔f2 ♖c6. This would mean that both players overlooked the simple 22.cxd6. We tend to think that the sequence given is more logical.

22.♔f2 ♔g7 23.g3 f6 24.f4 ♔f7 25. ♔e1 b5 26.b4 ♔e8 27.fxe5 dxc5 28.exf6 ♗xf6 29.bxc5 ♗e7 30.♖xd8+ ♗xd8 31.♖d6 ♖xd6 32. cxd6 ♗a5+ 33.♔d1 ♗b4 34.e5 ♗c3 35.e6 ♗e5 36.d7+ ♔e7 37.♗g4 ♗c7 38.♔c2 b4 39.♔d3 ♔f6 40.♔c4 a5 41.♔c5 h5 42.♗h3 g5 43.♔c6 ♗d8 44.♗g2 a4 45.♗d5 ♗a5 46.♔b7 a3 47.♔c8 ♔e7 48.♗c4 ♗d8 Draw

Besides Cuba, the other big stop for the Log Cabineers was Clinton, North Carolina. National Master Charles "Kit" Crittenden, one of the top players in the South in the 1950s, fondly recalls the match:

> Thanks for your inquiry about the match between the Log Cabin Chess Club and North Carolina, in 1956. That notable chess personality E. Forry Laucks was leader of the Log Cabin Team: "Forward Log Cabiners: Let's Schuss!"
>
> You are right about my status as a chess player in N.C. at the time: I was the highest rated player, having won the state chess championship several times by then. So I was #1 on the N.C. team. My opponent was not Bobby Fischer, #2 on the Log Cabin team, but Norman Whitaker! So I missed out on a chance to play Bobby Fischer because he was not ranked highly enough! I'd known of Bobby from my friends in New York City — I'd played in various U.S. Opens, & a U.S. Junior in Ft. Worth in 1949, and even been to N.Y. & played

chess there. I remember Bobby at the time — a gangly 12-year-old kid, in sneakers & (I think) a long-sleeved shirt of some kind. I asked him if he wanted to play some 5-minute chess, & he said OK, but somehow it never happened. Another lost opportunity!

Bobby played Al Jenkins, our #2, and won. Al has told me that he has many times looked for the score of their game, but has not been able to locate it. He's in his 70's now, going strong, and lives in Raleigh still.

Sometimes it happens that there are circumstances where I tell people that I won the N.C. Championship when I was 14 (in 1948). That sounds impressive. But then I tell them that Bobby Fischer won the U.S. Championship when he was 14!! That puts matters in perspective.

By the way, Larry Remlinger told me that on some occasion when they were both up & coming juniors, he played BF a lot of 5-minute chess, & they came out about even.

1956 U.S. Junior,
July 1-7 in Philadelphia

This was Fischer's first big breakthrough. He won his last round game versus David Kerman by an adjudication which took two hours of analysis by a panel of three referees. Arthur Feuerstein won the final of the U.S. Junior Blitz Championship. His score was 4.5 from five. Bobby was second at four, followed by William Lombardy at 3.5.

NM David Kerman, who still plays actively in the Los Angeles area, hasn't been able to find the game score for many years, but remembers that he was Black in a Winawer French and that the game was very close till the last few moves of the time control. The United States Chess Federation journal, *Chess Life*, which at that time appeared in newspaper format (11 by 8 1/2) with the banner *America's Chess Newspaper*, had the headline . . .

It's Fischer! In Junior

Setting a new record in the U.S. Junior Championship by winning the title at the age of 13 on his second try (Bobby placed 20th with a 5-5 score at Lincoln in 1955), Fischer becomes the youngest player to hold the U.S. Junior title. He has outdistanced two other players who also began their junior tournament careers at the age of 11— Ross Siemms and Larry Remlinger.

Siemms began his career in the Junior at Cleveland in 1947, placing fifth, placed second on S-B at Milwaukee in 1950 (losing the title to James Cross) and did not win the U.S. Junior title until Long Beach in 1954 after six attempts. Larry Remlinger placed eighth (winning the Dittmann Trophy for contestants under 15) in his first appearance in Kansas City in 1953. He placed second in 1954 at Long Beach and second again at Lincoln in 1955, but has yet to win the coveted title; he was not a contender this year.

The Eleventh Annual U.S. Junior Championship began auspiciously at Philadelphia with 28 participants, representing Canada, Texas, New York, Pennsylvania, California, Rhode Island, Michigan, Wisconsin, Illinois, New Jersey and Massachusetts. It was held at the Franklin Mercantile Chess Club with Bill Ruth as tournament director, assisted by D. A. Giangiulio.

1. R. Fischer	8.5-1.5
2. C. Henin	8-2
3. Feuerstein	8-2
4. S. Geller	7-3
5. G. Baylor	6-4
6. T. Levine	6-4

Bill Whisler writes in the April 1999 issue of Chess Life:

Bobby and I met in the 1955 U.S. Junior where we played to a draw. After the 1956 U.S. Junior we both went to the U.S. Open in Oklahoma City. I found a ride with someone and invited Bobby to come along with us. All I recall is that we were in a big luxury car, got to know each other better and had interesting conversations. It was a nice friendly trip and the last time I talked with him.

---

[13] *King's Indian Sämisch E87*
William Whisler–RJF
U.S. Junior Open, Philadelphia 1956

1.d4 ♘f6 2.c4 g6 3.♘c3 ♗g7 4.e4 d6 5.f3 O-O 6.♗e3 e5 7.d5 ♘h5 8.♕d2 f5 9.O-O-O f4 10.♗f2 ♗f6 11.♘ge2 ♗h4

This old-fashioned line, where Black tries to blockade the kingside, was Fischer's first favorite against the Sämisch.

12.♗g1 ♘d7

12...g5? 13.c5! g4 14.♘c1 gxf3 15. gxf3 ♘a6 16.c6! gave White a large advantage in Petrosian–Gligoric, Zurich 1953. Another try for Black is 12...b6, intending 13...a5. White is a little better in this line, but it's not easy to break through.

13.♔b1 ♗e7 14.♘c1 c5

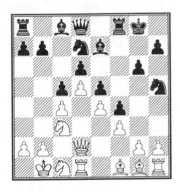

Bobby may have been influenced by Geller–Gligoric, Zurich 1953, which continued 14...♘c5 15. ♘d3 ♘xd3 16.♗xd3 ♗d7 17.♗c2 ♕e8 18.♗f2 a6 19.♖c1 ♔h8 with equal chances. A year after this game with Whisler, Bobby tried 14...♔h8 against the East Coast master Herbert Avram in a Log Cabin tournament, but was defeated in fine style – 15.♘d3 a6 16.♕c2 ♖f7 17.♘e2 ♕f8 18.♕c3 g5 19.c5! dxc5 20.h4 ♖g7 21.hxg5 ♖xg5 22.♖xh5! ♖xh5 23.♘exf4 and 1-0 in 43.

A recent attempt to rehabilitate this system for Black was seen in M. Gurevich–P. H. Nielsen, Taastrup 1992, but White was better after 14...♘hf6 15. g3 c5 16.♗h3 ♘b6 17. ♗xc8 ♕xc8 18.♕e2.

15.♗d3

An alternative plan was 15.dxc6 bxc6 16.♘b3, intending 17.c5.

15...♘df6 16.♘1e2 ♘e8 17.♖f1 a6 18.g4 ♘hf6 19.h4 h6 20.♘c1

This allows Black to keep the kingside closed. If White wants to have play on that side of the board, he has to sacrifice a pawn with 20.g5.

20...♘d7 21.h5 g5 22.♔c2

White would like to put his King on g2 and then play b2-b4, but he doesn't have the time to do this, as Black is ready to play ...b7-b5.

22...♘c7 23.♘b3

This clumsy-looking move blocks the break b2-b4, but allows White to answer 23...b5 with 24.♘a5, heading to c6.

23...♘f6 24.♕e2 ♗d7 25.♗f2 ♕e8 26.♖b1 b5 27.♘d2 bxc4 28.♘xc4
and eventually **0-1**

On this position Bill Whisler writes:

The final moves are missing — White eventually lost. I assume the last move was 28...♗b5 or 28...♘b5 instead of 28...♘c5 as I recorded on my scoresheet. I lost be-

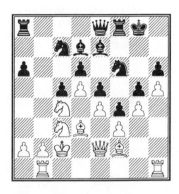

cause of a blunder (he forked my King and Queen, most likely with the Knight on d4), not because of some deep positional plan. Probably I was so upset with my own stupidity that I didn't bother to write down the last few moves, which may be the reason it never appeared in print. I hoped that over the years I might have a sudden 'flash' and remember what happened but, so far, no luck.

Source: *Chess Life*, April 1999, p. 16

U.S. Open, Oklahoma City July 16-28, 1956

Bobby Fischer, 13, who recently won the U.S. Junior Chess Championship at Philadelphia, continues as the center of attraction for the spectators and newspaper men. The brilliant Brooklyn youngster has been on two television programs and his portrait was featured by the local press. Bobby chews gum continuously, is a Dodger fan, likes Elvis Presley, and seems completely

unaffected by all the publicity he is getting. Unlike most chess prodigies, his manners are excellent. He has been playing chess for about seven years.

Mainly for publicity reasons, Bobby Fischer was paired in the first round with A. M. Swank of Oklahoma City, who is 78 years old and boasts a long, flowing beard. Mr. Swank was no match for the Junior Champion who is

Bobby (left) and Edmar Mednis play the last round of the Canadian Open. Mednis, who had the same score as Bobby in the 1956 U.S. Open, finished a half point ahead of him in Montreal.

playing with the strength of a master and has not lost a single game in nine rounds. His score of 6 points includes a win over Dr. Lapiken, California master, and draws with New York masters Santasiere and Owen. In the first eight rounds, all of Bobby's opponents, except Swank, were rated masters or experts. In the ninth round, Bobby was paired with Dale Ruth of Midwest City, Oklahoma, the most promising of the young local players. Ruth set a trap for Bobby, but it boomeranged and cost the Oklahoma player the game.

Source: 1956 U.S. Open bulletin

The twelve-round Swiss was won by Arthur Bisguier with a score of 9.5. James Sherwin, who had the same score, lost out on tiebreaks. Bobby and Anthony Saidy, who tied for fourth-seventh at 8.5, stayed at the

home of Dr. Ernest Gill, a former Oklahoma state champion.

Bobby next traveled to Montreal, Quebec, where he played in the first Canadian Open. The 88-player, ten-round Swiss, held August 30-September 2, was won on tiebreaks by Larry Evans over William Lombardy, both of whom scored 8-2. Bobby ended up in eighth-twelfth at 7-3 and, before leaving Canada, he gave a simul in Montreal on September 5, scoring +18 =1-0.

The following article by NM Allen Kaufman, now the director of the Chess-in-the-Schools program, gives an idea of how far Bobby had come in the past nine months. It appeared in *Chess Review* toward the end of 1956.

Chess Life in New York

Having returned from Washington D.C. with equal second prize in his pocket, Bobby Fischer resumed his rapid transit play at the Manhattan Chess Club with a victory in the weekly event. In Washington he tied with Rossolimo, Lombardy, Feuerstein, etc., behind Berliner. In New York he won the rapids ahead of local masters. Bobby has definitely arrived.

His style of play is difficult to describe. His moves are confident and aggressive. In the Rosenwald tournament he displayed tactical brilliance (vs. Byrne) as well as the ability to "kvetch" out a positional game (vs. Seidman).

His manner of kibitzing is clearer. All his opponent's moves are blunders, "Bobby keel!" he shouts. "Look at that move," he exclaims. "Boy is he weak!" But don't believe that Bobby is anything but a nice kid; his kibitzes are all in fun.

Away from the board, Bobby (known to his chess friends as "Baby Fuscher") is quite like other thirteen year olds. He is a Rock and Roll fan ("I like music with the Big Beat") and loves comic books and cookies. Witches scare him more than a powerful Kingside attack.

Rumor says he may play at Hastings in the Christmas tourney. He is a master player, and afraid of no one. Watch his results!

Third Lessing J. Rosenwald Trophy Tournament – New York, Oct.-Nov. 1956

This was a very impressive debut for 13-year-old Bobby, who showed he could hold his own with the best players in the country. This was the tournament in which he played his "Game of he Century" against Donald Byrne.

Bobby wasn't the only surprise. Arthur Feuerstein, who had drawn with Bobby in the U.S. Junior in Philadelphia during the summer, was outstanding, scoring plus two. The report in the December 5, 1956, issue of *Chess Life* says he would have finished second if he had not weakened in a favorable game against Edmar Mednis. The *Chess Life* reporter, Master Harold Sussman, described Feuerstein as fearless and original. Feuerstein was a member of the 1957 U.S. Student Team in Iceland and the first master scalp for a young Joel Benjamin!

Also scoring well was Abe Turner, who was heading toward a high prize until his fiascoes against Bisguier and Reshevsky in the last two rounds. Turner was a well-liked chess pro who spent Monday through Friday earning his keep as a chess hustler, and weekends writing plays.

One of the few players with a lifetime plus record against Bobby (two wins and a draw in 1956-57), Turner was also instrumental in helping Larry Evans early in his career. His life was senselessly ended when he was stabbed to death by fellow *Chess Review* employee Theodore Smith, who had been

Abe Turner vs. Bobby at the 1957 Rosenwald, which served as the U.S. Championship

released from a mental asylum only a few years before.

GM Larry Evans, in a heart-felt appreciation in *Chess Life*, December 1962 (p.281), pointed out the true absurdity of his death.

Never really in financial difficulty because of his numerous friends and chess students — "clients" as he called them — Abe did not need the income or respectability of a job. One can only wish that he had remained jobless, even

	1	2	3	4	5	6	7	8	9	10	11	12	
1. Sammy Reshevsky	♖	1	½	1	1	0	1	1	½	1	1	1	9.0
2. Arthur Bisguier	0	♖	½	½	0	½	1	1	1	½	1	1	7.0
3. Arthur Feuerstein	½	½	♖	0	1	0	0	½	1	1	1	1	6.5
4. Edmar Mednis	0	½	1	♖	1	1	1	½	½	0*	½	0	6.0
5. Sidney Bernstein	0	1	0	0	♖	1	0	½	1	½	1	½	5.5
6. Donald Byrne	1	½	1	0	0	♖	1	0	0	1	0	1	5.5
7. Abe Turner	0	0	1	0	1	0	♖	1	0	1	1	½	5.5
8. Robert Fischer	0	0	½	½	½	1	0	♖	1	0	½	½	4.5
9. Hebert Seidman	½	0	0	½	0	1	1	0	♖	0	½	1	4.5
10. Eliot Hearst	0	½	0	0*	½	0	0	1	1	♖	0	1	4.0
11. Max Pavey	0	0	0	½	0	1	0	½	½	1	♖	½	4.0
12. George Shainswit	0	0	0	1	½	0	½	½	0	0	½	♖	3.0

* The double loss for Mednis and Hearst is not a mistake. It was a double forfeit. Hearst overstepped at move 40 and Mednis had quit keeping score. According to the rules of the time, both players got a zero!

to endure the taunts of "chess bum." It is ironic, but had he not taken that fatal job he would be alive right now."

According to the tournament report, Eliot Hearst was under the psychological handicap of having just finished his Master's thesis and of preparing for the Armed Forces. Hearst, who is now a Professor of Psychology at Columbia University, has a fifty percent lifetime score against Bobby, but is the first to admit that his timing was good. "Of course, I played him hundreds of games, starting with my giving him Queen or Rook odds and ending up in the 1960s with our playing blitz with me having 4½ minutes and him 1½ minutes. We were about even at those odds."

Bobby analyzing at the Manhattan CC during the Rosewald tournament. Seated are (l-r) Bill Lombardy and Manhattan CC President Morris J. Kasper. Edward Lasker, President of the Marshall CC, is standing.

1957
The Big Breakthrough

Bobby started off 1957 slowly, but had an incredible summer, metamorphosing from promising master to one of the country's best. In autumn, he made the jump from one of the country's best to national champion!

Fischer played very little during the first half of 1957, probably because of school, but did tie for sixth-fourteenth at 4-2 in the 61-player Log Cabin Independent Open, held February 22-24. His losses were to Herbert Avram and Anthony Santasiere.

Here is one example of how fast Fischer was improving. On June 13, 1957, the Manhattan Chess Club celebrated its victory in the Met League by holding a special exhibition by Reshevsky. He played blindfold against ten strong players, one after another, at ten seconds a move. He won six (from Gresser, Guala, Rowe, Saxon and Shipman) and lost four (Heitner,

Bisguier, Feuerstein and Fischer). Less than six months later, Bobby was national champion and not taking odds from anyone!

---

[14] *King's Indian Classical   E91*
Samuel Reshevsky (blindfolded)–RJF
New York (10 sec./move) 1957

1.c4 ♘f6 2.♘c3 g6 3.♘f3 ♗g7 4.d4 O-O 5.e4 d6 6.♗e2 c6 7.O-O a6 8.♖e1 b5 9.b3 b4 10.e5 dxe5 11.dxe5 bxc3 12.exf6 ♗xf6 13.♗h6 ♕xd1 14.♖axd1 ♖e8 15.♗d3 ♘d7 16.♗e4 ♘c5 17.♗xc6 ♗f5 18.g4 ♗xg4 19.♔g2 ♗f5 20.♗xa8 ♖xa8 21.♘d4 ♘d3 22.♘xf5 ♘xe1+ 23.♖xe1 gxf5 24.♖d1 e5 25.c5 ♖c8 26.b4 f4 27.♔f3 ♗e7 28.♔e4 ♖c6 29.♖g1+ ♖g6 30.♖xg6+ fxg6 31.♔d3 ♔f7 32.♔xc3 g5 33.c6 ♔e6 34.♔c4 ♔d6 35.b5 axb5+ 36.♔xb5 e4 37.♔c4 ♗f6 38. h4 f3 39.hxg5 e3 40.♗f8+ ♗e7 41. ♗xe7+ ♔xe7 42.c7 ♔d7 0-1

U.S. Junior 1957

The newspaper *Chess Life* reported on the U.S. Junior, held July 8-14 in San Francisco, in its August 5, 1957, issue.

U.S. Junior to Fischer!

The Brooklyn master junior (or junior master) Robert Fischer gathered in the U.S. Junior title in stride at San Francisco with an 8½-½ score, drawing one game with California State Champion Gilbert Ramirez of San

Bobby gets his first place trophy from a representative of Spreckels Russell Dairy

Francisco, who placed second with 7½-1½, losing no games, but drawing with Richard Owen of Salt Lake City and Ronald Thacker of Richmond in addition to Fischer. Stephen Sholomson of Los Angeles, who has recently shot into prominence on the Pacific Coast, was third with 6½-2½, losing to Fischer and Ramirez, and drawing with Leonard Hill of Mt. View. Thacker was fourth with 6-3, losing to Fischer and Hill, while drawing with Ramirez and Ralph Clark of Long Beach.

Fifth to tenth on Median points with 5½-3½ each were Mike Bredoff of Redwood City, Leonard Hill, Arthur Wang of Berkeley, Ralph Clark, Robert Walker of Portland and Warren Miller of Albuquerque. Eleventh to fourteenth with 5-4 each were Rex Wilcox of Salinas, Andrew Schoene of Malaga, Thomas Heldt Jr. of Albuquerque and David Krause of Palo Alto.

Fred Wreden, aged 10, of San Francisco, won custody of the Independent-Press Telegraph Trophy for ranking players under 13 years; the Milwaukee Journal Independent Press Telegram Trophy for ranking players under 15 and the Hermann Dittman Trophy all went to 14-year-old Bobby Fischer.

In all, 33 juniors contested in the 9-round Swiss event directed by International Master George Koltanowski, held at the Spreckels Russell Dairy Co. auditorium in San Francisco. While most of these were Californians, there was one from Brooklyn, N.Y. (Fischer), one from Texas (James Bennett), one from Kansas (Howard Killough, Jr.), one from New Jersey (Andrew Schoene), one from Oregon (Robert Walker), one from Utah (Richard Owen) and two from New Mexico (Warren Miller and Thomas Heldt Jr.). California was ably represented by Ramirez and Sholomson, although, unfortunately, Larry Remlinger could not participate.

With George and Leah Kotanowski arranging matters, there was considerable outside activity for the players when they could be pried from the chessboards, including an evening as guests of the Fox Theater seeing the newest Pat Boone picture. Their hosts, the Spreckels Russell Dairy Co., served them chocolate milk and ice cream daily.

One of Bobby's victims in the tournament, Bill Haines of Vallejo, California, remembers that Fischer showed the other players in the tournament endgame studies. Here is one that he still remembers over forty years later.

U.S. Junior Championship

San Francisco, California   **8-14 July 1957**

		1	2	3	4	5	6	7	8	9	
1. Robert Fischer	Brooklyn, NY	+19	+12	+4	+16	=2	+3	+5	+9	+6	**8.5**
2. Gilbert Ramirez	San Francisco, CA	=20	+18	+9	+3	=1	+6	+16	+8	=4	**7.5**
3. Stephen Sholomson	Santa Monica, CA	+22	+7	+14	-2	+24	-1	+12	=6	+5	**6.5**
4. Ronald Thacker	Richmond, CA	+29	+15	-1	-6	+28	=8	+17	+16	=2	**6.0**
5. Mike Bredoff	Redwood City, CA	-14	+20	+28	+11	=7	+10	-1	+12	-3	**5.5**
6. Leonard Hill	Mountain View, CA	+27	-11	+23	+4	+16	-2	+7	=3	-1	**5.5**
7. Arthur Wang	Berkeley, CA	+31	-3	+26	+9	=5	-12	-6	+18	+13	**5.5**
8. Ralph Clark	Long Beach, CA	+30	=26	-19	+22	=10	=4	+14	-2	+20	**5.5**
9. Robert Walker	Portland, OR	+17	+13	-2	-7	+29	+11	+24	-1	=10	**5.5**
10. Warren Miller	Albuquerque, NM	+28	-16	=22	+26	=8	-5	+27	+15	=9	**5.5**
11. Rex Wilcox	Salinas, CA	+33	+6	-16	-5	+21	-9	=13	+17	=12	**5.0**
12. Andrew Schoene	Malaga, NJ	+21	-1	+29	+14	+19	+7	-3	-5	=11	**5.0**
13. Thomas Heldt Jr.	Albuquerque, NM	+23	-9	-15	+33	=17	+26	=11	+19	-7	**5.0**
14. David Krause	Palo Alto, CA	+5	+X	-3	=12	=15	=24	-8	+23	=16	**5.0**
15. Leighton Allen	San Francisco, CA	bye	-4	+13	-24	=14	=28	+21	-10	=19	**4.5**
16. William Haines	Sacramento, CA	+25	+10	+11	-1	-6	+19	-2	-4	=14	**4.5**
17. Robert Dickinson	Redwood City, CA	-9	+21	-24	+23	=13	+20	-4	-11	+26	**4.5**
18. Fred Wreden	San Francisco, CA	=32	-2	-20	-21	+30	+22	+29	-7	+24	**4.5**
19. James Bennett	Fort Worth, TX	-1	+27	+8	+32	-12	-16	+28	-13	=15	**4.5**
20. Richard Owen	Salt Lake City, UT	=2	-5	+18	-29	+22	-17	+26	+24	-8	**4.5**
21. Howard Killough Jr.	Russell, KS	-12	-17	+25	+18	-11	+23	-15	=27	+X	**4.5**
22. Ivan Vegvary	San Francisco, CA	-3	+X	=10	-8	-20	-18	+25	+31	+30	**4.5**
23. William Lee	San Francisco, CA	-13	bye	-6	-17	+25	-21	+30	-14	+31	**4.0**
24. James Schmerl	Piedmont, CA	-26	+30	+17	+15	-3	=14	-9	-20	-18	**3.5**
25. Don Sutherland	San Francisco, CA	-16	-29	-21	+31	-23	bye	-22	=30	+27	**3.5**
26. John Blackstone	San Jose, CA	+24	=8	-7	-10	+X	-13	-20	+28	-17	**3.5**
27. Allan Haley	Nevada City, NV	-6	-19	+31	-28	+X	+29	-10	=21	-25	**3.5**
28. Ray Hoppe	San Francisco, CA	-10	=31	-5	+27	-4	=15	-19	-26	bye	**3.5**
29. David Bogdanoff	Redwood City, CA	-4	+25	-12	+20	-9	-27	-18	bye	-F	**3.0**
30. Bruce Pohoriles	Larkspur, CA	-8	-24	-33	bye	-18	+31	-23	=25	-22	**2.5**
31. Jonathan Krug	San Rafael, CA	-7	=28	-27	-25	bye	-30	+X	-22	-23	**2.0**
32. Steve Joplin	Oakland, CA	=18	-F	bye	-19	-F	—	-F	—	—	**1.5**
33. Lincoln Fong	San Francisco, CA	-11	-F	+30	-13	-F	—	—	—	—	**1.0**

1.♘e7+ ♚h7 2.g6+ ♚h8 3.♔b4 e2 4.♔c5 e1=♕ 5.♔d6 **Draw,** as a lone Queen can't give checkmate.

Bobby watches Ramirez (left) vs. Thacker

Bobby Fischer Becomes Youngest Player To Win U.S. Open Championship event

At 14 years, Bobby Fischer, Erasmus High student of Brooklyn, becomes the youngest master to win the U.S. Open title. Fischer scored 10-2 in a games-won tie with U.S. Champion Arthur Bisguier, but gained the title on adjusted tie-breaking points, with Bisguier placing second. Donald Byrne, recent winner of the New Western Open, who was a strong contender throughout the race, finished in third place with 9½-2½.

Tied for fourth with 9-3 were Walter Shipman, Robert Byrne (Donald's older brother), Edmar Mednis and Anthony Santasiere. Scoring 8½-3½ were Anthony F. Saidy, Paul Brandts and J. Theodorovitch of Toronto, while 8-4 scores were compiled by Hans Berliner, Attilio di Camillo, Morton Siegel, Orest Popovych, Gerald Fielding of Re-

gina and William G. Addison. Scores of 7½-4½ were attained by Victor Guala, John W.Collins and Dr. Erich W. Marchand.

The event, which drew 175 players from 23 states, the District of Columbia, Mexico and Canada, was a thriller from the start. Donald Byrne climbed into the lead, showing the form that had won him the U.S. Open title in Milwaukee in 1953. But in the ninth round, Byrne suffered his first defeat from Bobby Fischer, and the loss catapulted Fischer into first place with 8-1 (no losses), while Donald Byrne dropped into a second place tie with his brother Robert.

Round ten, however, saw Donald Byrne climb to share the lead with Fischer, as Byrne defeated Walter Shipman, while Fischer was drawing with

Robert Byrne. This gave Donald Byrne and Fischer 8.5-1.5 each, while Robert and Bisguier were close on their heels with 8-2. Still in contention with 7.5-2.5 each were Addison, Saidy, Guala, Siegel, Mednis and Shipman. Round eleven saw the two leaders retain their place at the top, as Bobby beat Addison and Donald defeated Saidy, but the final day of the competition saw Bisguier beat Byrne, while Bobby drew with Shipman.

Bobby was declared the winner on tiebreak, which produced some hard feelings, but he clearly faced stronger opposition than Bisguier who had lost

to Addison in round six. Fischer drew with his co-winner, R. Byrne and Shipman, while beating D. Byrne, Mednis and Addison! The two winners each received $750 for their efforts.

Source: *Chess Life* 1956

Game anthologies give eleven of Bobby's twelve games from Cleveland. They will never find the last one, because Bobby won his first game on forfeit when H. Kemperer of Montreal, Canada, failed to appear (he didn't show up for subsequent rounds either).

Summer and Fall

Bobby completed a highly successful summer by winning the New Jersey Open over Labor Day Weekend. His 6½-½, included a draw with Dr. Ariel Mengarini, and earned him $125. In September, Fischer played an eight-game match with Filipino junior champion Rodolfo Cardoso, winning 6-2. Cardoso's second was future FIDE President Florencio Campomanes.

The notes by Fischer to the last game of the match come from the little-known, but excellent, *Leaves of Chess*, which appeared in the late 1950s and early 1960s.

[15] *Reti* A07
RJF–Rodolfo Cardoso
New York (8) 1957

1.♘f3

After seven Sicilians, with the last two drawn, I thought it was timely to change the opening.

1...♘f6 2.g3 d5 3.♗g2 ♗f5 4.0-0 e6 5.d3 ♗d6

The Bishop is misplaced on this square. Better was 5...♗e7.

6.♘bd2 h6?

Due to misplacement of the Bishop, Black has no time for this move.

7.e4!

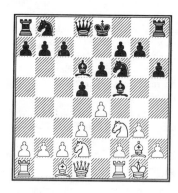

Careless playing of the opening by Black gives White unexpected

opportunities. For example, if 7...
dxe4 8.dxe4 ♘xe4 9.♘xe4 ♗xe4
10.♕d4, and White regains the
pawn with advantage.

7...♗g4

This is the only alternative to
7...dxe4, on account of the threat of
8.e5.

8.h3 ♗xf3 9.♘xf3 ♘bd7

If 9...dxe4 10.dxe4 ♘xe4 11.
♘d4 ♘c5 (11...f5 12.♘xe6) 12.
b4 wins.

**10.♕e2 dxe4 11.dxe4 ♗c5 12.e5 ♘d5
13.c4 ♘e7 14.♗d2 ♘f5 15.♔h2 c6**

Trying to strengthen himself on
the white squares, he weakens himself on the black ones. 15...a5 was
better.

16.b4 ♗e7 17.♗c3

Overprotecting e5, and making
way for the attack on the gaping
hole at d6.

17...g5?

In desperation at the unfolding
of White's plan, Black is dreaming of
an attack of his own on the kingside.

18.♘d2 ♕c7 19.♘e4 ♖g8

19...♘xe5 loses a piece after 20.
f4. White would also do well after
20.♘xg5.

20.c5 ♔f8

20...♘xe5 loses a piece after 21.
♘d6+

21.♘d6 b6

Black now weakens himself on
the White squares as well, while he is
thinking of trying to dislodge the
Knight. Meanwhile, White is not

planning to use the Knight for a
bind, but a breakthrough.

22.♘xf5! exf5 23.e6!

A crushing blow. Black's whole
center is demolished, and with all
White's pieces in play he can hardly
hope to survive.

23...♗f6 24.♖ad1 ♘e5 25.♖fe1

Black fights back gamely, but
this puts an end to his defensive resources.

**25...♘g4+ 26.hxg4 ♗xc3 27.♖d7
♕c8 28.♖xf7+ ♔e8 29.♖ed1**

29.♕d3 also wins, but I have
found that over the board it is better
not to make unnecessary sacrifices.

**29...♖g7 30.♖xg7 ♗xg7 31.gxf5 ♔f8
32.e7+ 1-0**

Reprinted with permission of *Leaves of
Chess*, July-October 1957, page 19
(Folios 4+5).

Fischer–Beninson

This is the most obscure of all
Bobby's matches. Fischer mentions it
in *Bobby Fischer's Chess Games*, giving the score as 3.5-1.5 in his favor.

Wade and O'Connell give September
of 1957 as the date and the Marshall
Chess Club as the likely venue.
Bobby's opponent, Dr. Daniel Benin-

son, an Argentine who worked at the United Nations for the Atomic Energy Commission, was a master-strength player.

Thanks to Michael "Mig" Greengard, who recently spoke with Beninson, we can add the following.

It was a training match, apparently one of several arranged for Fischer around this time. Neither player was paid. Beninson was one of the stronger players in the Manhattan CC and was friends with others like Lombardy. He also puts the score at 3.5-1.5, Fischer. He doesn't remember the progressive score, but is almost sure he didn't win any games. He said it was obvious to all that Fischer was going to be a star, that he

was something special. He described him as "terribly strong" by then.

They did stay in touch, Fischer's mother even calling ahead to ask Beninson to "take care" of Bobby while he was here on his first trip. Beninson is pretty sure that he talked with Fischer on each of his trips* minus his recent 1996 visit to promote FischerRandom.

Beninson is currently the president of the "Autoridad Regularia Nuclear." He almost never plays anymore, though he is familiar with most of the top Argentine players from his era (Sanguinetti, Najdorf, etc.).

* Fischer visited Argentina for chess in 1959, 1960, 1970, 1971 and 1996.

Bobby's First U.S. Championship 1957/58

This was Fischer's first game in his first U.S. Championship, which he won at the age of 14.

[16] *King's Indian Attack A08*
RJF–NM Arthur Feuerstein
U.S. Championship (1) 1957/58

Notes by Fischer from *Bobby Fischer's Games of Chess* and authors **(A)**.
1.e4 c5 2.♘f3 e6 3.g3 ♘f6 4.d3 d5 5. ♘bd2 ♗e7 6.♗g2 O-O 7.O-O ♘c6 8.♖e1 ♕c7 9.♕e2 ♖d8

Better is 9...♗d7. Then if 10.e5 ♘e8; followed by 11...f6.

(A) Better is 9...b5.

10.e5

(A) This is the key move in this type of position (when Black places his

pawns on d5 and e6). The pawn on e5 cuts Black's position in half and makes it difficult to maneuver the pieces between the queenside and kingside.

10...♘e8 11.c3

If immediately 11.♘f1, then 11...♘d4 12.♕d1 (12.♘xd4 cxd4 and Black has good play on the c-file) 12...♗d7 13.c3 ♘xf3+ 14. ♕xf3 ♗c6 or 14...b5 with a good game for Black.

11...b5

On the right path.

12.♘f1 b4 13.♗f4

Overprotecting the KP. Preventing ...f6 and preparing a King-side attack.

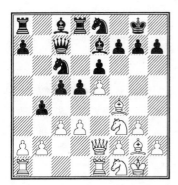

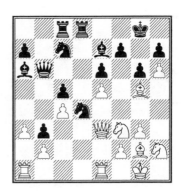

13...♕a5?

A strategic mistake. Correct is 13...bxc3 14.bxc3 ♖b8. As played, Black does not obtain enough play on the queenside to counterbalance White's coming attack on the other wing.

14.c4! ♘c7

Where is the Knight going?

15.h4

The key move to White's attack. White's plan is to (a) advance the h-pawn to h6, forcing a weakness at f6; (b) maneuver a Knight to g4; (c) trade off Black's KB. The outcome of the game depends on the execution of this plan.

15...♕b6 16.h5 b3

With the idea of artificially isolating White's c-pawn.

17.a3 dxc4 18.dxc4 ♗a6

Better is 18...♗b7 followed by 19...♘d4.

19.♘1h2 ♖ac8 20.h6 g6 21.♗g5 ♘d4

(A) A better try is 21...♗xg5 22. ♘xg5 ♘d4 23.♕e3 ♘f5 24.♕f4 ♖d4 25.♘g4 ♘e8 (not 25...♖xf4 26. ♘f6+ ♔f8 27.♘d7+) 26.♖e4 ♗xc4.

22.♕e3

22...♗xg5

If 22...♘c2, then 23.♕f4 with an overpowering attack.

23.♕xg5 ♘e8

Reinforcements. If 24...♗xc4, then 25.♘g4 with a strong attack.

24.♘g4 ♘f5 25.♖ac1 ♕c7 26.♘d2

(A) This Knight threatens both to take the b-pawn and to move to e4, aiming at the f6 square.

26...♖d4

If instead 26...♕b6, then 27. ♘e4 (threatening ♘gf6+, and Black's Queen is too far away to defend the kingside.

27.♘xb3 ♖xc4 28.♖cd1 ♖a4

(A) If 28...♖c2, then 29.♗e4 ♖xb2 30.♘f6+ or if 28...♕e7, then 29. ♕xe7 ♘xe7 30.♘e3 ♖a4 31.♖d7, winning. Possibly Black should try 28...♕b6 29.♘d2 ♖d4 30.♘f3 ♖xd1 31.♖xd1 ♕xb2.

29.♖e4!

With the indirect plan of dislodging Black's Knight on f5.

This brings White's Knight into the game with decisive effect. There is no adequate defense against 32. ♜xa4 and 33.♞e4.

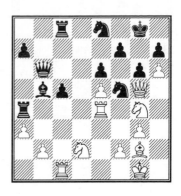

29...♝b5

(A) Black's best hope to hang on was 31...c4.

30.♜c1

In order to draw Black's Queen away from the defense of the kingside.

30...♛b6 31.♞d2

31...♜xe4 32.♞xe4 ♝d3

Loses flatly. The only way to avoid immediate disaster is 32...

U.S. Championship 1957/58

		1	2	3	4	5	6	7	8	9	10	11	12	13	14	
1.	**Robert Fischer**	♔	½	1	1	½	½	1	1	½	1	1	1	½	1	**10.5**
2.	**Sammy Reshevsky**	½	♔	0	0	1	1	1	½	1	½	1	1	1	1	**9.5**
3.	**James Sherwin**	0	1	♔	½	½	1	0	½	½	1	1	1	1	1	**9.0**
4.	**William Lombardy**	0	1	½	♔	½	½	½	½	0	1	0	1	1	1	**7.5**
5.	**Hans Berliner**	½	0	½	½	♔	0	0	½	½	1	1	1	½	1	**7.0**
6.	**Arnold Denker**	½	0	0	½	1	♔	0	1	½	0	1	0	1	1	**6.5**
7.	**Arthur Feuerstein**	0	0	1	½	1	1	♔	½	1	0	0	½	½	½	**6.5**
8.	**Edmar Mednis**	0	½	½	½	½	0	½	♔	0	1	½	½	1	1	**6.5**
9.	**Herbert Seidman**	½	0	½	1	½	½	0	1	♔	0	1	0	1	0	**6.0**
10.	**Sydney Bernstein**	0	½	0	0	0	1	1	0	1	♔	0	1	½	0	**5.0**
11.	**Arthur Bisguier**	0	0	0	1	0	0	1	½	0	1	♔	½	0	1	**5.0**
12.	**Atillio Di Camillo**	0	0	0	0	0	1	½	½	1	0	½	♔	0	1	**4.5**
13.	**Abe Turner**	½	0	0	0	½	0	½	0	0	½	1	1	♔	½	**4.5**
14.	**George Kramer**	0	0	0	0	0	0	½	0	1	1	0	0	½	♔	**3.0**

♕d8 33.♕xd8 ♖xd8 34.♖xc5, with an easy endgame win.

33.♘gf6+ ♔h8

If 33...♘xf6, then 34.♘xf6+ ♔h8 35.g4 ♘d4 36.♘e4 ♕d8 37.♖xc5, winning.

34.g4 ♗xe4 35.♗xe4 ♘d4 36.♘xe8 ♕d8 37.♕xd8 ♖xd8 38.♘d6 ♘e2+ 39.♔f1 ♘xc1

see diagram adjacent

40.♘xf7+ ♔g8 41.♘xd8 ♘b3 42. ♔e2 ♘d4+ 43.♔d3 ♔f8 44.♘c6 1-0

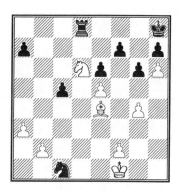

T.V. Chess

On May 11, 1958, WNTA (Channel 13) had a live telecast of Bobby Fischer playing 13 opponents simultaneously. When he did not finish in the allotted time, the station allowed the games to be played to a conclusion by delaying the next program for a few minutes. Fischer scored +12=1–0, with the lone draw going to Walter Harris.

[17] *Danish Gambit Declined C21*
RJF–Walter Harris
New York (simul) 1958

1.e4 e5 2.d4 exd4 3.c3 d5 4.♕xd4

The text is very unusual. White usually plays 4.exd5, but Bobby goes back to the past.

4...c6

Black has a wide range of choices, including 4...dxe4, 4...♘f6, 4...♗e7, 4...♕e7, 4...♘c6 and 4...♗e6, which was Alekhine's choice in his game against Gambin from Melilla 1945: 5. ♗b5+ c6 6.♗d3 ♘d7 7.♘f3 ♘c5 8. ♗c2 dxe4 9.♘g5 ♘f6 10.♗e3 ♕c7

with a clear advantage for Black. Harris' move leaves White with a small advantage due to Black's isolated Queen pawn.

5.exd5 ♕xd5 6.♕xd5 cxd5 7.♘f3 ♘f6 8.♗f4 ♘c6 9.♘bd2 ♗f5 10. ♘b3 ♗e7 11.♗b5 O-O 12.♗xc6

The plan of ♗b5xc6 is debatable, as White has no clear way to blockade the c5-square.

12...bxc6 13.O-O ♖fc8 14.♖fe1 ♘e4?!

Black would be doing fine after 14... ♗f8, intending ...c6-c5.

15.♘fd4 ♗e6 16.f3

The immediate capture on e6 gives White a big advantage, e.g., 16.♘xe6 fxe6 17.♘d4 ♔f7 18.f3 ♘c5 19. ♖e3, threatening 20.♖ae1 and 20.b4.

16...♘c5 17.♘xe6 ♘xe6 18.♘d4 ♗c5 19.♗e3 ♗xd4 20.♗xd4 ♘xd4 21.cxd4 ♖e8 22.♔f2 ♖xe1 23.♖xe1 ♔f8 24.♖c1 ♖c8 25.♔e3 g5 26.♖c5 f5 27.b4 f4+ 28.♔d2 ♔e7 29.♖a5 ♖c7 30.a4 ♔d6 31.♖a6 ♔e7 32.

♖a5 ♔d7 33.g3 ♔d6 34.gxf4 gxf4
35.♖c5 a6 36.♖a5 ♖a7?

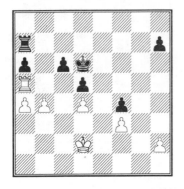

37.b5 cxb5 38.axb5 ♔c7 39.♖xa6?

Walking into a pin. The right way
to defend was the more active 36...
♖b7 37.♔c3 ♖b6.

The pawn ending is drawn. Bobby
should have played 39.bxa6 with a
healthy extra pawn.

39...♖xa6 40.bxa6 ♔b6 41.♔c3
♔xa6 42.♔b4 ♔b6 43.♔a4 ♔a6 44.
h3 h6 45.♔b4 ♔b6 46.♔a4 ♔a6 47.
h4 h5 Draw

Bobby visits the Soviet Union

Fischer visited the Soviet Union
only once. On March 26, 1958, Bobby
appeared on CBS-TV's "I've got a
Secret" program and emcee Gary
Moore had a special secret for Bobby
— two round-trip airplane tickets.

Chess Review (May 1958, p.132) reported that Bobby could now accept
the Soviet government's offer to play
a series of exhibition matches in Moscow this June and July. In addition, he
would also be able to use the same
ticket to represent the United States in
the Interzonal in August, as his tickets
on the Belgian airline Sabena allowed
for stopovers.

Fischer went with his sister Joan to
Moscow, but he didn't enjoy himself.
The planned exhibition matches never
came off. Bobby felt slighted that the
reigning World Champion, Vassily
Smyslov, never met him. The Russians had all sorts of sightseeing

planned for him, but he preferred to
spend his time at the Moscow Central
Chess Club. There he crushed one
Soviet master after another. Finally,
Petrosian was brought in, but even
against the great "Tiger" Bobby won
some games.

One of the masters Bobby beat during his blitz session was GM-to-be
Evgeny Vasiukov. The following anecdote by GM Taimanov sheds some
light on Bobby's exceptional memory.

His memory was amazing. Just
one more example. It happened in
Vancouver, Canada, in 1971. At the
closing of my infamous match against
Fischer, Fischer and I were sitting
with fellow-grandmasters at a ban-
quet and were talking peacefully after the preceding storms (curiously,
we communicated in Serbian, which
both of us knew). The conversation
revolved around the match until my

"I Have a Secret" host Garry Moore handing Bobby plane tickets to the USSR

second, Yevgeny Vasiukov, suddenly turned to Fischer.

"Bobby, do you remember that in 1958 you spent several days in Moscow and played many blitz games against our chessplayers? I was one of your partners."

"Of course, I remember," Fischer replied.

"And the result?" Vasiukov asked.

"Why only the result?" Fischer responded. "I remember the games. One was a French."

And he rattled off all the moves!
Source: Taimanov in *Russians Versus Fischer*, page 58

Vladimir Bagirov, writing in the book *White Fischer* (p.25), relates:
[W]hen the chess officials found yet another opponent for Bobby with a less familiar surname than the American expected, he got angry. They explained to him that there were hundreds of good chessplayers in the Soviet Union that could play decently.

Bobby answered, "There are only about a dozen players in the Soviet Union that can play decently."

Fischer vs. Matulovic

Fischer's match with Milan Matulovic is shrouded in mystery. The basic details are known. That it was held July 20-26, 1958, at the Chess Club Slavia in Belgrade alongside a match between Bent Larsen and Milan Vukcevic. Bobby won the match 2.5-1.5, but only the first game, a win by Matulovic, has surfaced. The results of the final three games are not known, though game four had Bobby as White in a French that went fifty moves.

Yugoslav magazines of the time had very little on the match, which was held prior to Bobby's participation in the Interzonal. Matulovic doesn't seem to have his game scores. A few years ago he was offered 1000 Deutsche Marks (roughly $600) by IM Robert Wade for the three missing games, but even with that motivation he was unable to find them.

1960-1965

Student Olympiads

One of the greatest triumphs of American chess in the post-World War Two era, was the victory of the United States at the Student Team Olympiad at Leningrad in 1960. The USSR was the dominant country in the Olympiads of the 1950s and 60s, but it had a dearth of young talent in the late 1950s and early 1960s, in part due to the losses suffered during the Second World War. Boris Spassky won the World Junior Championship in 1955, but it was to be 14 (!) years before another Soviet youngster, Anatoly Karpov, took the title.

The 1959 Student Team Championship in Budapest was won by Bulgaria with 40.5 points to the Soviet Union's 39. The United States didn't participate. Future GMs Nikola Padevski and Georgy Tringov won the individual silver and gold medals, on boards one and two. The Soviet team performed very well lower down, with fourth board Yuri Nikolaevsky and second reserve Vladimir Liberzon winning gold medals, and first reserve Anatoly Volovich taking the silver. The latter, incidentally, has lived for many years in New Jersey. But boards one through three — Bukhuiti Gurgenidze (6/10), Alexander Nikitin (6.5/10) and Aivars Gipslis (7.5/10) — couldn't keep pace with their Bulgarian counterparts.

The following summer the disgrace was even worse for the Soviets, as they lost on their homeground to the Americans at the height of the Cold War. The American team of Lombardy, Kalme, Weinstein, Saidy, and Mednis was in exceptionally good form and scored an outstanding 41 points from 52. The USSR finished second with 39.5, while Yugoslavia was third at 37 (with Cleveland's Milan Vukcevich playing a key role) and the Czechs, fourth with 31.5. Imagine if Bobby had been playing! The only other time the United States has finished first ahead of the Russians was the 1993 World Team Championship in Lucerne.

The following year the Soviets got their revenge by winning in Helsinki: 1. USSR 39.5, 2. USA 34.5, 3-4. East Germany and Czechoslovakia 31. The Soviets showed up with a new team, while the Americans were missing only Saidy. The United States, which lost to the Soviets 3-1, had great results from Lombardy and Weinstein on first and second board (each won silver medals for 9/11 scores). Fourth board Kalme had 7.5/10, Mednis, the first reserve, had 5.5/8, and second reserve Larry Gilden won both his games. Unfortunately, third board James Sherwin, an Interzonalist in 1958, was in uncharacteristic form and scored only a single draw from six games.

Anthony Saidy

One of the finest young players in the country is Anthony Saidy, a 24-year-old medical student from New York. The current Canadian Open champion, Saidy has long been considered a threat in any event in which he competes. He has placed high several times in the U.S. Open, and last year at St. Louis, Tony defeated both the winner (Byrne) and the runner-up (Benko) and seemed headed for the title when a loss to Poschel in the 11th round ruined his chances and brought him down to a tie for fourth prize. Undaunted, Tony, a month later, scored his first major tournament win, the Canadian Open at Kitchener, Ontario.

Saidy has competed on the U.S. Student Team no less than four times, with consistently fine results. He was high scorer for the team in Iceland (1957) and Bulgaria (1958) and scored 4.5-2.5 on board four in the team's victory last year at Leningrad. Against Soviet opposition, Tony holds an even score, despite a loss to a comparative unknown in 1956 — M.Tal.

Tony was born in Los Angeles, but has lived in New York since age 10 . . . [H]is father, Fred Saidy, [is] a well-known playwright, who has penned many fine shows, including the delightful "Finian's Rainbow." Tony learned chess from his father, whom he says is a poor player, but good at bridge. At 11, he joined the Marshall Chess Club and was one of the "Marshall Juniors," whose past ranks have included many of the country's leading players. Tony obtained his B.S. at Fordham, is currently

Captain and USCF President Jerry Spann, Ray Weinstein and Bill Lombardy (l-r) head for the 1960 World Student Team Championship in Leningrad

in his fourth year at Cornell University Medical College in New York and will soon be Dr. Saidy.

Saidy is husky and rugged looking, appears poised and confident both on and off the chessboard. He captained the U.S. Student Team twice, and was a key organizer as ICIA president, which involved the not inconsiderable task of collecting the funds necessary for the team's existence.

Saidy has an aggressive, positional chess style which together with a fine knowledge of openings and a sharp eye for combinational possibilities make him a very dangerous opponent. He generally thinks deeply in the early stages of the game and as a result often gets into time trouble. Though a fine blitz player and an expert at "time pressure swindles," Tony often pays the penalty for trying to cheat the clock. In the recent U.S. Championship, Saidy came tantalizing close to being the first American in four years to defeat Fischer, when a blunder just before the time control cost him the game.

Charles Henin, *Chess Life*, 1961 (page 258).

Caracas, Venezuela, 1960

Fischer played in several GM tournaments in South America during 1959 and 1960. In Caracas, Venezuela, he gave an exhibition on August 6, 1960. Little is known about this simul other than that Roderick C. Vizenetz beat Bobby in 27 moves.

Bobby also played in a blitz event, placing second to Spanish IM Antonio Medina, who came to Venezuela in 1955, attracted, like many at the time, by the strong oil-fueled economy. He stayed till 1962 when he won the U.S. Open in San Antonio on his way home. The crosstable for the event appeared in *Ocho y Ocho* in 1994 (p. 44).

	W	D	L
1. Antonio Medina	9	0	0
2. Bobby Fischer	7	0	2
3. Celso Sanchez	6	0	3
4. Laszlo Tapaszto	6	0	3
5. Manuel Belmonte	4	1	4
6. Leon Schorr	4	0	5
7. Salvador Diaz	4	0	5
8. A. Sadde	2	1	6
9. Isidoro Cherem	1	0	8
10. Pedro Galarraga	1	0	8

During the 1999 U.S. Open in Reno, Nevada, NM Leon Schorr of Caracas kindly shared his recollections of this event. According to Schorr, the event was a five-minute tournament and an eleventh player started the tournament, but didn't finish it. Legendary GM Miguel Najdorf, who lived in Venezuela from 1958-60 and sold insurance there, lost to Bobby in the first round and then withdrew!

Najdorf and Isidoro Cherem were responsible for bringing Bobby to Venezuela. Cherem, who first met Bobby at Buenos Aires 1960, which ended on July 21, was to become a good friend. He tried, in 1975, to help negotiate a match with Karpov. Cherem was also responsible for bringing GMs Herman Pilnik and Julio Bolbochan to Venezuela (they are both buried there)..

Fischer lost two games in the blitz tournament, one to Medina, the other to NM Laszlo Binet Tapaszto. Tapaszto was born in Hungary in 1930. A contemporary of future GMs Pal Benko (b. 1928), Istvan Bilek (b.1932) and prodigy Lajos Portisch (b.1937), he was one of the young stars of Hungarian chess in the early 1950s. His rise was cut short by the Revolution in 1956 which caused him to emigrate, but in Venezuela he had few opportunities to realize his potential as a chess player. Tapaszto played with success in U.S. Swiss System events in the 1960s and 1970s. He now lives in Rochester, New York, where he sports a 2400 USCF rating at age 69.

Venezuela has hosted a few big events, the Caracas 1970 Grandmaster tournament with Anatoly Karpov, Leonid Stein and Borislav Ivkov, being the most significant. Traditionally, Olympiads and Zonals have offered aspiring Venezuelan players their main opportunities for international experience. Such has been the case for Schorr, who was chosen for four Olympiads and who tied for third in the 1967 Central American Zonal. The latter result would be good for the International Master title today, but the rule which awards an automatic IM title for a two-thirds score in a Zonal had not then been approved.

Tandem Simul

The following games are rarities. They appear to be from Bobby's only tandem simul (the two exhibitors alternate moves). But sometimes two brains aren't better than one! The two simul givers can often have different ideas about the position, leading to strange situations. [This author (J. D.) gave a team simul at a chess camp in Bloomington, Illinois, with GM Alex Yermolinsky and IMs Jeremy Silman and Josh Manion. Many games were comical, with the masters engaged in a fair amount of muttering as their lines got crossed.] Here Bobby and GM Larry Evans face a strong opponent and after a series of indifferent moves find themselves in a very unpleasant situation.

How do you rate the tandem performance of (say) Fischer (2664) and Evans (2553) against say Gersch (2198)? If Gersch wins, is it an upset, or is Gersch "up" for the encounter, or is there more art than logic in chess? Tandem chess certainly shouldn't detract from the logic of a game and, according to Bobby, he and Evans weren't just fooling around that night, "Gersch just played a good game." Actually, this is the way the facts read and you can't get more factual than the score. The following is the well-played positional game Gersch won against the team of Fischer and Evans. — Ed.

Source: *Chess Life*, Sept. 1963, p. 220

Larry Evans believes this game was played at John Fursa's Chess and Checker Club (a.k.a. the Fleahouse) near Times Square.

[18] *QGD Cambridge Springs   D52*
RJF & Larry Evans–L. Gersch
New York (tandem simul) 1960

1.d4 d5 2.c4 e6 3.♘c3 ♘f6 4.♗g5 ♘bd7 5.♘f3 c6 6.e3 ♕a5

The venerable Cambridge Springs, named after a western Pennsylvania resort, is enjoying a resurgence.

7.♘d2

This is the traditional answer to Black's counterplay based on ...♗b4 and ...♘e4, but more critical is *7. cxd5*. If Black answers 7...exd5, he finds himself in a QGD Exchange variation where his Queen on a5 is misplaced. The latest word in the preferred line, *7...♘xd5*, is Kramnik–Ivanchuk, Novgorod 1995, where *8.♕d2 ♗b4 9.♖c1 h6 10.♗h4 c5!* (the modern interpretation of the Cambridge Springs is based more on ...c5 than ...e5) *11.a3 ♗xc3 12.bxc3 b6* led to a sharp, unbalanced position. The game continued *13.e4 ♘5f6 14.♗d3 ♗b7 15. d5 c4 16.dxe6 cxd3 17.exd7+ ♘xd7 18.♕xd3 g5 19.♗g3 ♘c5 20.♕d6 Draw*. The players assessed 20... ♘xe4 21.♕c7 O-O 22.♕xb7 ♘c5 23.♕c6 ♘d3+ 24.♔e2 ♖ac8 25. ♕xh6 ♘xc1+ 26.♖xc1 ♕b5+ 27. ♔e1 ♖fe8+ 28.♗e5 ♖xe5+ 29. ♘xe5 ♕xe5+ as unclear.

7...♗b4

GM Yasser Seirawan of Seattle is a big fan of 7...dxc4, winning the Bishop pair. After 8.♗xf6 ♘xf6 9.♘xc4 ♕c7, both sides have chances.

8.♕c2 ♘e4

Ivanchuk prefers the fluid 8...c5.

9.♘dxe4 dxe4 10.♗f4

The retreat to h4 is more popular, as White doesn't want to have to answer ...e5 with dxe5.

10...O-O 11.♗e2 e5 12.dxe5?!

This natural-looking move spoils White's game, as it takes all the pawn tension out of the position. Correct was 12.♗g3.

12...♘xe5 13.O-O ♗xc3 14.bxc3

This position has seldom been reached, and for good reason: White's Bishops have few prospects and his queenside pawns are weak. Ed. Lasker–Em. Lasker, New York 1924, varied with 14.♕xc3, but White fared no better, as his pawns were easy targets in the endgame: 14...♕xc3 15.bxc3 ♖e8 16.c5 ♘d7 17.♗d6 b6 18.cxb6 axb6 19.♖fd1 ♗a6 20.♗xa6 ♖xa6 21.a4 ♖ea8 22.♔f1 f5 23.♖ab1 ♖8a7 24. g4 (Desperation. Black threatened to make a few more consolidating moves and then take some pawns for free.) 24...fxg4 25.♖b4 ♘f6 26.♗b8 ♖a8 27.♖d8+ ♔f7 28.♗c7 ♖xa4 29.♖xa8 ♖xa8 30.♖xb6 ♘d5 21.♖b7 ♔e6 32.c4 ♘e7 with a winning endgame.

14...♗f5 15.♕b3 b6 16.♖fd1 ♖fd8 17.♖d4 ♘d3 18.♗g3 c5 19.♖d5 ♗e6 20.f3

White had to play 20.♖xd8+, but after 20...♖xd8 the position is far from pleasant.

20...♗xd5 21.cxd5

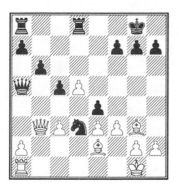

21...c4! 22.♕xc4 ♕xd5 23.♕xd5 ♖xd5 24.fxe4

When Tarrasch said that two Bishops and a Rook are equal to two Rooks and a Knight, he wasn't thinking of this position! Gersch mops up in efficient fashion.

24...♖5d8 25.e5 ♖ac8 26.♖d1 ♖xc3 27.♗h4 ♖d7 28.♗e1 ♖c1 29.♖xc1 ♘xc1 30.♗c4 ♖c7 31.♗d5 ♘d3 32. ♗d2 ♖c2 33.e6 ♖xd2 34.e7 ♖d1 Mate

Source: *Chess Life*, Sept. 1963, p.220

A second game from the tandem simul has recently emerged. Carl Wagner of Durham, North Carolina, sent this game to "Evans on Chess," GM Larry Evans monthly question-and-answer column in *Chess Life*. Wagner recalls that Bobby played the odd-numbered moves.

[19] *Guioco Piano   C53*
RJF & Larry Evans–Carl Wagner
        New York (tandem simul) 1960

1.e4 e5 2.♘f3 ♘c6 3.♗c4 ♗c5 4. O-O ♘f6 5.c3 O-O?

Black has to capture the e-pawn. The position after 5...♘xe4 has a surprisingly old history dating back to at least the early 1860's. Today it's still seen on rare occasions. A recent example is Okhotnik–Eisterer, Balatonbereny 1996, which continued 6.♗d5 (Best, 6.d4 is easier for Black to meet, e.g., Keres–Raud, Tallinn 1935: 6...d5 7.♕e2 exd4 8.cxd4 ♘xd4 9.♘xd4 ♗xd4 10.♘c3 ♗xc3 11.bxc3 ♗e6 and White didn't have enough compensation for the missing material) 6... ♘f6 7.♗xc6 dxc6 8.♘xe5 O-O 9.d4 ♗d6 (9...♗e7 10.♘d2 ♗e6 11.♘df3 equal, Barua–Koshy, Calcutta 1996) 10. ♗g5 ♗xe5 11.dxe5 ♕xd1 12.♖xd1 ♘d7, equal.

6.d4

Larry Evans

Now White is allowed to build a classical center for free.

6...exd4 7.cxd4 ♗b6 8.e5?!

Much better is 8.d5 ♘a5 9.♗d3 c5 10.♘c3 with a large advantage.

8...♘e8?

Correct is 8...d5 9.exf6 dxc4 10.d5 ♘b4 11.fxg7 ♔xg7 with a playable position for Black.

9.d5 ♘e7 10.♘c3 d6 11.e6 fxe6 12. dxe6 d5?

A better try is 12...♘f6, but after 13.♗g5 h6 14.♗h4 White is still on top.

13.♘xd5 ♗xe6 14.♘xe7+?

White's still winning after the text, but 14.♘xb6 just wins a piece.

14...♕xe7 15.♖e1?

Correct is 15.♕e2 ♖f6 16.♖e1 ♗xf2+ 17.♕xf2 ♕f7 18.♗xe6 ♖xe6 19.♗g5 with a winning position.

15...♗xf2+ 16.♔xf2?

The momentum is changing hands in drastic fashion. White could have kept an equal position by 16.♔h1 ♗xe1 17.♕xe1 ♖f6 18.♗g5 ♕d6 19. ♗xf6 ♗xc4 with compensation for the pawn.

16...♕c5+ 17.♗e3 ♕xc4 18.♔g1 c6 19.♘g5 ♗g4

Somewhat better is 19...♗f5.

20.♕b3

An interesting alternative was 20. ♖c1 ♗xd1 21.♖xc4 ♗h5 22.♖b4 trying to maintain White's pawn structure and activate the Rook.

20...♕xb3 21.axb3 a6 22.h3 ♗h5 23. ♘e6 ♖f7 24.♗d4 ♘c7?

Walking straight into a tactic. Much better is 24...♗g6.

25.♘xg7 ♘b5 26.♘xh5 ♘xd4 27. ♖ad1 ♘xb3 28.♖e5 b6

20...♖af8 is much more active. The text weakens Black's queenside pawns.

29.♖d6 ♘a5?

The correct way to defend the c-pawn is 29...♖c8.

30.b4 ♘c4 31.♖g5+ ♔h8 32.♖xc6 b5 33.♖gc5 ♖7f8 34.♖h6 ♖f7??

Black overlooks the weakness of his back rank. He was still very much in the game with 34...♖a7

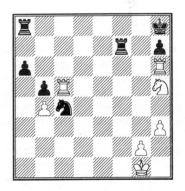

35.♖xa6 ♖7f8 36.♖xa8 ♖xa8 37. ♖xb5 1-0

Source: *Chess Life*, Aug. 1999, p. 12

Los Angeles, 1961

Bobby's trip to Southern California in summer 1961, for the second half of his match with Sammy Reshevsky, is well known. What is not, is that he made a visit to the Southland earlier in the year. The March 20, 1961, issue of *Chess Life* (p. 88) reports, "Bobby was in California briefly last month and was a guest at USCF Membership Chairman Lina Grumette's home." A few issues later (May, p. 148), "Jerome B. Hanken writes that he is now teaching in a camp for wayward children and that Bobby Fischer visited the boys and gave an exhibition while in California."

NM Hanken, organizer of the 1993 U.S. Championship, adds that Bobby was interested in prisoners and prisons at the time. Camp Afflerbaugh in Laverne, just outside Pomona, wasn't exactly a prison, and the youths weren't really prisoners, but the 18-year-old Fischer seemed satisfied and he was a big hit with the kids.

Bobby gave a public performance at the Hotel Ambassador on February 1. Facing 50 players, with an equal number turned away for lack of space, Fischer scored +40=7–3. The winners were Antonio Loera, D. C. McKenna and Robert W. Moore with Robert Cooper, Hebert Goldhammer, Kenneth Hense, Robert Katz, Tauno Saila, Wasily Skriabin and Kurt Smith splitting the point. NM Harry Borochow served as referee. Players paid $3.50 for the privilege of facing Bobby and spectators, $1.50.

Ken Hense, rated 1965 on the April 1961 USCF rating list provides this up-and-down struggle.

[20] *Ruy Lopez Steinitz Deferred   C76*
RJF–Kenneth Hense
Los Angeles (simul) Feb. 1, 1961

1.e4 e5 2.♘f3 ♘c6 3.♗b5 a6 4.♗a4 d6 5.c3 ♗d7 6.0-0 g6 7.d4 ♗g7 8.d5 ♘b8

Black can play 8...♘ce7 and after 9.c4 ♘f6 10.♘c3 O-O 11.♗xd7 ♘xd7 we reach the same position as in the game after Black's 11th move.

9.c4 ♘e7

ECO gives only 9...♘f6, but the text has been tried a few times.

10.♘c3 O-O 11.♗xd7

An alternative plan for White is 11.b4 followed by 12.c5.

11...♘xd7 12.♘e1 f5 13.♘d3 f4

13...♘f6 14.f3 fxe4 15.fxe4 ♕d7 16.♗g5 was better for White in Leko–Veroci, Sydney 1992.

14.f3 g5

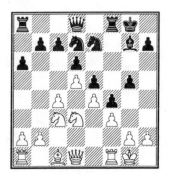

This position resembles a typical King's Indian, but the exchange of light-squared Bishops favors White. His bad Bishop is gone, while Black has difficulties getting in ...g5-g4.

15.♗d2 ♕e8

Black plans to transfer his Queen to g6 to support the advance ...g5-g4. The alternative was 15...♖f7, intending ...♗f8 and ...♖g7.

16.b4 ♕g6 17.c5 h5 18.♖c1

Bobby provokes complications. He could have maintained a safe advantage with 18.♘f2 ♘f6 19.h3, shutting down ...g5-g4.

18...g4 19.c6 bxc6 20.dxc6 ♘f6 21. ♔h1 h4 22.♖g1 ♘h5 23.h3

Better is 23.fxg4.

23...gxh3 24.gxh3 ♕e6 25.♖g4 ♘f6 26.♖g2 ♘xc6?!

26...♕xh3+ 27.♖h2 is about equal.

27.♘d5

27...♘xe4?

This combination ends up costing Black a piece. The best chance is 27... ♘d4. White gets nothing after 28. ♘xc7 ♕xh3+ 29.♖h2 ♕xf3+. Critical is 28.♘3xf4 exf4 29.♘xf4 ♕f7 30.♗c3 ♘e6 31.♘e6 ♖fb8 32.♕e1 with a strong attack. White will follow up with ♕xh4 and ♖cg1.

28.fxe4 ♕xh3+ 29.♔g1 ♕xd3 30. ♖xc6 ♖f7 31.♖xc7 ♖xc7 32.♘xc7 ♖a7 33.♘e8 h3 34.♖g5 ♔f8 35. ♕h5 ♕d4+ 36.♔h1 ♕xd2?

Black would have but a small disadvantage after 36...♕xe4+ 37.♔h2 ♕d5 38.♘xg7 ♖xg7 39.♕h8+ ♖g8 40.♕f6+ ♔e8.

37.♘xg7 ♕e1+ 38.♔h2 ♕f2+ 39. ♔xh3 ♕f1+ 40.♔g4?!

Correct is 40.♔h2 ♕f2+ 41.♖g2, completely winning. But the text cannot be criticized too severely, since White is still winning.

40...♕e2+ 41.♔h4?

White could have returned to the winning path with 41.♔h3 ♕f1+ 42. ♔h2 ♕f2+ 43.♖g2.

41...♕h2+ 42.♔g4 ♕e2+ Draw

White must repeat moves with 43. ♔h4 ♕h2+, as 43.♔f5 is met by 43...♖f7+.

Source: original scoresheet

Consultation Game

Bobby never played in a tournament in England. Scheduled to participate in Hastings in December of 1957, he changed plans when the U. S. Championship was organized on roughly the same dates. This was Bobby's debut and the first Championship in four years. Adding to its importance were the two qualifying spots for the 1958 Interzonal up for grabs. History was well served: Bobby won the Championship in his first try and then had a sensational result in the Interzonal, qualifying for the Candidates.

This is not to say that Fischer never played in England. He did, at least once. Rumors persist that he gave an impromptu simul in London in the early 1960s, but it's been difficult to track down. The following game appeared on British radio on the BBC's Third Network and appeared in print in *Chess Treasury of the Air*, pages 124-132, edited by Terence Tiller. It appears to be the only consultation game that Bobby ever played. The two teams played in different studios and their discussions were recorded and broadcast. The result was a most interesting program. But what happened to the tape of this game?

Fischer's partner, Leonard Barden, was joint British Champion in 1963 and represented England in several Olympiads. Jonathan Penrose was, for many years, England's best player. He is now ranked among the world's best at correspondence chess. His teammate, Peter Clarke, was one of England's top players in the 1960s, and is the author of several excellent books on the game.

---

[21] *Sicilian Keres Attack   B81*
RJF & Leonard Barden
GM Jonathan Penrose & Peter Clarke
London 1961

1.e4 c5 2.♘f3 e6 3.d4 cxd4 4.♘xd4 ♘f6 5.♘c3 d6 6.g4 h6 7.h3 ♘c6 8.♗e3 ♗d7 9.♕d2 ♘xd4 10.♕xd4

♕a5 11.O-O-O ♗c6 12.♔b1 ♗e7 13.♗g2 O-O 14.♕d2 ♖fd8 15.♘d5 ♕xd2 16.♘xe7+ ♔f8 17.♗xd2 ♔xe7 18.♖he1 ♖ac8 19.c4 ♘d7 20.b3 e5 21.♗e3 ♘c5 22.f3 b6 23.h4 ♘e6 24. ♗f1 f6 25.h5 ♗e8 26.♔b2 ♗f7 27. a4 ♖b8 28.a5 ♘c5 29.♖a1 ♖d7 30. ♔c3 bxa5 31.♗xc5 dxc5 32.♖xa5 ♖c7 33.♖ea1 ♖bb7 34.♖b1 ♗e8 35. b4 cxb4+ 36.♖xb4 ♖xb4 37.♔xb4 ♖b7+ 38.♔c3 ♗f7 39.♗d3 ♔d7 40. c5 ♖b3+ 41.♔c2 ♖b7 42.♗b5+ ♔d8 43.♗c6 ♖c7 44.♗d5 ♗e8 45.♔b3 ♗d7 46.♔c4 ♔e7

At Broadcasting House, no agreement could be reached on the proper result. Penrose and Clarke were claiming a draw, which was flatly rejected by Fischer: "What's the matter with you guys — are you dreaming or something?" So an independent adjudicator was sought —no less a player than former World Champion Dr. Max Euwe. In the meantime, Jonathan perhaps remembering the adjudication that went against him as a junior in the Glorney Cup, put in some serious homework. "I spent a lot of time on it, wrote it all down and sent it to Dr. Euwe. I wondered if, today, computers would find something wrong with my analysis"

Source: *Chess*, August 1998, p. 35.

Listeners were encouraged to send in their analyses of the position. Some of the material which follows first appeared in *Chess Treasury of the Air*. Former World Champion Max Euwe, in his role as adjudicator, writes:

There are two types of chess position. In the first it is possible to prove a clear win or draw within reasonable time. In the second type this is not possible.

One should not worry if the term "reasonable" is a little vague. For the time required for such a proof increases, after a certain limit, at an inordinate rate. If the mathematical proof for a win or draw cannot be supplied within two weeks, it may take years or even a century. An extreme case is the starting point of the game of chess. This "problem" would take more than a million years to solve mathematically.

The adjourned game *Fischer and Barden v. Penrose and Clarke* belongs to the second category of positions. This could be expected. If four strong players, at least two of them world class, cannot come to a mutual understanding about the given position, one may be sure that the position does not contain a clear win or a clear draw.

All this may sound disappointing to you, and there is certainly reason to ask, "If there is no proof of the result, what can you offer us instead?"

No more than a presumption, an appraisal, an evaluation which is based on an overall view of the position and on a number of variations.

Further, naturally, on my experience as a chessplayer.

I cannot avoid my judgement being subjective; it is certainly debatable, but can hardly be refuted. For others, one can no more disprove my adjudication than I can prove it. I hope there are no serious mistakes in my illustrative variations, but even if I have made any they should not necessarily affect my general considerations of the result.

You certainly have a right to consider all this very unsatisfactory, but please do not blame me; I cannot alter the nature of chess.

Let us now look at the position. I need hardly say there are only two possible results: either White wins or Black reaches a draw. A loss for White, of course, may be ruled out.

I begin with a few general remarks. The first is that should White succeed in bringing his c-pawn to c6 and his King to c5, the game must be won for him. An example, 47.♖a6 ♔d8 48.c6 ♔e7 49.♔c5. The position now reached is not worth analysing. It is a clear win for White. I trust you agree. But, of course, Black should not permit this.

I have one more general remark. Should the White Rook succeed in definitely reaching the seventh or eighth rank, Black is lost in that case, too. By "definitely," I mean "without Black's being able to oppose the White Rook with his own Rook."

An example: 47.♖a1 ♔d8 48. ♖b1 ♔e7 49.♖b8, etc. Perhaps this is a little more complicated. White threatens 50.♖g8; and should Black close the eighth rank by playing 49...♗e8, he soon comes into

Zugzwang after White's 50.♖a8. On the other hand, if Black (after the penetration) tries to oppose the White Rook by ...♖c8, then White answers ♖b7 thus occupying the seventh rank, which is equally fatal for Black. Again: Black is not forced to accept any of these possibilities. A last general remark has to be made. Should White at some moment exchange rooks, a dead draw will result in almost all cases.

With these three remarks in mind, we try the following variations, starting from our initial position: *47.♖a6 ♗c8 48.♖a2 ♗d7* (stopping the advance of the c-pawn) *49.♖b2* (threatening to penetrate to the eighth rank) *49...♔d8* (meeting 50.♖b8+ with 50...♖c8 and if 51.♖b7, then 50...♖c7) *50. ♖f2* (angling for the advance f3-f4) 50...♔e7 51.f4 ♗xg4? 52.♖g2 ♗xh5 53.♖xg7+ ♔d8 54.♖g8+ ♔e7 55.fxe5 fxe5 56.c6! ♔d6 57. ♖d8+ ♔e7 58.♖h8 followed by ♔c5 with a winning position.

Does this mean that White is winning? No! The culprit was the capture of the g-pawn which allowed White's Rook to become incredibly active. Black can improve his position greatly by substituting *50...♖c8* for 50...♔e7.

Now 51.f4 exf4 52.♖xf4 a5 53.♖f2 ♔c7 54.e5 ♗xg4 55.exf6 gxf6 56. ♖xf6 ♗xh5 57.♖xh6 ♗e2+ 58. ♔d4 ♖d8 with a draw.

Dr. Euwe again:

It was a pleasure to go over the different entries for the final adjudication . . . I have found in these entries many more possibilities than I had seen myself, and especially in the analysis sent in *hors concours* by Penrose and Clarke.

Having studied the position again and again, I have returned to the conclusion already given in my first talk: Black with best play will manage to reach a draw. However, there are still a few difficult points to treat.

One of the listeners came up with an interesting winning attempt for White . . . After 47.♖a6 ♗c8 he varies with 48.♖c6 and after 48... ♖xc6 49.♗xc6 ♗a6+ 50.♔d5 Black's position is not so easy, but he can hold with 50...♗e2 51.♗a4 ♗xf3 52.c6 ♗xg4 53.c7 ♗c8 54. ♔c6 f5 55.exf5 ♗xf5 with a draw due to White's wrong-colored Rook-pawn.

Another tricky try is the pawn sacrifice g5 followed by h6. For example, after *47.♔b4* (instead of 47.♖a6) *47...♔e8 48.♖a2 ♔e7 49.♖c2 ♗e8 50.♖c1 ♗c6* (50... ♗d7? 51.c6! followed by 52.♔c5) *51.♗xc6 ♖xc6 52.♖d1 a6 53. ♖d5 ♔e8 54.♔c4 ♔e7 55.♖d1 ♔e8*

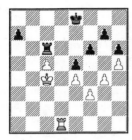

56.g5!? hxg5 (56...fxg5? 57.♔d5) 57.♖h1 ♔e7 58.h6 gxh6 59.♖xh6 ♖c7! 60.♖h7+ ♔d8 61.♖h8+ ♔e7 62.♖a8 ♖d7 63.♖xa6 ♖d4+ 64.♔b5 ♖d3 65.♔b6 ♖xf3 66. ♖a7+ ♔e6 67.c6 ♖b3+ and White cannot win. A narrow escape for Black!

I repeat my adjudication: with best counterplay by Black, a draw must result.

Blitz in New York

SM Asa Hoffman, in his game collection *Chess Gladiator*, offers the following game, a very rare win for him over Bobby. We suspect the venue was the Flea House, the popular name for the since defunct Chess and Checker Club of New York. Located on Times Square at 212 West 42nd Street, the Flea House was open all hours of the day, with upwards of 200 people cramming into its two main rooms to play chess and other games. Players often played for stakes and Asa was one of several hustlers happy to "give their customers a trim."

The following anecdote by Stewart Reuben, writing in *The Chess Scene* (pp.221-222), may apply to this game.

Bobby used to be willing to play five-minute chess at the stakes of a dollar a game. Working this out to be 7 dollars per hour at worst, it was hardly exuberant [*sic*]. I played him several times at this, receiving 10 to 1 money odds, and even managed to draw one game.

Desperate for a game one evening, he gave a good friend of mine, Asa Hoffman, 20 to 1 odds. I found this very irritating, as Asa was much stronger than me, but Bobby did not agree. Asa did not want to take the whole dollar for himself, so I had 25 cents as did other spectators to make it up to a dollar. In an Evans Gambit, Bobby played badly and lost the first game. Quickly, he shelled out the 20 dollars, but could only succeed in giving away 19 dollars. We had been so miserly that only 95 cents had been staked!"

---

[22] *Evans Gambit C52*
Asa Hoffman–RJF
New York (blitz) 1963

1.e4 e5 2.♘f3 ♘c6 3.♗c4 ♗c5

Bobby didn't answer 1.e4 with 1...e5 often, and, when he did, his opponent would play the Ruy Lopez. His only tournament game defending 3.♗c4 was versus Edmar Mednis in the 1963/1964 U.S. Championship.

4.b4

Mednis chose 4.c3 ♘f6 5.d4 exd4 6.cxd4 ♗b4+ 7.♗d2 ♗xd2+ 8.♘bxd2 ♘xe4! and got the worst of it when he failed to capture on f7 immediately. Instead, 9.♕e2 d5 10.♘xe4 O-O gave Black a nice pull.

4...♗xb4 5.c3 ♗a5 6.d4 exd4 7.O-O dxc3

Hoffman writes:

This is the Compromised defense. Fischer studied all of the nineteenth century games, and enjoyed testing his defensive skills in some difficult variations.

8.♕b3 ♕f6 9.e5 ♕g6 10.♘xc3 ♘ge7 11.♗a3 O-O 12.♖ad1 ♖e8 13.♘e4!

ECO gives only 13.♗d3 ♕h5 14. ♘e4 ♘xe5 15.♘xe5 ♕xe5 16.♗b2 ♕e6 17.♕b5 with a clear advantage for White (Lasker).

Fischer looked at this move with some suspicion! Could this be the latest Russian analysis? The move, in fact, is given in *Common Sense in Chess* by Emanuel Lasker. The continuation given is 13...♕xe4 14.♗xf7+ ♔f8 15.♗g8 d5 16.exd6 ♘xg8 17. ♘g5 ♕g6 18.♕f7+! ♕xf7 19.♘xh7 mate! (Hoffmann).

13...h6 14.♘g3 ♗b6?

Here 14...♖f8 15.♗d5 wins the Exchange. The most interesting try was 14...b5. What about 14...♘d8? If 15.♕a4 ♗b6 16.♗d3 ♕e6 17.♗c4 ♕c6 18.♗b5 is equal.

15.♘h4 ♕g5 16.♗xf7+ ♔f8 17. ♘g6 Mate

Unusual Annotations

Paul Keres had some critical comments in the British Magazine *Chess* to some of Fischer annotations in *Chess Review*.

---

[23] *Sicilian Closed   B25*
J. F. Reinhardt–RJF
                    Western Open 1963

1.♘f3 ♘f6 2.g3 g6 3.♗g2 ♗g7 4. O-O O-O 5.d3 d6

"Believe it or not," Black stands better! Now, whatever White does, Black will vary it and get an asymmetrical position and have the superior position due to his better pawn structure!

                                    Fischer

We just don't believe it! — **Keres**

6.e4 c5 7.♘c3 ♘c6 8.h3 ♖b8 9.♗e3 b5 10.e5

Nine out of ten grandmasters, including Petroshan, Botvinnik, Keres and Smyslov would have played this move, yet it loses by force. — **Fischer**

With such a mentality, he can hardly be surprised if, in his next serious attempt at the highest honours, he again falls short of complete success. — **Keres**

10...dxe5 11.♗xc5

With a weak and doubled King pawns, and a weakened queenside position, one could assume that Black is lost. This position occurred in Mednis-Fischer, 1958-59 U.S. Championship, with QRP's traded off, which is actually an improvement for White, but it is not enough to save the game. — **Fischer**

11...b4

Now Black's plan becomes clear. By forcing the QN to leave c3, Black gains control of d5 for his own Knight, after which the Bishop on c5 will be left stranded. Mednis played the Knight

to a4, but here, after ...♘d5, White has a lost game. — **Fischer**

12.♘e4

This opens up lines for Black's pieces. 12.♘e2 might be better.
12...♘xe4 13.dxe4 ♕a5 14.♗e3 ♗a6 15.♖e1 ♖fd8 16.♕c1

Unpleasant as it is, ♕b1 was probably the best move. — **Fischer**

Possibly best is 16.♘d2. White's best chance for counterplay is to break with a2-a3 and this is the only way to do it. Play could continue 16...♕c7 17.a3 ♖d6 (if 17...♕c8, then 18.♕b1) 18.axb4 ♘xb4 19.♗f1 ♗xf1 20. ♖xa7 ♕xc2 21.♖xf1 ♖bd8 22.♕xc2 ♘xc2 23.♘c4 with advantage to Black.

16...♘d4 17.♔h2

After this it is all over but for the demonstration. What White should have played is 17.♘xd4 exd4 18.♗d2, relying on the threat of a3. However, Black's course would have been ...♕b6; and if a3, ...b3; or if not a3, then ...d3 etc. — **Fischer**

Perhaps a better try is 17.♗xd4 exd4 18.♗f1 ♗xf1 19.♖xf1 ♖bc8 19. ♕d2 f5 20.♖fe1 ♕a4 21.♖ac1 ♕c6 with advantage to Black.

17...♖bc8 18.♘xd4

A bitter pill to swallow. Black's strategy, beginning on the tenth move, has triumphed. White is left with only bad alternatives. Since there was no way to defend the c-pawn, White was forced to undouble Black's king pawns and unleash the full fury of his position. — **Fischer**

18...exd4

19.♗g5 d3 20.a3 ♖xc2 21.axb4 ♕b6 22.♕e3 ♗d4 23.♕f3 ♖xf2 24.♕g4 d2 0-1

Source: *Chess Life* 1963, pages 216-217

New York 1963

[24]   *Modern*   *B06*
RJF–W. Beach
            Poughkeepsie 1963

1.e4

Before this game began, when I asked Mr. Beach how to spell his name, he remarked that we had met over the board on a previous occasion some years ago and that I had beaten him on the White side of a Pirc Defense. I had absolutely no recollection of that game.

[An earlier Fischer–Beach game has yet to surface and appears to have been lost, as have many of Fischer's tournament games prior to 1958. GM Alex Sherzer and NM Lael Kaplan met with Bobby several times in Budapest in the mid-1990s, and often quizzed Fischer as they relaxed in one of Budapest's famous medicinal baths. They report they he still had a phenomenal recall of his games going back to at least the early 1960s. It appears that the famous Fischer memory may be confined to when he became a GM, that his recall for games at the dawn of his career — when they would understandably be less logical — is not as strong.]

1...g6

. . . but this it: the Pirc or "Rat" Defense, as I have heard people call it in some of the chess clubs.

2.d4 ♗g7 3.♘c3 d6 4.f4 c6

Too passive. Black must reserve the advance of this pawn until it can be played to c5 at the right moment.

5.♘f3 ♗g4

Once again bad policy. Up until now White's only advantage was one of space, but by this move Black prepares to give up the minor exchange. 5...b5 would have been consistent, but bad. White would answer with 6.♗d3. Best for Black seems 5...♘f6, although, strategically, he already has a lost game.

6.♗e3 ♘d7

On 6...♕b6, Fischer planned 7.♕d2.

7.h3 ♗xf3 8.♕xf3 e6

8...♘f6 would be met by 9.e5.

9.O-O-O ♘e7 10.g4

The rest is just more or less technique. All White need do is force a breakthrough somewhere — almost anywhere — and then his superior development and dynamic Bishops will do the rest.

10...♕a5 11.♔b1 ♖b8

Apparently Black is dreaming about an attack on the b-file. He should have castled — either on the King- or Queenside.

12.e5

Of course: the breakthrough. As Sammy would say, "Black has little choice." 12...d5 is strongly answered by 13.♗d3 and f5. Of course, Black's next move has the disadvantage of allowing White's Knight to enter the game via e4.

12...dxe5 13.dxe5 ♘d5 14.♘e4 ♗f8

Fischer gives 14...O-O 15.♗d2 ♕c7 as better, although then he would play h4-h5 or g5 followed by bringing the Knight to f6.

15.♗c1

15.♗d2 followed by c4 was the "positional" way to do it. I purposely

allowed Black his little counter-demonstration on the Q-side, since, by doing this, he would be too occupied to consider the safety of his own King.

15...b5

According to Fischer, 15...♘c5 offers more resistance.

16.f5 b4

If 16...♘xe5, then 17.♕g3 ♕c7 18. fxe6 fxe6 19.♘g5 ♘f7 20.♕xc7 ♘xc7 21.♘xf7, winning.

17.fxe6 fxe6 18.♗c4 ♘xe5 19.♕g3 ♗g7

If 19...♕c7, then 20.♗xd5 exd5 21. ♗f4 ♗g7 22.♘g5 or if 19...♘d7, then 20.♗xd5 cxd5 21.♘f6+ ♘xf6 22.♕xb8+.

20.♗xd5 cxd5 21.♗h6

Just when Black thought he was out of the woods — the end comes.

21...♕c7

If 21...O-O, then 22.♗xg7 or if 21... ♗xh6, then 22.♘f6+ ♔f7 23.♕xe5.

22.♘d6+ ♔d8

If 22...♔f8, then 23.♕xe5.

23.♗xg7 ♕xd6 24.♕xe5 1-0

Source: *Chess Life*, Feb. 1964, p.44

The Last Swiss Game

The round seven game against NM Matthew Green from of the 1963 New York State Championship is the last game that Fischer ever played in a Swiss System event and the only tournament game from the 1960s which does not appear in a standard Fischer anthology. It was published in Al Horowitz's column in the *New York Times* shortly after the event.

Going into the last round, Fischer was a point ahead of the field, but

gave no thought to locking up first place with a quick draw.

---

[25] *Sicilian Paulsen   B42*
RJF–Matthew Green
                    Poughkeepsie (7) 1963

1.e4 c5 2.♘f3 e6 3.d4 cxd4 4.♘xd4 a6 5.♗d3 ♘c6 6.♘xc6 bxc6 7.O-O d5 8.exd5 cxd5 9.c4

Fischer's treatment is similar to that used against Petrosian in game seven of their Candidates match. That game,

eight years later, began: 1.e4 c5 2.
♘f3 e6 3.d4 cxd4 4.♘xd4 a6 5.♗d3
♘c6 6.♘xc6 bxc6 7.O-O d5 8.c4
♘f6 9.cxd5.

9...♘f6 10.cxd5 ♘xd5 11.♗e4 ♗d6?!
11...♗e7 looks safer.

12.♘c3 ♘xc3

13.♗c6+!

This *Zwischenschach* keeps the
Black King in the center, as 13...♗d7
is met by 14.♕xd6.

13...♔e7

14.bxc3

An automatic recapture? No, Bobby
had to consider the unusual *14.♕g4!?*,
which works brilliantly if Black tries

to hang onto material, e.g., 14...♖b8
15.♕xg7 or 14...♘d5 15.♗xa8. The
only reply is *14...♘e2+*, when 15.♔h1
♖b8 16. ♕xg7 ♘xc1 leaves White a
piece down with insufficient compensation. Critical is *15.♕xe2* ♖b8 16.
♗e3 ♗xh2+ 17.♔h1 ♕c7 18.♖fc1
♗f4, when White has compensation
for the pawn. The try 16.♕g4 arrives
at a position similar to the game, but
with one small difference — White's
pawn is on b2 and not c3.

14...♖b8 15.♕g4 ♖g8?

Under pressure, Green pitches material. The cold-blooded 15...g6 should
have been played, after which Black
has surprising defensive resources,
e.g., 16.♗h6 f6 17.♕f3 ♕a5! 18.
♗g7 ♕e5 19.g3 ♖d8 20.♖fe1 ♕f5
and Black is hanging on.

**16.♕h4+ f6 17.♕xh7 ♗b7 18.♗xb7
♖xb7 19.♖e1 ♕c8 20.h3 ♔f7 21.
♕h5+ g6 22.♕f3 ♖b5 23.a4 ♖f5 24.
♕e2 ♗c5 25.♗e3 ♖e5 26.♕f3 ♖d8
27.♖ab1 ♗xe3 28.♖xe3 ♖xe3 29.
♕xe3 ♖d7 30.♕h6 f5**

31.c4!

Taking advantage of Black's unpro-
tected pieces.

31...♛d8 32.♔h2 a5 33.f4 ♔f6

33...♛f8 offered better chances to resist.

(see diagram next column)

34.♖b7!

Exploiting the loose position of Black's King.

34...♖e7

If 34...♖xb7, 35.♛g5+ picks up the Queen.

35.c5 1-0

After 33...♔f6

Reuben Fine

The active playing careers of Reuben Fine and Bobby Fischer didn't overlap, but that didn't prevent them from going at it in 1963. Lou Hay's *Bobby Fischer: Complete Games of the American World Chess Champion* gives three blitz games played between them (Fischer 2-1) as well as the skittles game Bobby chose for his classic *My 60 Memorable Games*. In the preface to that game GM Larry Melvin Evans wrote: "Having become one of the leading players in the world, Fine quit chess at the height of his career (1945) to become a practicing psychoanalyst; but he has lost none of his love for the game and little of his brilliance. The following is one of seven or eight offhand games played at his home in New York. As far as can be ascertained, Dr. Fine very nearly held his own."

The following game, which appeared in the second issue of the excellent, but short-lived, *ChessWorld*, is another one of the offhand games. The magazine had this to say about the game:

> *ChessWorld* takes great pleasure in publishing on its cover a game that does in fact transcend time to a slight degree, a game played between the two greatest champions of their day, though decades apart: Bobby Fischer (Black) and Reuben Fine (White).
>
> The game was played in New York City in March of 1963 without a chess clock, and is here presented to the public for the first time. We draw no conclusions, make no excuses, offer no qualifications. We let the reader decide on his own.

[26] *Sicilian Sozin   B87*
Reuben Fine–RJF
   New York (offhand), March 1963

1.e4 c5 2.♘f3 d6 3.d4 cxd4 4.♘xd4 ♘f6 5.♘c3 a6 6.♗c4 e6 7.♗b3 b5 8.♛e2 ♗e7 9.g4?

Fine's move is not given by *ECO* which offers only 9.♗e3, 9.f3 and 9.

♗g5. It doesn't work well with 6. ♗c4, as Black is able to get in a quick ...d5.

9...b4 10.♘b1 d5 11.e5 ♘fd7 12. ♗f4 ♕b6 13.♘f3 a5!

(see diagram next column)

The twin threats of 14...a4, trapping the Bishop, and 14...♗a6, preventing castling, are very hard to meet.

14.♗a4 O-O 15.♗e3 ♕c7 16.♗d4 ♗a6 17.♕e3 ♘c5 18.♗xc5 ♗xc5 19.♘d4? ♕b6 0-1

White loses decisive material after 20.c3 bxc3 21.bxc3 ♕b2.

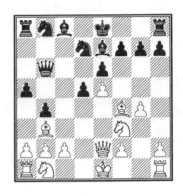

After 13...a5!

Simul at the United Nations, 1965

One of Bobby's more unusual exhibitions was held at the Church Center of the United Nations on May 21, 1965. Results for the event are contradictory. *Chess Review* has Bobby facing 26 players with a score of 23 wins plus losses to Vladimir Vakula of the USSR and club secretary Luis Loayza of Peru and a draw with Evgeny Zhukov of the USSR. *Chess Life* and Zhukov have it +18=1–2. Neither of these may be right, as the two games from the event which have surfaced are both draws! It doesn't make things any clearer to know that *Chess Life* gives Ivan Grischenko, not Vakula, as a winner.

The event was sponsored by games manufacturer TAG, Inc., and its newly designed Manchurian chess tables and chessmen were used. From the look of the photo published on page 196 of the July 1965 issue of *Chess Review*,

Bobby must have finished the exhibition with an aching back: the tables were less than two feet off the ground! His eyes might also have been sore — the Manchurian pieces were definitely not based on the Staunton design.

[27] *Ruy Lopez Møller   C78*
RJF–F. Snitzer
New York (simul) May 21, 1965

1.e4 e5 2.♘f3 ♘c6 3.♗b5 a6 4.♗a4 ♘f6 5.O-O b5 6.♗b3 ♗c5

Snitzer is 30 years ahead of his time. This sequence has become very popular in the mid-1990's.

7.♘xe5 ♘xe5 8.d4 d6?

This isn't the reason for the popularity of 6...♗c5. Correct is 8...♗xd4 9. ♕xd4 d6 10.f4 ♘c6 11.♕c3 ♗b7 12. e5 ♘e4 13.♕e3 ♘a5 14.♘d2 ♘xb3 15.axb3 ♘xd2 16.♗xd2 Draw, Svidler–Shirov, Groningen 1996.

9.dxc5 dxc5 10.f4?!

10.♕xd8+ ♔xd8 11.f4 ♘eg4 12.
e5 c4 13.exf6 is clearly better for White.
**10...♕xd1 11.♖xd1 c4 12.fxe5 cxb3
13.♘c3**

This leads to an equal position, but
13.exf6 bxc2 14.♖e1 cxb1=♕ 15.fxg7
♖g8 16.♖xb1 ♖xg7 is, at most, only
slightly better for White.
**13...bxc2 14.♖d2 ♘g4 15.♘d5 O-O
16.♖xc2 ♘xe5 17.♗f4 ♘g6 18.♗xc7
♗b7 19.♘b6?**

19.♖ae1 is equal.
19...♖a7?

Correct is 19...♗xe4!
20.e5 ♖e8 21.♖e1 ♘f4 22.♗d6

22...♗xg2??!

22...♘d5 is equal. The extremely
resourceful text is not quite sound.
23.♖xg2??

Correct is 23.e6! ♘xe6 24.♔xg2,
winning material.
**23...♖b7 24.♖g4 ♖xb6 25.♖d1 ♘g6
26.♖c1 h6 27.♖e4**

27.♖c5 is better, although Black has
a big advantage.
**27...f6 28.♖c7 ♘xe5 29.♗xe5 ♖xe5
30.♖xe5 fxe5.**

The position should be an easy technical win for Black, but . . .
**31.♔f2 ♖e6 32.♔e3 e4 33.♖a7 ♔h7
34.b3 h5 35.a4 bxa4 36.bxa4 ♔g6**

**37.a5 ♔f6 38.♖b7 g5 39.h3 g4 40.
hxg4 hxg4 41.♖b6 ♔e5?**

41...g3! wins.
42.♖b8?

There was nothing wrong with 42.
♖xe6+ ♔xe6 43.♔xe4 with a drawn
pawn ending. The text should lose.
42...♖c6 43.♖g8 ♖c3+ 44.♔e2 Draw

44...g3 is still winning.
Source: *New York Times*, July 1, 1965.

Evgeny Zhukov remembers that the
U.N. Secretariat had a pretty strong
chess club and that Fischer impressed
him as being modest, but confident.

[28] *French Rubinstein   C10*
RJF–Evgeny Zhukov
New York (simul) May 21, 1965

**1.e4 e6 2.d4 d5 3.♘c3 dxe4 4.♘xe4
♘d7 5.♘f3 ♘gf6 6.♗d3 ♗e7 7.
♕e2 c5 8.♘xf6+ ♘xf6 9.dxc5 ♕a5+
10.♗d2 ♕xc5 11.O-O-O ♗d7**

Deviating from the theoretical path
which indicates 11...O-O.
**12.♘e5 ♗a4 13.g4 ♖c8 14.b3 ♗c6
15.♘xc6 bxc6 16.g5 ♘d5 17.♕e5
O-O 18.♔b1 a5 19.h4 ♘b4 20.
♕xc5 ♗xc5 21.♗xb4 axb4 22.f4
♗e3 23.f5 e5 24.♖de1 ♗d4 25.h5**

25...h6

Black should have tried 25...♗c3 (or the immediate 25...♖a8) 26.♖e4 ♖a8 (threatening 27...♖xa2!), hoping for 27.♖c4? ♖xa2! 28.♖xc3 ♖fa8 winning. White has to play 27.a4 bxa3 28.♔a2 with drawing chances.

26.gxh6 gxh6 27.f6 ♔h8 28.♗c4 ♖c7 Draw

Black should have played 28...♖a8 to double Rooks, leaving Bobby to deal with the threats against his a-pawn.

Source: *Shakhmatny Vestnik*, 1993, 11:15

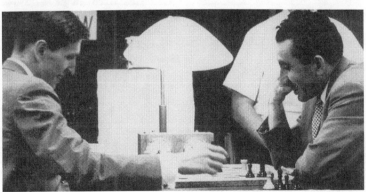

Top: GM Miguel Najdorf vs. Bobby
Bottom: Bobby vs. GM Tigran Petrosian
at Santa Monica 1966

Fischer's 1964 Transcontinental Tour

The December 1963 issue of *Chess Life* published an article under the headline:

Fischer Plans Tour

United States Champion Bobby Fischer has announced plans for his first transcontinental tour. He will be available for simultaneous exhibitions and lectures from February through May of 1964 and colleges, chess clubs, and private groups who are interested in having him appear to play and lecture should immediately contact *Chess Tours*, 3560 Broadway, New York, N.Y. 10031.

Mr. Fischer has announced that his fee is $250 for a 50-board exhibition and lecture. Full details are available from Chess Tours at the above address.

Cross-country chess tours had long been a fixture of American chess when Bobby planned his trip. Lasker, Capablanca and Alekhine all made big simul extravaganzas across the United States in the twenty-year period covering roughly 1915-1935. During the Great Depression, many top American players used the proceeds from such events to stay in chess. I. A. Horowitz, one of the founders (with GM Kashdan) of *Chess Review*, used to keep the magazine afloat by traveling the country simuling, lecturing, and selling books and subscriptions to his journal.

American chess had changed a lot by the 1960s. Before the Second World War, chess clubs were the glue that held U.S. chess together. Many cities had good clubs and prominent individuals were often members. Most major cities had chess columns in the big daily newspapers.

This was no longer true in 1964. Whether this was due to changes in the American lifestyle, or the rapidly emerging dominance of weekend tournaments, is not clear, but it makes the success of Bobby's tour all the more remarkable, especially when you realize that Fischer was asking for an unprecedented fee.

A few years before Bobby's trip, the U. S. Chess Federation announced a cross-country tour by GM William Lombardy. The former World Junior Champion (Toronto 1957) and first board for the gold-medal-winning U. S. Student Team (Leningrad 1960) was offering to play forty boards for $100. Bobby's asking price was $250 for fifty boards plus travel expenses.

Today, when corporate sponsorship makes it possible for Garry Kasparov to receive $30,000 a simul, Bobby's fee might seem puny, but it was big bucks in 1964. The 1964 Amsterdam Interzonal had a first prize of $750. As one observer pointed out, he could make more giving a few simuls than for three-week's work against the world's best.

American chess players were more than happy to pay for the opportunity to listen to and play Fischer. I (J. D.) have dealt with the tour at length in *A Legend on the Road*. What follows are new games, reports and reminiscences, plus expanded annotations to some key games.

Detroit - February 9
+47=2-2

---

[29] *French Winawer   C19*
RJF–H. Kord
Detroit (simul) February 9, 1964

1.e4 e6 2.d4 d5 3.♘c3 ♗b4

"I may be forced to admit that the Winawer is sound.   But I doubt it! The defense is anti-positional and weakens the kingside."— Fischer, *My 60 Memorable Games*.

4.e5 ♘e7 5.a3 ♗xc3+ 6.bxc3 c5 7.a4 ♛a5 8.♗d2 ♘bc6 9.♘f3 c4!?

Conventional wisdom holds that Black should hold off on this move and maintain the tension in the center, while developing with 9...♗d7. The text has had a bad reputation since the 1940's, but is not an easy nut to crack.
10.♘g5

The classical way of answering 9...c4, but 10.g3 is probably equally good.
10...h6 11.♘h3 ♗d7

Black can try to cut across White's plan of ♘h3-f4-h5 with 11...♘g6, but after 12.♗e2, intending 13.♗h5, White has the advantage.

12.♘f4 O-O-O 13.♗e2

This move is natural, but 13.♘h5, attacking g7 and restraining ...f7-f6, is more thematic. Black might then try 13...♛c7, meeting 14.♘xg7 with 14...♘xe5. White should answer 13...♛c7 with 14.♗e2 and a slight edge.

13...f6 14.exf6 gxf6 15.O-O e5 16.♘h5 ♖df8 17.♔h1 ♔b8 18.♖ab1 ♔a8 19.♛c1 ♛c7 20.♗xh6 ♖f7 21. dxe5 ♖h7 22.♗g7 ♖xh5 23.♗xh5 ♖xh5 24.♗xf6 ♘xe5 25.♛f4 ♘7g6

26.♗xe5 ♕xe5 27.
♕xe5 ♘xe5 28.a5
♔b8 29.h3 ♔c7
30.♔g1 b5?

This allows White
to get rid of his
weak a-pawn. Bet-
ter was 30...♘c6
31.♖a1 d4 with a
complicated strug-
gle. White has three
connected passed
pawns on the king-
side, but Black's
minor pieces are
very active.

31.axb6+ axb6 32.
f4 ♘f7 33.♖f3 b5
34.g4 ♖h8

35.♔g2?
Asking for trouble
on the diagonal. Bobby
should have played 35.
♖d1 ♗c6 36.♖e3.
35...♗c6 36.♖e1 ♘d6
37.♖e7+?
This check leaves
both of White's Rooks
under attack. Instead,
Fischer had to play
37.♔h2.
37...♔d8 38.♖a7 d4
39.f5
The last chance to continue fighting
was 39.cxd4.

39...d3 40.cxd3 cxd3 41.♖a6 d2 42.
♖a1 ♗xf3+ 43.♔xf3 ♖xh3+ 44.♔f4
♖xc3 45.♖ad1 ♘c4 0-1

Source: original scoresheet.

Waltham, Mass. - February 20
+39=1-0

While researching *A Legend on the
Road*, I (J.D.) was unable to pin down
the details of Bobby's visit to Brandeis University in Waltham, Massachusetts. Since then, two participants
in the event, George Colman and Richard Lunenfeld, have stepped forward
and helped fill in the gaps.

The exhibition, sponsored by the
university and organized by Lunenfeld, was held on February 20. Bobby
scored 39 wins and one draw against
the 40-player field composed primar-
ily of Brandeis students. Among his
victims was NM Robin Ault. The two
had played in the 1959/60 Championship (as U.S. Junior Champion, Ault

was a seed); so it was a little unusual
for Ault to be taking a board at Brandeis. Even a little more unusual was
that the top five players (Ault was first
board) on the university chess team
had the first move against Bobby!
Lunenfeld asked Fischer if some of the
players could have White, and Bobby
agreed, after a little reflection, to five
boards.

Ault lost quickly after getting a bad
opening, but Lunenfeld used the first
move to good advantage. Aided by an
opening surprise, he was slightly better in the early middlegame and lost
his way only towards the end of the
game.

[30] *Sicilian   B54*
Richard Lunenfeld–RJF
Waltham (simul) February 20, 1964

1.e4 c5 2.♘f3 d6 3.d4 cxd4 4.♘xd4 ♘f6 5.♗c4?!

According to Lunenfeld, this rare gambit, which isn't given in any standard reference work, was accidentally played by U.S. Women's champion Lisa Lane a few years before this game.

5...♘xe4 6.♕h5

Stronger than Lane's try. Now Bobby thought for a few minutes.

6...e6 7.♗xe6!?

Tricky, but 7.♗b5+ was probably a better try.

7...♗xe6 8.♘xe6 ♕e7 9.O-O ♕xe6 10.♖e1 ♗e7?

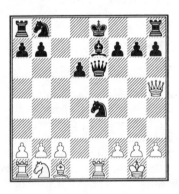

Black could have kept an advantage with 10...d5, making White work to recover the piece. Now Lunenfeld obtains a small advantage.

11.♕b5+ ♕d7 12.♕xd7+ ♘xd7 13. ♖xe4 ♘f6 14.♖e2 ♔d7 15.♘c3 ♖hc8 16.♗g5 ♘g8 17.♗f4!?

White would maintain his small advantage with 17.♗xe7, but he starts to

drift, as Bobby, having already finished off many opponents, comes around faster and faster.

17...♗c4 18.♗g3 ♖ac8 19.♖d1 ♖8c6 20.♖ed2 ♘f6 21.♖d4 ♘h5 22.♖xc4

White should save his Bishop either here, or on the next move, with 22. ♗e5 or 23.♗e5.

22...♖xc4 23.♖d2? ♘xg3

Bobby has always been a masterful exponent of the Rook-and-Bishop-vs.-Rook-and-Knight ending.

24.hxg3 ♗g5

The text tries to force weaknesses in White's position.

25.f4 ♗f6 26.♘d1 b5

Black grabs space on the queenside, while White can only sit.

27.♔f2 b4 28.♔e3 a5 29.♔d3 ♖c5 30.♔e4 h5

Fischer fixes the White pawns on f4 and g3 as targets.

31.c3?

White finally cracks in a difficult position. The text not only loses a pawn, but violates the rule of opening lines on the side of the board where one stands worse.

31...bxc3 32.bxc3 ♝xc3 33.♖c2 ♝b4 34.♖xc5 dxc5 35.♔d5 ♝e1 36.♔xc5 ♔e6 37.♔b5 ♝xg3 38.♔xa5 ♝xf4 39.♔b6 g5 40.a4 h4 41.a5 ♝h2 42.

a6 ♝g1+ 43.♔b7 g4 44.a7 ♝xa7 45. ♔xa7 f5 46.♔b6 ♔e5 47.♔b5 ♔d4 48.♔c6 f4 49.♘f2 h3 50.gxh3 g3 0-1

Montreal - February 23
+46=4–5

[31] *Vienna* *C26*
RJF–G. Jobin
Montreal (simul) February 23, 1964

1.e4 e5 2.♘c3 ♘f6 3.g3 d5 4.exd5 ♘xd5 5.♕e2!?

A novelty that has escaped the attention of theory. White normally plays 5.♝g2. On 5.♘ge2, Tartakower analyzed 5...♝g4 6.♝g2 ♘xc3 7. bxc3 ♘c6 8.d4 ♕f6 as clearly better for Black.

5...f6?!

The more natural way to defend the e-pawn is by 5...♘c6. One trick behind 5.♕e2 is that 5...♘c6 6.♝g2 ♘xc3? is met by 7.♝xc6+! bxc6 8. ♕xe5+, winning a pawn. However, Black has a much stronger continuation in 6...♘db4! This move attacks c2 and threatens ...♘d4.

6.♝g2 ♘xc3 7.bxc3 ♝e7 8.♘f3 ♘d7 9.d4 O-O 10.O-O ♝d6 11.c4 exd4 12. ♘xd4 ♘c5 13.♝a3 c6?!

This weakens Black's position. A more solid continuation was 13...♖e8 14.♕f3 ♕e7.

14.♖ad1 ♕c7 15.♘b3 b6 16.♕d2 ♝e7 17.♘xc5 bxc5 18.♕e3 ♝f5 19. ♝xc5 ♖fe8 20.♝xe7 ♖xe7 21.♕c5 ♝xc2 22.♖d2 ♝g6 23.♝xc6!?

The mundane 23.♕xc6 was probably more effective. The text allows

for some flashy tactics, but unnecessarily complicates.

23... ♖e6

It looks like Black is winning material, but Fischer has seen further.

24.♖d6!

A nice shot by Bobby. Now 24... ♖xd6?? is met by 25.♝d5+, winning Black's Queen, or 24...♕xd6 25.♕xd6 ♖xd6 26.♝xa8.

24...♖ae8 25.♝xe8 ♕xc5 26.♖xe6 ♝f5?

The immediate 26...♕xc4 is better.

27.♖e3 ♕xc4 28.♖fe1?!

The more patient 28.a3, preserving the pawn, was the right way to go.

28...♕xa2 29.♖e7 ♝g6 30.♝xg6 hxg6 31.♖b7 a5 32.h4 a4??

Black completely loses his sense of danger. He had chances to draw with 32...♔h7, meeting 33.♖ee7 with 33...♕a1+ 34.♔g2 f5 and 33.♖e8 with 33...g5 34.h5 g4.

33.♖e8+ ♔h7 34.♖bb8

The Black King is caught in a mating net.

(See diagram next column)

34...g5 35.h5 g6 36.♖e7+ 1-0

After 34.♖bb8

Montreal Clock Simul - February 24
+10=0–0

Fischer gave only two clock exhibitions during his tour. All the games from Davis, California, have been preserved, but the following sharp struggle is the only specimen that has been saved from Montreal. Initially, we thought that the Montreal clock simul might be a treasure chest of Fischer gems — advance publicity suggested the field would be strong and Bobby figured to be out for blood after a sub-par result the night before (+46=4–5) — but conversations with two of the participants have not borne this out.

Denis Allan and Tony Cayford both remember the strength of the players being in the 1700-2100 range, as some masters had decided not to play at the last moment. Cayford, who was then an expert, but is now one of America's top correspondence players, no longer has his game score, but clearly remembers that his game with Bobby was the last to finish; the time control was 40 moves in 2 hours.

The story of Fischer's game with Denis Allan is more intriguing. Today, Allan is a strong master who represented Canada in the 1987 Interzonal in Szirak, Hungary, but back in 1964 he was an expert. When Bobby published the following game in 1964, he listed Black as "Opponent," and subsequent Fischer game anthologies have used N.N. It seems likely that the organizers didn't preserve a record of the games and that Bobby just relied on memory. Now we know Black's real identity!

Denis Allan writes:

Yes, I am indeed "N.N." I have your book — *A Legend on the Road* — which I bought, because it includes this game, which seems to be surfacing in various places, such as the November 1996 issue of *Chess*.

After the simul, I was in Ben's Delicatessan (an institution in Montreal) with Fischer, Leslie Witt and Moe Moss, a chess columnist who was involved in the organization of the Montreal visit. We looked briefly at the game and Fischer commented that 10...e4 was a new move. It certainly was to me . . . I had little knowledge of the Two Knights at that time, other than that ...b5 and ...♘d4 were playable. Consequently, I had used a great deal of time before . . . playing [13]...♘f4, which I did fairly quickly, as it seemed obvious and strong.

I don't recall looking at the game after and lost the scoresheet. Several times when I lived in Toronto in the late sixties, an oldtimer from Montreal would say to me, "Allan, you missed a win in that game with Fischer," and I would say, "No, we looked at it afterward in the restaurant and if there was a win for Black, we would have seen it." In 1974, while killing time at the St. Catharine's library while my car was being fixed, I came across a book with all of Fischer's known games, and was surprised to see a section of about 30 exhibition games at the end, the first one being my game, and with a diagram showing the missed win. To my knowledge, no one had the score of the game. Later, I saw it in Estrin's book in Russian on the Two Knights, with comments attributed to Fischer.

One of the things I remember Fischer saying while he was in Montreal was "you can learn something from any patzer." Obviously, this was a case in point, where the famous player studies and learns from a game he plays in a simul, while the patzer, who should treasure the experience, forgets it!

Incidentally, Witt did not play in the clock simul — there may have been a place reserved which he gave to me, as I had just recently arrived in Montreal, but I don't remember. Fischer did give an interview on a youth television program his first day in Montreal, which culminated with his playing a two-minute game against Witt. Fischer played 4...♕h4 against the Scotch and got a winning position, but Witt was an excellent speed player, certainly one of the best in Canada then, and he won the game.

I remember they played about a dozen five-minute games one night before Witt eventually won one. They played for some small amount, with Fischer giving money odds, I think 3 to 1. I recall him saying that money odds were all he would give — that material or time odds changed the nature of the game, which he would not do.

This game appeared with in-depth notes by Fischer in the Spring 1964 issue of the *American Chess Quarterly*.

[32] *Two Knights C57*
RJF–Denis Allan
Montreal (clock simul) Feb. 24, 1964

1.e4 e5 2.♘f3 ♘c6 3.♗c4 ♘f6 4.♘g5 d5

Here Fischer notes,

More usual is 4...♕e7? 5.♗xf7+ ♔d8 6.♗b3 h6? 7.♘f7+ and 8.♘xh8 — in simultaneous exhibitions, at least!

5.exd5 ♘d4

After 5...♘xd5 6.d4! and White already practically has a won game! I guess I must have won, at the very least, 100 games or so with this line on my first chess tour, which took me across Canada and the United States. The move actually played is Ulvestad's Gambit—sharp but unsound.

Technically, 5...♘d4 is the Fritz variation, named after German player Alexander Fritz (1857-1932). According to *The Oxford Companion to Chess*, Fritz suggested it to Carl Schlechter, who analyzed it in the *Deutsche Schachzeitung* 1904. The Ulvestad variation actually starts with 5...b5, but the two lines are highly transpositional.

Olaf Ulvestad, a first-rate analyst, established his reputation with his *Chess Charts* in 1941. The highlight of his career was splitting a pair of games with David Bronstein in the 1946 USA–USSR match. For the next 45 years, he divided his time between the Pacific Northwest (Washington, Oregon and British Columbia) and Europe, pursuing his twin passions of chess and music. Today, he lives in retirement in Retsil, Washington.

Players looking for a sharp, albeit not airtight, answer to White's main line of the Two Knight's may wish to consider the following variation: *5... ♘a5 6.♗b5+ c6 7.dxc6 bxc6 8.♗e2 h6 9.♘f3* (Bobby would, of course, play 9.♘h3.) *9...e4 10.♘e5 ♕d4* (The games of NM William Schill of Washington state first brought this line to our attention. Spassky's old trainer Vladimir Zak has recommended it.) *11.f4 ♗c5 12.♖f1 ♕d8* (getting out of the way of c3 and b4 and preparing to make use of the weakened d8-h4 diagonal) *13.c3*.

The usual verdict is that Black must grovel, but, if he is prepared to sacrifice a piece for a few pawns, a loose White King and development, interesting things may happen. One encouraging example is Formenko–Radchenko, USSR 1967, which saw Black

win with a beautiful sacrificial attack: *13...♘d5 14.♕a4* (played not so much to attack, as to give the King the d1-square) *14...O-O 15.b4 ♕h4+ 16. ♔d1 ♖d8 17.♔c2 ♗f5 18.bxc5 e3+ 19. ♔b2 ♖db8+ 20.♔a3 ♕d8 21.♗b2 exd2 22.♖d1 ♗c2! 23.♕xc2 ♘b3! 24.♘c4 ♘xa1 25.♕xd2 ♕b6 0-1*

White can also try *13.d4* which got an outing in Mednis–van Oosterom, Antwerp 1955. The battle between the future GM and future multi-millionaire chess patron saw the former emerge with a winning advantage after 13...♗b6 14.c3 ♘d5 15.♔f2! O-O 16. ♔g1 c5 17.dxc5 ♗xc5+ 18.♔h1 ♗e3? 19.b4!, as 19...♗xc1 is met by 20. ♕xc1 ♘b7 21.♖d1 with the unstoppable threat of 22.c4. Van Oosterom would later go on to own the largest software company in his native Holland. He now lives in Monaco where he sponsors numerous events, including the annual Melody Amber and the Ladies-vs.-Veterans events.

6.c3 b5 7.♗f1 ♘xd5 8.cxd4

The main line is 8.♘e4.

8...♕xg5 9.♗xb5+ ♔d8 10.♕f3 e4?

Fischer gives this move an exclamation mark, praising it for drawing the White Queen out into the open where it will be a target for Black's better developed pieces. This assessment was made at a time when a strong resource for White had yet to be discovered.

A better try for Black is *10...♗b7*, which led to Fischer's shortest loss on the tour after *11.O-O* (11.♘c3 is held to be a better try) *11...exd4* (11...♖b8 12.♕g3!? ♕xg3 13.hxg3 exd4 was equal in Shabalov–A. Ivanov, U.S. Championship 1996) *12.♕xf7??* (12. d3 ♕e5! gave Black good play in Paoli–Robatsch, Venice 1967) *12...♘f6 0-1*, Fischer–R. Burger, San Francisco 1964. (See game 58.)

Anyone can blunder in a simul, and Bob Burger was one of the stronger players in California at the time. Fischer indirectly includes this game in his commentary to Black's tenth move.

> By this dynamic move Black gives up a second pawn in order to give his pieces maximum scope, and also he hopes to catch White off guard by drawing the Queen out into the open. 10...♗b7 would be weaker, but it contained (N.B.: Fischer uses the past tense, as the *American Chess Quarterly* came out in the end of May and the San Francisco exhibition was in April) a cute trap, i.e., 11.O-O exd4 and if White is naive enough to go Pawn-grabbing — 12.♕xf7 (11. d3 is correct) 12...♘f6; and he loses a piece.

11.♕xe4 ♗d6 12.O-O?

After this move, Bobby ends up in serious trouble. Correct was 12.h4!, when White is doing very well.

12... ♗b7

Note the ominous portent of four Black pieces ready to explode in White's face! As an old chess friend once explained to me, "Three pieces are a mate — but four pieces!"

13.d3?

According to Fischer, the best try was 13.♖e1!, forcing ...c6 and, in so doing, taking some of the pressure off White's position by closing the diagonal. Bobby notes that 13.♘c3 was well met by 13...♖b8, when, after 14. d3 ♕h5, Black would win a piece.

13...♘f4?

Brilliant! Brilliant! The only trouble is that it loses! With 13... ♗xh2+!! Black could have pulled off a neat win.

Because 14.♔xh2 (14.♔h1 ♗f4!) 14...♘f4! 15.♗xf4 (15.♕xf4 ♕xg2 mate; 15.♕xb7 ♕h4+ 16.♔g1 ♘e2 mate) 15...♕h4+ 16.♔g1 ♗xe4 17. dxe4 ♕xf4 leaves White too far down in material.

14.♗xf4

Black's point was that after 14. ♕xb7, he had at least a perpetual by 14...♘h3+ 15.♔h1 ♘xf2+!, etc.

14...♕xb5 15.d5

Sidestepping 15.♕e3? ♕d5! 16.f3 ♖e8!, winning a piece.

15...♕xb2?

Allan misses the last chance to put up strong resistance. He had to play 15...♖e8 16.♘c3 ♕xb2 17.♕c4 ♗xf4 18.♖ab1 ♕d2 19.♖fd1 ♗a6 20.♕c6. Black is forced to bail out with 20... ♗xh2+ 21.♔xh2 ♕h6+ 22.♕xh6+ gxh6, when White's better pawn structure gives him the advantage.

16.♗xd6 cxd6 17.♖e1! ♕f6

Black should have tried to head for an endgame with 17...♕e5.

18.♘c3 ♖c8 19.♕b4!

Fischer is the master alchemist who knows how to transform his advantage. Here he allows simplification with 19...♖xc3 20.♕xb7 to get at Black's King.

19... ♖e8? 20.♕a5+

This wins at least the Exchange.

20...♔d7 21.♕a4+ 1-0

Quebec City - February 25
+48=0-0

[33] *Sicilian   B32*
RJF–M. Tordion
Quebec City (simul) February 25, 1964

1.e4 c5 2.♘f3 ♘c6 3.d4 cxd4 4.♘xd4 ♘xd4?!

Black trades off his only developed piece and brings White's Queen to a powerful position.

5.♕xd4 e6 6.♘c3 ♕c7?

Safer is 6...d6, but White is still much better because of his lead in development.

7.♘b5 ♕xc2 8.♗f4?

Bobby starts to make things messy. He could have obtained an overwhelming position by 8.♗d3 ♕c6 9.♗f4 with threats of 10.♘c7+ and 10.♖c1.

8...♗c5 9.♕d2

White could also have tried 9.♗d3 ♗xd4 10.♗xc2 ♗b6 11.0-0-0, when White's development gives him excellent compensation for the pawn.

9...♕xe4+ 10.♗e2?

Necessary is 10.♔d1 ♔f8 with a slightly better position for White.

10...♗b4 11.♘d6+ ♗xd6 12.♗xd6 ♘f6?

Black misses his chance against the great Bobby. Correct is 12...♕xg2 13.♖f1 ♘f6 with a big plus for Black. After the text, the position is about equal.

13.0-0 ♕d5 14.♕f4 ♕e4 15.♕g3 ♕g6

Bobby in Wichita, Kansas, on April 4, 1964. He is flanked by (L-R): (L) Keith Carson, Bob Michaelson and (R) D LaPierre Ballard, Charles Wayne Carson

Black continues to try to trade Queens. If 15...♕xe2?, then 16.♕xg7 is crushing.

16.♕a3 ♕g5

Better is 16...♘e4 17.♗d3 f5, intending ...♔f7, with equal chances.

17.♖ac1

White might have considered 17. ♗f3 to keep Black's Knight out of e4.

17...♘e4 18.♗b4 a5 19.♗f3 ♘d2 20.♗xd2 ♕xd2 21.♕c5 ♕b4?

Correct is 21...♖f8 to avoid what comes next.

22.♕xc8+ ♖xc8 23.♖xc8+ ♔e7 24. ♖xh8 h6 25.♖b8 b6 26.♖b7 ♕xb2 27.♖d1 ♕xa2 28.♖dxd7+ ♔e8 29. ♖e7+ ♔d8 30.♖bd7+ ♔c8 31.♗b7+ ♔b8 32.♖e8+ ♔a7 33.♖a8+ mate

[34] *Falkbeer Countergambit   C31*
RJF–A. Bilodeau
Quebec City (simul) February 25, 1964

1.e4 e5 2.f4 d5 3.exd5 e4

Fischer played the King's Gambit many times, but to the best of our knowledge this is only time that he accepted the Falkbeer Countergambit. In 1971, Bobby met Jorge Szmetan's 2...d5 with 3.♘f3.

4.♘c3

4.d3 is much more common.

4...♘f6 5.♕e2

This position can also be reached by the Vienna Game move order 1.e4 e5 2.♘c3 ♘f6 3.f4 d5 4.exd5 e4 5.♕e2, as in Suttles–Lengyel, Belgrade 1969.

5...♗g4

More commonly seen are 5...♗d6 and 5...♗f5. An example of the latter is Kavalek–Zinn, Polanica Zdroj 1964, which saw sharp complications arise after 6.h3 h5 7.♘f3 ♗c5 8.♘e5 O-O 9.g4 ♗h7 10.♕c4 ♘bd7 11.♘xd7 ♘xd7 12.♔d1 ♕h4 13.d4 ♕f2.

6.♕e3

Worth considering is 6.♕b5+ ♘bd7 7.♕xb7. Taubenhaus–Alapin, Frankfurt 1887, saw White get butchered: 7.d4 exd3 8.♗xd3 ♗c5 9.h3 ♕e7 10. ♔f1 ♘h5 11.♘ge2 ♗xe2+ 12.♘xe2 ♕h4.

6...♗f5 7.h3

White retains an advantage with 7. ♗b5+ c6 8.dxc6 bxc6 9.♗c4.

7...♘xd5 8.♘xd5 ♕xd5 9.g4 ♗c5 10.♕b3?

The offer to trade Queens looks logical, but better is 10.♕c3 ♗e6 11.♕xg7 ♗d4 12.♕g5 ♘c6 13.♗b5.

10...♗e6 11.f5

Another option was 11.♕xd5 ♗xd5 12.♘e2, meeting 12...e3 with 13.♖h2.

11...♕d4 12.♕g3 ♗d6 13.♕g2 ♗d5 14.♘e2 ♕c5 15.♘c3 O-O 16.b4 ♕d4 17.♗b2 ♗xb4 18.O-O-O ♘c6

Although Black retains some advantage after the text, 18...♗xc3 19.♗xc3

♕a4 20.f6 g6 21.♕e2 ♘a6 would have given him a large advantage.

19.f6 g6 20.h4 h6

Black should have captured on c3 again: 20...♗xc3 21.dxc3 ♕e3+ 22. ♕d2 ♕xd2+ 23.♖xd2 ♗xa2 with advantage.

21.g5 h5 22.♗e2

22.♘xd5 would have offered White better chances.

22...♘e5 23.♘b5

Again, White should play 23.♘xd5.

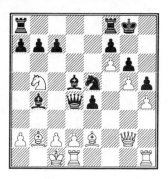

23...e3?!

Much stronger is *23...♕c5! 24. ♗xe5* e3 25.♕g3 exd2+ 26.♔b1 ♖fe8 27.♗d4 ♗xa2+ 28.♔b2 (28.♔xa2 ♕xc2+) 28...♕d5 or *24.♕g1 ♘d3+ 25.♗xd3 exd3 26.♕xc5 ♗xc5* with a substantial plus for Black.

24.♗xd4 ♗xg2 25.♖h2 exd2+?!

Better is 25...♗xd2+ 26.♔b1 ♘c6 27.♖xg2 a6 with an unclear position.

26.♔b2 ♘c4+?

Correct is 26...♘f3. After 27.♖xg2 ♘xh4 28.♖f2 ♘f5, Black has fighting chances.

27.♗xc4 ♗f3 28.♗e2 ♗xe2 29. ♖xe2 ♖ae8 30.♖xe8 ♖xe8 31.c3 a6 32.♘xc7 ♖e4 33.♖xd2 ♗a5 34.♘d5

♔f8 35.♗c5+ ♔e8 36.♖d4 ♖xd4
37.♗xd4 ♔d7 38.♔c2 ♔d6 39.♘e3
♗c7 40.♔d3 b5 41.♔e4 ♔c6 42.
♗e5 ♗xe5 43.♔xe5 a5 44.♘f5 ♔d7

45.♘d6 b4 46.cxb4 axb4 47.♘b7
1-0

Source: *New In Chess* #7, 1998 (Originally
published in *L'action catholique*, 1964)

Richmond - March 5
+44=2–4

Report by Spencer Matthews:

In the late afternoon of March
5, 1964, I traveled from Charlottesville to Richmond with a fellow
graduate student, Jack Wright. A
law student, Richard Callaghan,
who was a member of the Charlottesville and University chess
clubs attended also, but traveled
separately. We had dinner in Richmond and arrived at the site of
the exhibition well ahead of the
scheduled hour. I must confess, I
cannot now remember either the
scheduled time or the site. What I
do remember is that Fischer was
very late. I think his plane had
been delayed leaving New York and/
or Washington by snow. The assembled company feared that the
exhibition might have to be called
off. When we finally got word that
Fischer had left Washington, Jack
and I went to the Richmond airport to wait for him. We had him
to ourselves, so to speak, for the
roughly 20-minute drive back to
the site. You can imagine what a
high point that was for us. He
was genial, but uncommunicative
about any subject outside chess.
When he talked about chess, his
sentence structure got very intri-
cate and precise. Jack was partial
to the Slav Defense and Fischer
offered to open 1.d4 against him,
but Jack declined the favor telling
Fischer that he also liked the Pet-

roff. Fischer played the Vienna
against Jack!

It was about 11:00 p.m. when
Fischer began to address the players. I had imagined that he would
do something to keep the length
of the event manageable; but he
began with a lecture as adver-
tised. It took the form of a running commentary on one of his
tournament games. The game he
chose is #29 in *My 60 Memorable
Games*, Fischer–Geller, Bled 1961.

My recollection is that it was
about midnight when the exhibition actually began and close to
3:00 a.m. when it ended. It was
explained that Fischer would permit each of us two "passes" during the evening if we needed extra
time for particular moves. Otherwise, we were to wait until he arrived at the board and then make
the move we selected. One elderly
gentleman near me apparently was
hard of hearing and repeatedly
waved Fischer by. After several
such instances, Fischer stood before the board, tapped on the table
and said, "C'mon, fella, move! This
ain't postal chess!"

---

[35] *Sicilian Dragon   B76*
RJF–Spencer Matthews
Richmond (simul) March 5, 1964

**1.e4 c5 2.♘f3 d6 3.d4 cxd4 4.♘xd4
♘f6 5.♘c3**

Against 5...♘c6, Fischer preferred 6. ♗c4 over 6.♗g5.

Recently in a skittles game someone tried 6...g6!? against me. The game continued: 7.♘xc6 bxc6 8.e5 ♘h5? (Correct is 8...♘g4. Not 8...dxe5 9.♗xf7+, winning the Queen — that was another skittles game!); 9.♕f3! e6 10.g4 ♘g7 11. ♘e4 ♕a5+ 12.♗d2 ♕xe5 13. ♗c3, Black resigns. — Fischer in *My 60 Memorable Games*, p. 87.

Black tried 8...♘d7 in Fischer–Wilkerson, Davis (clock simul) 1964, but White quickly won after 9.exd6 exd6 10.0-0 d5 11.♘xd5 ♘c5 12.♕d4 cxd5 13.♗b5+ ♗d7 14.♗xd7+ ♕xd7 15.♕xh8 f5 16.♖e1 ♘e6 17.♕f6. That made the score 1:1 between the players: three days prior, Wilkerson had beaten Bobby in a simul in San Francisco in the famous Mechanics Institute Chess Club, one of the oldest and nicest in the United States. Max Wilkerson managed this club for many years before retiring in 1996.

5...g6 6.♗e3 ♗g7 7.f3 0-0 8.♕d2 ♘c6 9.0-0-0

Fischer deviates from his normal 9. ♗c4.

9...d5 10.♘xc6 bxc6 11.h4!?

This is rare move has been tried only a handful of times. White usually follows 10.♘xc6 with 11.♗h6. GM Sergey Tiviakov, in his *Chess Informant* monograph on the Dragon covering B75-76 (the Yugoslav Attack without ♗c4), gives 11.h4 ♕a5 as unclear and suggests 11...♗e6!? This got a tryout in Sorri–Arnaudov, Kharrachov 1967, where Black got good play for the Exchange after 12.e5 ♘d7 13. ♗h6 ♗xe5 14.♗xf8 ♕xf8. A simi-

lar idea was seen in Maiorov–Gaponenko, Krasnodar 1995, after 11...e6 12. e5 ♘d7 13.♗h6 ♗xe5. Matthews opts for the same theme of sacrificing the Rook for the dark-squared Bishop plus a pawn.

11...♕a5 12.e5 ♘d7 13.♗h6 ♗xe5 14.♗xf8 ♘xf8 15.h5 ♖b8 16.♖e1 d4 17.♖xe5 ♕xe5 18.♘e4 ♗f5 19.♗d3 ♗xe4 20.♗xe4 c5 21.hxg6 hxg6 22. ♗d3 ♘e6 23.♗c4 ♘f4 24.g3 d3

24...♘h5 may be stronger, as after the text White has 25.♗xf7+ ♔xf7 26.♕xf4+ with approximate equality.

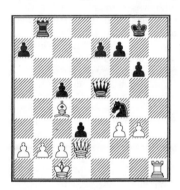

25.cxd3? ♘e2+ 26.♔b1 ♘d4?!

26...♘xg3 was a better try for the advantage.

27.♕h6??

Completely overlooking Black's threat. Correct was 27.f4 with equality.

27...♖xb2+ 28.♔xb2 ♘f5+ 0-1

Naturally, I was high as a kite. I almost ran the car off the road on the way back to Charlottesville thinking about the game. If Jack hadn't warned me, I'd have hit a car pulling out on to the road from a country driveway. Jack and I had classes the next day (oops, I mean later that day) and so we were anxious to get back. Until I read your account, I had no idea Fischer had been dumped beside the highway to flag down a bus; but in those days in rural Virginia, that was a common way to get to cities. Fischer was very gracious in signing the scoresheet. I put the damn thing away so carefully when I moved from Charlottesville that I've never been able to find it again.

I can't document it, but I have the very clear memory that Fischer played 44 games, won 37, drew 4, and lost 3. The reason the memory is so strong is that soon after the event, I read that he'd gone undefeated in a large exhibition "up north," so I felt pretty good about Virginia chess. Actually, my memory is that he went 64-0 in Buffalo, N.Y. I see from your book's schedule of exhibitions that he never even played in Buffalo, so maybe I dreamed the whole thing up.

Even though I don't have Fischer's signed score, I kept a good, legible copy to share with my friends, so I'm very confident of the accuracy of the game. I've often wondered whether Fischer "let" me have the win because of the lateness of the hour and because of the acquaintanceship we had on the ride from the airport. Clearly 28.♔xb2 is the only move that doesn't allow mate in a few, so when he played it he might have intended to play on and force me to demonstrate that I could hold up under the pressure. Probably, I couldn't have. He wasn't so considerate of everybody. Sometime during the evening, a nearby player who had a Queen against two Rooks in an ending (I can't remember the details of the posi-

tion) asked Fischer, "Can you win this?" Fischer said, "Yes." And the player said, "Okay, I resign." I wondered what Fischer's answer would have been if the question had been framed, "Is this a win?"

NM Macon Shibut of Virginia received gold in "a stack of old papers and archival junk pertaining to chess in Virginia." He found a photocopy of a newspaper clipping on which the date " 'March 10, 1964' had been rubber-stamped." Unfortunately, the provenance of the article which follows could not be determined.

Confidence Paid Dividend

by Charles Ashworth

The national chess champion knocked his king on its side. Although he moves so quickly that he frequently knocks over pieces, in this case it was for keeps. His king stayed on its side and Robert Fischer of New York acknowledged defeat by resigning. The winner was Charles Powell, the Richmond chess champion.

The victory came last Thursday at the Virginia Home here. Fischer came to Richmond to play chess with 50 Virginians simultaneously.

Earlier in the evening, before the games started, Powell had fidgeted uneasily behind his card table. His black pieces were before him. The white were beside an aisle to be used by Fischer.

The national champion arrived four hours late at 11:10 p.m. and gave a brief lecture on chess. At 12:10, the competition began, and, at 1:25 a.m., Fischer acknowledged that Powell had beaten him. Confidence had come to Powell during the game. Less than an hour after the match started, Fischer was willing to declare a draw. Powell decided to play on. "I just thought I could beat him. We both ended up attacking each other's King, and it was a question of who got the other guy's King first." More than an hour after the Powell victory, the games concluded with three last-minute victories by Virginians: S. G. Matthews of Charlottesville, Julian Allen of Richmond and Carl R Nichols of Richmond. Two other players, Bob Vassar and Jesse Burke, both of Richmond, achieved draws.

Carl Stutz, a member of the club, later asked Fischer if such victories were common. Fischer indicated not, although, he said, there have been wins in several of his multi-game exhibitions.

Powell, 19, was graduated from Thomas Jefferson High School last June. He is now a freshman at Randolph-Macon College in Ashland. He plans to major in mathematics or physics. He learned chess from his father, B. G. Powell of 3106 Rendale Ave. He has been a member of the Richmond Chess Club for three years and is an avid promoter of the club.

He ran through the winning game the other day for a reporter. While moving the pieces with great agility and rapidity, he kept up a running commentary on the game, interspersed with plugs for the club. If it's not too much, Powell said, he would like the story to mention that the 1964 city championships will begin at 7 p.m. Saturday at the Virginia Home and will continue on Thursday and Saturday nights for two weeks.

Having said this, his hand was on his queen, which had the opposing king in check. Although the game could have been prolonged, checkmate of his opponent was only a few moves away.

At that point the real game had ended. Powell mentioned that the Richmond Chess Club would like more members, put his chessmen away, folded his board and departed.

New Orleans - March 26
+70=2-3

Andrew Lockett was a legendary figure in Louisiana chess for many years. During the period 1917 to 1937, Lockett was the dominant player in the state, though he considered himself more of a problemist than a player. He was also a major organizer. He faced many top players in simuls over the years including Capablanca, Torre, Edward Lasker, Denker, Horowitz, Emanuel Lasker, Dake, Reshevsky, Bisguier, Evans, and Koltanowski.

Lockett was 68 years old when he faced Bobby.

[36] *Modern   B07*
RJF–Andrew Lockett
New Orleans (simul) March 26, 1964

1.e4 d6 2.d4 g6 3.♘c3 ♗g7 4.f4

Another interesting possibility is 4.h4, which I have played in some skittles games. For example, Fischer–N.N. went 4.h4 h5? 5.♘h3! ♗xh3? (a common mistake in this line) 6.♖xh3 c5? 7.dxc5 dxc5 8. ♗b5+ ♘c6 9.♖d3 ♕a5 10.♗d2 with a won game for White. If Black answers 4.h4 with 4...h5, then 5. ♗e2 c5 6.dxc5 ♛a5 7.♔f1! ♛xc5 8.h5 O-O with a double-edged game. I beat Tal in a five-minute game with this line.

Source: "Fischer talks Chess," *Chess Life*, February 1964, p.44

4...♘c6

4...c6 5.♘f3 ♗g4 6.♗e3 ♘d7 7. h3 ♗xf3 8.♛xf3 e6 9.O-O-O ♘e7 10. g4 ♛a5 11.♔b1 ♖b8 12.e5 dxe5 13. dxe5 ♘d5 14.♘e4 gave White a significant advantage in Fischer–Beach, New York State Open 1963.

5.♘f3 ♗g4 6.♗e3 ♗xf3 7.gxf3 e6 8. ♛d2 a6 9.O-O-O d5 10.h4 h5 11.f5 gxf5 12.exd5 exd5 13.♗h3 ♘ce7 14.♖hg1 ♗f8 15.♘e2 ♛d6 16.♔b1 O-O-O 17.♘g3 ♗h6 18.♘xf5 ♘xf5 19.♗xf5+ ♔b8 20.♗xh6 ♘xh6 21. ♗d3 ♛f6 22.♖g5 ♛xd4 23.♖xh5 ♘g8 24.♖xh8 ♛xh8 25.♖h1 ♛h6 26.♛xh6 ♘xh6 27.♖g1 ♖e8 28.b4 b5 29.♖g5 c6 30.♔b2 ♖e6 31.♔c3 ♖f6 32.♔d4?

Correct is 32.♖h5 with an equal position.

32...♖xf3 33.♔c5 ♔c7 34.♖e5 ♔d7 35.♔b6 ♖f4 36.♖h5 ♖f6?

Better is 36...♘g4 with advantage to Black.

37.♔xa6 ♔c7 38.♔a5 ♖d6 39.a4 ♖d8

39...bxa4 is correct. White would then have a slight advantage after 40.♔xa4.

40.♗xb5 cxb5 41.♖xh6 bxa4 42. ♔xa4 ♖f8 43.♖f6 ♔d7 44.b5 ♖a8+ 45.♔b4 ♔e7 46.♖f2 ♖h8 47.b6 ♖xh4+ 48.♔c5 ♖c4+ 49.♔xd5 ♖b4 50.♔c5 ♖b2 51.♔c6 ♔d8 52.b7 f6 53.c4 ♖b4 54.c5 1-0

Source: *Louisiana Chess Association Bulletin*, June 1971.

Wichita - April 4
+37=2-1

D LaPierre Ballard has this to say about the exhibition:

Bobby played 40 games that night at the University of Wichita Campus Activities Center. He lost to me, drew with Dan Pritchard and Robert Hart and won the rest. His most notable game was against Keith Carson, who was the best player in Oklahoma at the time. Bobby played the Vienna. Eventually an ending was reached in which Bobby had an f-pawn and an h-pawn. Keith had studied this Rook and Pawn type of ending previously and thought he could draw. Bobby played like Capablanca and by constant maneuvering managed a win.

I went with the man who organized the exhibition to pick up Bobby. I cannot remember that man's name. He had been a Colonel. Bobby was very late — 45 minutes, I recall. On the way to the simul, I sat with him and chatted.

I asked him about his recent article in the magazine *Chess World*, which only lasted three issues. He had listed the ten best players of all time. He had put Morphy as first . . . The great accumulation of knowledge since 1860 would be assimilated and mastered by Morphy very quickly and then, were he alive in 1964, he would have been the best.

I asked him about Petrosian. He rattled off an ending from a game of Petrosian's and said, "The man obviously did not know how to play that ending."

Before the simul Bobby gave a talk about his famous game at Bled 1961 where he had beaten Geller in 22 moves. Bobby had White in a Steinitz Deferred Ruy. Bobby started the talk by showing 1.e4 on the board. He then said, "I always play pawn to King four for my first move just like Steinitz did before he got old!"

During my game, Bobby made no comments until the end. He said after he turned over his King

Bobby in Wichita with *Shakhmatny Bulletin* 1/1964 and **D LaPierre Ballard**

that 32.♕h7+ would have been much better than what he played. He did not say, "I resign." I noticed that when he played a pawn or Bishop that he thoughtfully screwed it into the board, i.e., he twisted it between his thumb and forefinger.

It cost $5 to play Bobby. That was a lot for a 19-year-old college student then. I figured it was my one and only chance in my whole lifetime; so I put a big effort into it. My game ran over three hours and I did not move a muscle the whole time, except to play my moves.

[37] *Sicilian Accelerated Dragon*   *B35*
RJF–D LaPierre Ballard
Wichita (simul) April 4, 1964

1.e4 c5 2.♘f3 ♘c6 3.d4 cxd4 4.♘xd4 g6 5.♘c3 ♗g7 6.♗e3 ♘f6 7.♗c4

O-O 8.♗b3 ♘g4 9.♕xg4 ♘xd4 10.
♕d1 ♘xb3 11.axb3 b6 12.♗d4 f6
13.h4

The obvious 13.♗xf6 ♗xf6 14.
♕d5+ e6 15.♕xa8 ♗xc3+ 16.bxc3
♕c7 17.O-O a5! 18.♖a4 d5! 19.exd5
♗b7 20.♕a7 exd5 21.♖e1 ♖a8 is
winning for Black, Kotkov–A. Zaitsev, USSR 1962.

Ballard was familiar with all this,
having just read the article on this
variation by Vladimirov and A. Geller
in the January 1964 issue of *Shakhmatny Bulletin*.

13...♗b7 14.h5 ♔f7

A move unknown to theory in 1964.
Today the focus is on 14...d5 (see Shabalov–Rausis, Riga 1989, *NIC Year-
book 14*, p.33).

15.♕g4 d5 16.exd5 ♗xd5 17.O-O-O
♗e6 18.♕g3 ♕b8 19.♕f3 ♕c8 20.
♘e4?

Fischer loses his sense of danger
and blunders the Exchange in an equal
position.

20... ♗g4 21.hxg6+ hxg6 22.♕d3

On 22.♘g5+, Black has 22...♔g8 23.
♕e4 ♗f5! (23...♗xd1?? 24.♕xg6) 24.

♕e2 e5! (24...fxg5? 25.♗xg7 ♔xg7
26.♕xe7+ ♖f7 27.♖h7+ wins) 25.
♗c3 fxg5 and it's all over.

22...♗xd1 23.♖xd1 ♕c6 24.♖h1
♖ac8 25.c3 ♖h8 26.♖e1 ♖hd8 27.f4
♕d5 28.♔b1 ♕xb3 29.f5

According to Ballard, who gives the
move a double exclam, White now
dominates the light squares. Actually,
Black is just winning.

29...gxf5 30.♘g5+ fxg5 31.♕xf5+
♗f6

32.♗xf6

According to Fischer, White should
have played 32.♕h7+ (Ballard), but
after 32...♔e8 33.♕g6+ (33.♗xf6
♖d1+ 34.♖xd1+ ♕xd1+ 35.♔a2 exf6)
33...♔d7 34.♗xf6 exf6 35.♕xf6 (35.
♕g7+ ♔c6, heading for b5 and a6)
35...♖c5!, Black's King has a safe haven on c8.

**32...♖d1+ 33.♖xd1 ♕xd1+ 34.♔a2
♖c5 0-1**

White soon runs out of checks. *Inside Chess* reader Gordon Gribble gives
35.♕h7+ ♔xf6 36.♕h6+ ♔f7 37.
♕h7+ ♔e8 38.♕h8+ ♔d7 39.♕h3+
g4 and it's all over.

The following games from Wichita come from an old mimeographed souvenir bulletin of the event, kindly supplied to us by Robert Hart.

---

[38] *Alekhine   B03*
RJF–Mechem
Wichita (simul) April 4, 1964

1.e4 ♘f6 2.e5 ♘d5 3.d4 d6 4.c4 ♘b6 5.exd6 exd6 6.♘c3 ♗f5 7.♘f3 a6?

This move just loses time.

8.♗d3 ♗xd3 9.♕xd3 ♗e7 10.0-0 O-O 11.♖e1 ♘8d7 12.b3 ♖e8 13.♗f4 ♘f8 14.♖e2 ♘g6 15.♗g3 ♕d7 16.♖ae1 ♗f8

17.h4! ♖xe2 18.♖xe2 h5

This is a difficult decision. Black creates a target on the kingside with this move, but passive defense with 18...♘e7 19.a4 ♖e8 20.a5 ♘c8 wouldn't be to everyone's taste.

19.♘g5 ♕g4 20.♖e4 ♕f5 21.♕e2 ♘d7

This lets Black's kingside get shredded, but 21...f6 22.♘e6 followed by d5 is no picnic either.

22.♘d5 ♘f6 23.♘xf6+ gxf6 24.♘f3 ♖c8 25.d5 ♘e5 26.♘d4 ♕g6 27.♖f4 ♘g4

A spirited try. The immediate 27...♕b1+ allows 28.♕f1 ♕xa2 29.♖xf6. The text covers f6 and h2.

28.♘f5 ♘e5 29.♘d4 ♘g4 30.♖f5

Bobby doesn't want to draw.

30...c5

Black isn't giving up. Now he wants to dislodge the Knight.

31.dxc6 bxc6 32.♕f3 ♖e8

32...c5 is tricky, but White keeps the advantage with 33.♘e2 (not 33.♘c6 ♖xc6 or 33.♘c2 ♘h6) 33...♘h6 34.♖xh5.

33.♔f1 ♖e6?

This is the fatal mistake. Necessary was 33...c5, when 34.♘c6 is forced. The position is complicated, but still looks like White for choice: 34...♘h6 35.♖d5 (forced) 35...♕b1+ 36.♕d1 ♕xa2 37.♗xd6. Nonetheless, this was Black's best try.

34.♕d3

Bobby doesn't fall for the trap, 34.♘xe6 fxe6, when the Rook is attacked and ...♕b1+, followed by mate, looms.

34...♘e5 35.♗xe5 ♖xe5 36.♖f3 ♕xd3+ 37.♖xd3 ♗e7?

It's not pretty, but 37...♖c5 was the last chance to prolong the struggle.

38.♖e3

There's nothing wrong with 38.♘xc6, but Bobby prefers to simplify to a completely won Knight-vs.-Bishop ending.

38...♖xe3 39.fxe3 c5 40.♘f5 ♗f8 41.♘g3 1-0

Bill McLaughlin was one of the people responsible for bringing Bobby to Wichita. An annual memorial tournament is held here every year in his honor.

---

[39] *Two Knights   C59*
RJF–Bill McLaughlin
   Wichita (simul) April 4, 1964

1.e4 e5 2.♘f3 ♘c6 3.♗c4 ♘f6 4. ♘g5 d5 5.exd5 ♘a5 6.♗b5+ c6 7. dxc6 bxc6 8.♗e2 ♗c5?

This avoids Bobby's favorite 8...h6 9.♘h3, but at a terrific cost. White now has the opportunity to bolster his Knight with 9.d3. Black is a pawn down for nothing, as his play against the g5-Knight, the idea behind this line, is gone.

9.d3 h6 10.♘f3 ♕d6 11.♘c3 ♗f5 12.O-O O-O 13.♘d2 ♖ad8 14.♘b3 ♘b7 15.♘xc5 ♘xc5 16.♗e3 ♖d7 17.♗f3 ♖fd8 18.♕e2 ♘e6 19.♖fe1 g5?

Black stands badly, but this self-inflicted wound only hastens the end.

20.g3 ♘d4 21.♗xd4 exd4 22.♘e4 ♗xe4 23.♗xe4 ♖e8 24.♕f3 ♖de7

25.♕g2?

The natural 25.♖e2, followed by doubling Rooks, was indicated.

25... ♔g7?

Black misses his chance, i.e., 25... ♘xe4 26.dxe4 ♕g6! 27.f3 f5 with good counterplay.

26.♖e2 ♘d5

26...♘xe4 was still the best, though current circumstances were not as favorable.

27.♖ae1 g4

27...f5 had to be played. Now Bobby has it all his way.

28.♕f1 ♘c7 29.♗f5 h5 30.h3 ♖xe2 31.♖xe2 ♕f6 32.hxg4 ♖h8 33.♕g2 hxg4 34.♗xg4 ♕g5 35.♕e4 ♖e8 36. ♕xd4+ ♔g8 37.♖xe8+ ♘xe8 38.♗d7 ♘g7 39.♗xc6 ♕c1+ 40.♔g2 ♕xc2 41.♗e4 ♕c7 42.b4 ♘e6 43.♕e3 a5 44.b5 ♘c5 45.♗c6 ♕d6 1-0

---

[40] *Sicilian Dragon   B76*
RJF–Munzlinger
   Wichita (simul) April 4, 1964

1.e4 c5 2.♘f3 ♘c6 3.d4 cxd4 4.♘xd4 d6 5.♘c3 g6 6.♗e3 ♗g7 7.♕d2 ♘f6 8.f3 ♗d7 9.O-O-O a6?!

This plan is too slow. Black normally castles on move eight, but 8... ♗d7 is possible if Black follows up with 9...♖c8.

10.g4 b5?! 11.h4 b4?

11...♖c8 looks a little better.

12.♘d5

White trades off the Knight that defends Black's King.

12...♘xd5 13.exd5 ♘e5 14.h5

Bobby is after much bigger fare than the b-pawn. There's not much Black can do at this point.

14...gxh5 15.♖xh5 a5 16.♗h6 ♗xh6
17.♕xh6 ♘g6 18.♕g7 ♗a4 19.♗d3
♖f8 20.♖xh7 ♗xc2 21.♗xc2 ♖c8 22.
♔b1 ♔d7 23.♗f5+ ♔e8 24.♗xg6
♕c7 25.♗xf7+ ♖xf7 26.♕xf7+ 1-0

[41] *French Alekhine-Chatard   C13*
RJF–Self

Wichita (simul) April 4, 1964

1.e4 e6 2.d4 d5 3.♘c3 ♘f6 4.♗g5
♗e7 5.e5 ♘fd7 6.h4 a6 7.♕g4 f5
8.♕h5+! g6 9.♕h6 ♗xg5 10.hxg5
♕e7?!

10...♔f7 11.♘ge2! ♘f8 12.O-O-O
♖g8 13.g4, Yanofsky–Gudmundsson,
Reykjavik 1947, gives White a small
edge.

11.♘h3 ♘c6 12.O-O-O ♕f8?

If Black wants to show the worth of
10...♕e7, he must continue with 12...
♘d8 to stop 13.♘f4, as 13...♘f7 hits
the Queen and the g5-pawn. Play
might continue 13.♔b1 ♘f8. White
is better, but with the position closed,
and no sacrifices on d5 in the air,
Black can play.

13.♕h4

Bobby has a nice alternative in 13.
♘f4, but prefers to play for the attack.

13...♕e7

This walks straight into an uppercut.
It takes good nerves to play 13...h5, but
it makes sense to block the position.
After 14.♘f4 Black must play 14...
♕g8. This is hardly pretty, but much
better than what happens.

14.♘f4 ♘f8

15.♘cxd5!

This sacrifice is very common in the
Alekhine-Chatard. The central pawns
will roll right over Black.

15...exd5 16.♘xd5 ♕d8 17.♘f6+
♔e7 18.d5 ♘xe5 19.♖e1 ♔f7 20.
♖xe5 ♘d7

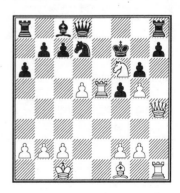

21.♕xh7+! ♖xh7 22.♖xh7+ ♔f8 23.
♖h8+ ♔f7 24.♖xd8 ♘xe5 25.f4 ♘g4
26.♗c4 b5 27.♗b3 ♔e7 28.♖e8+
♔d6 29.♘xg4 fxg4 30.f5 ♔d7 31.
♖h8 gxf5 32.g6! ♗b7 33.♖xa8 ♗xa8
34.g7 1-0

[42] *Evans Gambit C51*
RJF–Travis
Wichita (simul) April 4, 1964

1.e4 e5 2.♘f3 ♘c6 3.♗c4 ♗c5 4.b4
♗xb4 5.c3 ♗e7 6.d4 d6?

A mistake that was played quite
often against Bobby.

7.♕b3

Later in the tour Bobby found the
most effective way of dealing with
6...d6, i.e., *7.dxe5 ♘xe5 8.♘xe5 dxe5
9.♕h5!* (see game 61). Maybe Black
can improve with 7...♗g4!? intending
to meet 8.♕b3 with 8...♗xf3 9.
♗xf7+ ♔f8 10.gxf3 ♘xe5 11.♗c4
♘xf3+ 12.♔e2 ♘e5, which seems
fine for the second player.

Fischer–Dillard, Toledo (simul) 1964,
saw 7...dxe5 8.♕b3 ♘f6 9. ♗xf7+
♔f8 10.♘g5 ♗d6 11.0-0 b6 12.
♘d2 ♘a5 13.♕b5 a6 14.♕d3 ♕e7
and now, in a much superior position,
Bobby let down his guard and blundered a piece with 15.♗d5? ♘xd5 16.
♕xd5 ♗b7 attacking both Queen and
Knight. Instead 15.♗b3 leaves White
with a substantial advantage.

7...♘a5

Here Fischer–Boatner, Houston (simul) 1964, had a quick finish: *7...♘h6
8.♗xh6 gxh6 9.♗xf7+ ♔f8 10.♗h5
1-0.* Black can drag things out with
10...d5, but loses several pawns.

8.♗xf7+ ♔f8 9.♕a4 c6 10.♗xg8
♔xg8 11.dxe5 b5

Black might have considered 11...
dxe5 12.♘xe5 ♗e6.

12.♕c2 dxe5 13.♘xe5 ♗f6

Once again, ...♗e6 was the right
move to put up resistance.

14.♘f3 ♗e6 15.0-0 ♕c7 16.♘bd2
c5 17.e5 ♗e7 18.a4 ♘c4?

Black's position wasn't pretty, but
he shouldn't have given up a second
pawn for nothing. He should have
played 18...a6.

19.axb5 ♘b6 20.c4 h6 21.♘e4

Angling for some fireworks. The
prosaic 21.♗b2 was also good.

21...♘xc4 22.♖a6 ♘b6

23.♘f6+ ♔f7

Black refuses the gift. If 23...gxf6
then 24.♕g6+ ♔f8 25.exf6 ♗d6 26.
♗xh6+ ♖xh6 27.♕xh6+ with ♘g5
to follow, leaves White with an overwhelming position. After 23...♗xf6,
White has 24.exf6 gxf6 25.♖d1 with a
decisive initiative.

24.♘h5 g5 25.♘d4! ♕xe5 26.♘xe6
♕xe6 27.f4 ♔g8 28.fxg5 hxg5 29.
♘f6+ ♔g7 30.♗b2 ♕e3+ 31.♔h1
♖xh2+ 32.♔xh2 ♗d6+ 33.♔h1 ♖h8+
34.♘h5+ ♔h6 35.♗xh8 ♔xh5 36.

♕h7+ ♔g4 37.♕f5+ ♔h5 38.♖xa7 ♗e7 39.♕f7+ **1-0**

---

[43] *French Alekhine-Chatard   C13*
RJF–Wilson
Wichita (simul) April 4, 1964

1.e4 e6 2.d4 d5 3.♘c3 ♘f6 4.♗g5 ♗e7 5.e5 ♘fd7 6.h4

Fischer's favorite answer to the Classical French. He played the Alekhine-Chatard several times on the '64 tour.

6...c5

Black's main try. The more cautious 6...a6, preventing ♘b5, was seen in Fischer–E. Bone, Houston (simul) 1964, where the future USCF rating director, escaped with a win after a rare Fischer howler: **6...a6 7.♕g4 f5 8.♕h5+ g6 9.♕h6 ♗xg5 10.hxg5 ♕e7 11.♘h3 ♕f8 12.♕h4 c5 13.♘f4 ♕f7 14.O-O-O cxd4 15.♘cxd5! exd5 16.e6 ♕g8 17.♘xd5 ♔d8 18.exd7 ♕xd5 19.♖xd4 ♕xa2 20.♖a4 ♕e6 21.♕d4??** (21.dxc8=♕+ ♔xc8 22. ♗d3 leaves White with a decisive advantage due to Black's exposed King) **21...♕e1+ 0-1.**

7.♘b5!?

A calculated bluff or does Bobby have a big surprise in store? The line played by Fischer is trappy, but is considered to lead to a draw by force. The main theoretical continuation is 7.♗xe7.

7...♕b6?

The right way to take advantage of White's seventh move was *7...f6!*, leading, after colorful play, to a draw by perpetual check: *8.♗d3 a6 9.♕h5+ ♔f8 10.♖h3* (This might be where Bobby had something up his sleeve. The little known game Platz–Fulop, New York 1942, saw *10.♘d6!? ♗xd6 11.exd6 fxg5 12.hxg5 ♕e8 13.♗g6 hxg6 14. ♕xh8+ ♔f7 15.♕h7 cxd4 16.O-O-O ♘c6 17.♖h3 ♘de5 18.♖h4 ♘e7 19. dxe7 ♕xe7 20.♕h8 1-0) 10...axb5 11. ♗h6 ♕a5+* (11...gxh6+ 12.♕xh6+ ♔f7 13.♕h5+ is a draw by perpetual check) *12.♗d2 ♕c7 13.♖g3 cxd4 14.♘f3 ♘xe5 15.♖xg7! h6!* (forced, as 15...♔xg7? 16.♗h6+ mates and 15...♘xf3+? is met by 16.♔d1!) *16. ♗h7!* (16.♗xh6? ♖xh6 17.♕xh6 ♗b4+ wins for Black. A new attempt to breathe life into the position was seen in Pavlovic–Züger, Mitropa Cup 1990: 16.♖g3 ♘xf3+ 17.♖xf3 ♘c6 18.♔f1 ♕e5 19.♕g6 f5 20.♖g3 ♗xh4 21.♖h3 ♗g5 22.f4 ♗xf4 23. ♖e1 ♗xd2 24.♖xe5 ♘xe5 25.♕f6+ ♘f7 26.♗xb5 ♖xa2 27.♕xd4 ♗xg5 28.♖xc3 ♖a1+ 29.♔e2 ♖a8 30.♖c7 ♖g8 31.♕c3 ♗e7 32.♖xc8+ ♖xc8 33.♕xc8+ ♘d8 with a draw a few moves later.) 16...♔xg7 17.♕xh6+ ♔f7 18.♕h5+ draw, Rossetto–Ståhlberg, Vina del Mar 1947.*

8.♕g4 ♕a5+?

This check is pointless. The only way to play was 8...f6.

9.c3 h5 10.♕g3 g6 11.♗xe7 ♔xe7 12.♘f3 ♘c6 13.dxc5 a6 14.♘d6 ♕xc5

15.♕g5+ ♔f8 16.♕f4

Winning, as there is no good way to guard f7. If 16...♖h7 then 18.♘g5.

16...♘dxe5 17.♘xe5 ♘xe5 18.♕xe5 ♖h7 19.♗d3 ♔e7 20.♘e4 ♕b6 21. ♕f6+ ♔d7 22.♘g5 ♕xb2 23.♖b1 1-0

---

[44] *Alekhine   B03*
RJF–Robert Hart
Wichita (simul) April 4, 1964

1.e4 ♘f6 2.e5 ♘d5 3.d4 d6 4.c4 ♘b6 5.exd6 exd6 6.♘c3 ♗f5

More common is 6...♗e7, hoping to be able to play ...♗g4 after ♘f3. White often takes time out to play h3 to stop the pin.

7.♘f3

7.♗e2 ♗e7 8.♗e3 ♘8d7 9.♘f3 O-O 10.b3 with a small edge for White, Maroczy–Tartakower, New York 1924.

7...♗e7 8.♗d3 ♗xd3 9.♕xd3 ♘c6 10.O-O O-O 11.♖e1 ♕d7 12.b3

A typical solid move for a simul. A sharper try is 12.d5, which leads to complications that favor White after 12...♘b4 13.♕e2 ♖ae8 14.a3 ♘a6 15.♗e3.

12...♖fe8 13.♗b2

13.a3 was worth considering, though the text seems more natural.

13...♘b4 14.♕d2 ♕f5 15.♘e4?!

This throws away much of White's advantage. Instead, 15.♘b5! is strong, as Black has nothing better than 15... ♘a6: if 15...♘c2?, 16.♘xc7 ♘xe1 17.♖xe1 is winning.

15...d5 16.♘g3

A more active alternative is 16.♘c5, as 16...♘c2 is met by 17.♖e5.

16...♕c2 17.c5 ♕xd2 18.♘xd2 ♘d7 19.♖ed1 ♗f6

Threatening both 20...♘xc5 and 20...♘c2. Clearly, the initiative has changed hands.

20.♘f3

If 20.♘h5, then 20...♘d3 21.♗c3 ♖e2 is very strong for Black.

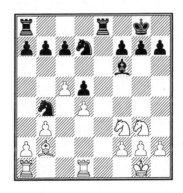

**20...♘xc5 21.♘h5 ♘e4 22.♘xf6+
♘xf6 23.♘e5 ♖e6 24.♖ac1 c6 25.a3
♘a6 26.f3 ♖d8 27.b4 ♘d7?!**

Overlooking a tactical resource for
White. The correct way to consolidate
was 27...♘e8, intending ...♘d6.

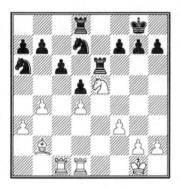

28.b5! ♘ab8

If 28...cxb5??, then 29.♘xd7 ex-
ploits Black's weak back rank.

29.a4?! ♘xe5?!

29...cxb5 30.axb5 ♖b6 wins a second pawn for Black.

**30.dxe5 ♘d7 31.bxc6 bxc6 32.♗d4
♘xe5 33.♗xe5**

Fischer feels that his best chance to
draw lies in the double Rook endgame.

**33...♖xe5 34.♖xc6 g6 35.♖c5 ♔g7
36.♔f2 ♖d7 37.♖d2 ♔f6 38.♖a5 d4
39.♖a6+ ♖e6 40.♖a5 ♔e7 41.♖d3
♖c6 42.♖e5+ ♔f6 43.f4 ♖e6 44.♖a5**
Draw

White has some compensation for
the pawn with his active Rook on a5,
but Black should make him prove it.

[45] *Sicilian Sozin   B87*
RJF–Aker
Wichita (simul) April 14, 1964

**1.e4 c5 2.♘f3 d6 3.d4 cxd4 4.♘xd4
♘f6 5.♘c3 a6 6.♗c4 e6 7.0-0 b5
8.♗b3 ♗b7 9.f4 ♘bd7 10.f5**

White has an interesting alternative
in 10.♖e1.

10...♘c5?

The first move out of theory and the
losing move. The forced 10...e5 11.
♘f3 ♘c5 12.♗g5 ♘xb3 13.axb3
♕b6+ 14.♔h1 ♘xe4 15.♘xe4 ♗xe4
16.f6 led to unclear play in Honfi-
Kadar, Pecs 1976.

**11.fxe6 ♘xb3 12.axb3 b4 13.♘d5
♗xd5 14.exd5 ♗e7 15.exf7+ ♔xf7
16.♘e6 ♕b6+ 17.♔h1 ♔g8 18.♗g5
h6 19.♗xf6 ♗xf6 20.♖xf6 1-0**

[46] *Ruy Lopez   C60*
RJF–Briggs
Wichita (simul) April 4, 1964

**1.e4 e5 2.♘f3 ♘c6 3.♗b5 ♕f6 4.
♘c3 ♕d6 5.0-0 ♘f6 6.♗xc6 dxc6
7.d4 ♘g4 8.d5 ♗d7 9.h3 ♘f6 10.
♕e2 b5 11.dxc6 ♗xc6 12.♘xb5
♕d8 13.♖d1 ♕b8 14.♘c3 ♗d6 15.
♘d5 ♘xd5 16.exd5 ♕b5 17.c4 ♕b6
18.dxc6 0-0 19.♕e4 ♖ad8 20.♗e3
♕xb2 21.♘g5 g6 22.♕h4 h5 23.g4
e4 24.gxh5 ♗e7 25.hxg6 ♕g7 26.gxf7+
♖xf7 27.♖xd8+ ♗xd8 28. ♖d1 ♗f6
29.♔h1 ♔f8 30.♘e6+ ♔e7 31.♕xe4
♕h8 32.♖d7+ ♔e8 33.♘xc7+ ♔f8
34.♕e8+ ♔g7 35. ♕xf7+ 1-0**

[47] *Vienna   C29*
RJF–Keith Carson
Wichita (simul) April 4, 1964

1.e4 e5 2.♘c3 ♘f6 3.f4 d5 4.d3

The game continuation is more commonly reached via 4.fxe5 ♘xe4 5.d3 ♗b4.

4...♗b4 5.fxe5 ♘xe4 6.dxe4 ♕h4+ 7.♔e2 ♗g4+ 8.♘f3 ♗xc3 9.bxc3 dxe4 10.♕d4! ♗h5 11.♔e3

11.♔d2! ♕g4 12.h3 ♕f4+ 13. ♔e1 ♕g3 14.♕f2 is a slightly better for White; 12...♕f5!? is interesting.

11...♗xf3 12.♗b5+

A necessary move to clear the back rank. If 12.gxf3, then 12...♕e1+ 13. ♔f4 ♕h4+ leads to a draw by perpetual check.

12...c6 13.gxf3 cxb5

Normally played, but Black has experimented with 13...♕h6+, trying to keep the White King as a target. Two examples after 14.♔xe4 ♕g6+ 15. ♔e3 cxb5 are:

A 16.♕d3?! ♘c6 17.♕xb5 O-O 18.f4 ♘xe5! 19.fxe5 ♖fe8 20.♗b2 ♕g5+ 21.♔e4 f5+ with a winning attack, Hayden–French, corre. 1993;

B 16.♗a3 ♘c6 17.♕d5 ♕xc2 18.♖ac1 ♕f5 19.♖he1 ♖d8 20.♕xb5 a6 21.♕b1 ♕g5+ 22.f4 ♕g2 23.♗d6 ♕h3+ 24.♔e4 f5+ 25.♔d5 ♕g2+ 26.♔c4 b5+ 27.♔d3 ♕f3+ 28.♔c2 ♕f2+ 29.♔b3 ♖c8 30.♖c2 ♕xf4 31. ♔b2 ♘a5 32.♔a1 ♕c4 33.e6 ♘c6 34.♕d1 h5 35.♖g1 ♖h7 36.♖xg7 1-0, Chigorin–Caro, Vienna 1898. The old masters really knew how to play with their Kings!

14.♕xe4 ♕e7

Should Black exchange Queens or stay in the middlegame? The traditional move, 14...♕xe4+, leads to an endgame that's difficult to assess. Blackburne–Zukertort, London 1887, continued 15.♔xe4 O-O (before White

has time to play ♗a3) 16.♖b1 a6 17. ♖d1 ♘c6 18.♗a3 ♖fe8 19.f4 f6 with a good game for Black. If, instead of 15...O-O, Black tries 15...♘c6, White can develop a strong initiative by 16. ♖b1 a6 17.♖g1 g6 18.a4 bxa4 19. ♖xb7, Himanen–Korhonen, corre. 1989.

15.a4 ♘d7

Black improves on Wayte–Oxoniensis, London 1883, where 15...bxa4 was strongly met by 16.♗a3 ♕c7 17.♕xa4+ ♘d7 18.♗d6 ♕xc3+ 19. ♔e2 a6 20.♖hd1 and the Black King was stuck in the center forever.

16.♗a3 ♕xe5 17.axb5 O-O-O 18. ♕xe5 ♘xe5 19.♗c5 ♖he8 20.♗d4 ♖d7 21.♔f2 b6 22.♖he1 ♖de7?

Carson has played wonderfully to this point, but here he falters. The right way to continue was 22...f6, when 23.f4 ♘g4+ 24.♔f3 ♖xe1 25. ♖xe1 ♘h6 26.♖e8+ (White has nothing better because of his inferior pawn structure) 26...♖d8 27.♖e7 ♖d7 with a draw by repetition in the offing. Note that Black cannot sidestep this with 26...♔c7 because of 27.♖h8. Carson's plan is to head for the notorious Rook vs. Rook plus f- and h-pawn. This ending is drawn, but it demands great accuracy from Black.

23.♖xe5 ♖xe5 24.♗xe5 ♖xe5 25. ♖xa7 ♖xb5 26.♖xf7 ♖b2?!

Black is still thinking about the Rook plus f- and h-pawn ending, but he had a much simpler draw in 26... ♖h5! 27.♔g2 g6. White's King is tied down and he has no easy way of producing a passed pawn.

27.♖xg7 ♖xc2+ 28.♔g3 ♖xc3 29. ♖xh7 ♔d8 30.h4 ♔e8 31.♖b7 ♔f8

Black decided several moves ago that he wanted to defend the f- and h-pawn ending. Carson faces two handicaps here: 1) he's playing the greatest player of all time; 2) the simul format means there are very few games left.

32.♖xb6

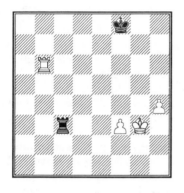

32...♖c1 33.♖b7 ♖h1 34.f4 ♖g1+ 35.♔f3 ♔g8 36.f5 ♔f8 37.♔f4 ♖c1 38.♔g5 ♖c6 39.h5 ♔g8 40.h6 ♔h8 41.f6 ♖c8 42.♔g6 ♖g8+ 43.♖g7 ♖f8 44.♖h7+ ♔g8 45.f7+ 1-0

---

[48] *French Winawer   C17*
RJF–Dockery
Wichita (simul) April 4, 1964

1.e4 e6 2.d4 d5 3.♘c3 ♗b4 4.e5 c5 5.a3 cxd4 6.axb4 dxc3 7.♕g4 cxb2 8.♗xb2 g6 9.♘f3

9.h4 h5 10.♕f4 ♘c6 11.♘f3 ♗d7 12.♘g5 ♘h6 13.b5! gave White a clear advantage in Batik–Skoda, Czechoslovakia 1961.

9...♘h6 10.♕f4 ♘f5 11.♗d3 ♘d7

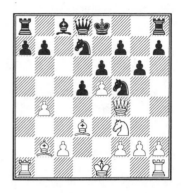

12.h4 b6 13.h5 ♕c7 14.hxg6 fxg6 15.♘g5 ♘b8?

Black's position isn't pretty, but 15...♘f8 would put up more resistance. After 16.g4 h6, Black meets 17.gxf5 by 17...hxg5, since ♖xh8 is no longer check! White should play 17.♘f3 ♘g7 18.♖xh6 with a big advantage. **16.g4 ♘g7 17.♗xg6+ ♔d8 18.♘f7+ ♔d7 19.♘xh8 hxg6 20.♕f7+ ♔c6 21.♕xc7+ ♔xc7 22.♖h7 ♘c6 23. ♖xg7+ ♗d7 24.b5 ♘b4 25.♔d2 ♖xh8 26.♖xa7+ ♔c8 27.♖a8+ 1-0**

---

[49] *King's Gambit Declined   C30*
RJF–Edgington
Wichita (simul) April 4, 1964

1.e4 e5 2.f4 ♘c6 3.♘f3 ♗d6 4.♘c3 ♘f6 5.♗b5 ♕e7 6.0-0 0-0 7. ♗xc6 dxc6 8.fxe5 ♗xe5 9.d4 ♗d6 10.e5 ♖d8 11.exf6 ♕xf6 12.♗g5 ♕f5 13.♗xd8 ♕f4 14.♗h4 ♗g4 15. ♗g3 ♕e3+ 16.♔h1 ♗xg3 17.hxg3 h5 18.♕e1 ♕xh6 19.♕e5 f6 20.♕xc7 ♖c8 21.♕xb7 ♖f8 22.♕xc6 h4 23. gxh4 ♗xf3 24.♖xf3 ♕xh4+ 25.♖h3 ♕xd4 26.♕e6+ ♖f7 27.♖e1 g6 28. ♕e8+ ♖f8 29.♕xg6+ 1-0

[50] *French Winawer   C16*
RJF–Fusco
Wichita (simul) April 4, 1964

1.e4 e6 2.d4 d5 3.♘c3 ♗b4 4.e5
♘c6 5.f4 ♕e7?

Black's strategy is best served by
leaving this square for the Knight.
Correct was 5...♘e7 or 5...♕d7.

6.♘f3 b6 7.♗d2 ♗b7 8.♗d3 O-O-O
9.O-O f6?! 10.♘e2! ♗xd2 11.♕xd2
♘b4?

Going from bad to worse Black
squanders two more tempi.

12.a4 ♘c6 13.c3 ♔b8 14.b4 ♕d7
15.a5

Bobby has the sort of automatic attack he could play in his sleep.

15...♘ge7 16.axb6 cxb6 17.♘c1
♘g6 18.♘b3 ♕c7 19.♖a3 ♗a8 20.
♖fa1 fxe5 21.fxe5 ♖hf8 22.b5 ♘ce7

23.♖xa7 ♕xa7 24.♖xa7 ♔xa7 25.
♘g5 ♘f4 26.♗xh7 g6? 27.g3 ♖fe8
28.gxf4 ♘f5 29.♗xg6 ♖g8 30.♗f7
♖h8 31.♗xe6 ♘h4 32.♔f2 ♖h6 33.
♔g3 ♘g6 34.f5 ♘h8 35.h4 ♖e8 36.
♕a2+ ♔b8 37.♕a6 ♖e7 38.♕xb6+
♖b7 39.♕d6+ ♖c7 40.b6 1-0

[51] *King's Gambit Declined   C30*
RJF–Greer
Wichita (simul) April 4, 1964

1.e4 e5 2.f4 f6 3.fxe5 ♘c6 4.d4 fxe5
5.♘f3 ♗b4+ 6.c3 ♗d6 7.♗c4 ♘f6
8.O-O ♘xe4 9.♕e2 ♘f6 10.dxe5
♗c5+ 11.♔h1 d5 12.exf6+ ♗e7 13.
fxe7 ♕xe7 14.♕xe7+ ♘xe7 15.♗d3
O-O 16.♖e1 ♘g6 17.♘bd2 ♘f4 18.
♗f1 b5 19.♘b3 ♘e6 20.♗xb5 ♖b8
21.♗c6 ♗b7 22.♖xe6 ♗xc6 23.
♖xc6 ♖be8 24.♔g1 h6 25.♖xc7 ♖f6
26.♖xa7 g5 27.h3 ♖g6 28.♘bd4 g4
29.hxg4 ♖xg4 30.♗xh6 ♔h8 31.
♖e1 1-0

[52] *Sicilian   B32*
RJF–K. Isely
Wichita (simul) April 4, 1964

1.e4 c5 2.♘f3 ♘c6 3.d4 d6 4.dxc5
dxc5 5.♕xd8+ ♘xd8 6.♘c3 ♘f6 7.
♘b5 ♘e6 8.♘g5 a6 9.♘xe6 ♔d7 10.
♘xf8+ ♖xf8 11.♘c3 e6 12.♗e3 1-0

[53] *Sicilian   B32*
RJF–Q. Isely
Wichita (simul) April 4, 1964

1.e4 c5 2.♘f3 ♘c6 3.d4 cxd4 4.♘xd4
e5 5.♘b5 ♘f6 6.♘1c3 ♗e7?

The only good move in this position
is 6...d6, transposing into the Svesh-
nikov variation.

7.♘d6+ ♗xd6 8.♕xd6 a6?

This move stops 9.♘b5, but costs
valuable time. The immediate 8...♕e7
was stronger.

9.♗g5 ♕e7 10.♕xe7+ ♘xe7 11.
O-O-O

White's lead in development and Bishop pair give him a pronounced edge.

11...b5 12.♗xf6 gxf6 13.♖d6 f5 14.f4
fxe4?

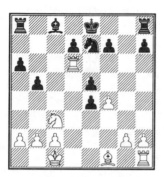

This brings White's Knight into the game. A better try was 14...exf4
15.fxe5 ♗b7 16.♗e2 O-O-O

Black might have considered 16...♖g8 with the idea of ...♖g5, trying to get counterplay.
17.♖f1 ♘g6 18.♖xf7 ♘xe5 19.♖f5 ♔c7 20.♖d4 ♖he8 21.♘d5+ ♗xd5 22.♖xd5 ♘c6

If 22...d6, then 23.a4! is strong.
23.♖f7 ♘e7?

Understandably, Black wants to advance his d-pawn, but this isn't feasible. Better resistance was offered by 23...h6, intending to use the e-pawn for counterplay.

24.♖h5 d5 25.♖hxh7 ♔d6 26.♖f6+ ♔e5 27.♖xa6 ♘f5 28.♗xb5 ♖e7 29. ♖h5 ♔f4 30.♖f6 ♖e5 31.g3+ ♔g4 32.♗e2 mate

[54] *Two Knights   C57*
RJF–Heckathorn
Wichita (simul) April 4, 1964

1.e4 e5 2.♘f3 ♘c6 3.♗c4 ♘f6 4.♘g5 d5 5.exd5 ♘xd5 6.d4 ♗e7 7.♘xf7 ♔xf7 8.♕f3+ ♔e8?

8...♔e6 9.♘c3 ♘b4 10.♕e4 c6 11.a3 ♘a6 12.♕e5+ (12.♗f4!? Euwe) 12...♔f7 13.♘xd5 cxd5 14.♗xd5+ ♔f8 15.O-O and White is better (Leonhardt).
9.♗xd5 ♘xd4 10.♕f7+ ♔d7 11.O-O h6 12.♘c3 ♕f8 13.♕h5 ♕f5 14. ♕d1 ♕xc2 15.♕g4+ ♕f5 16.♕xg7 ♕f6 17.♕g4+ ♔d8 18.♕d1 ♕g6 19. ♗e3 c6 20.♗e4 ♕f6 21.f4 c5 22.♘d5 ♕g7 23.b4 ♖g8 24.♘xe7 ♔xe7 25. fxe5 ♗h3 26.♖f2 ♖ad8 27.♕h5

The score was reconstructed from this point on and may not be accurate.
27...cxb4 28.♕xh3 ♕xe5 29.♕h4+ ♔d7 30.♗xd4 ♕xd4 31.♗f5+ ♔c7 32.♕xd4 ♖xd4 33.♖c1+ ♔b6 34. ♖b2 ♖f8 35.g4

and Fischer won.

Houston - March 28

Fischer wins 51 Games, Loses 3, Draws 3 Here

by George H. Smith
Houston Chronicle **Chess Columnist**

Chess in the United States received a tremendous boost over the Christmas holidays when Robert J. Fischer won the national title for the sixth time with a record-breaking 11-0 performance. This was well illustrated last Saturday night at the Shamrock Hilton Hotel where Fischer played in a simultaneous exhibition. He was scheduled to meet 50 players but when seven extra showed up, he graciously consented to play all comers. About 40 spectators also attended. This writer can recall no other exhibition so well attended here.

Fischer opened with a fine lecture on the difference between today's master play and that of Paul Morphy's day. He said Morphy's dynamic qualities would have enabled him to easily hold his own today.

Grandmaster Fischer's score in the simultaneous exhibition was 51 wins, three draws and three losses, with nearly all of the best in the Houston area competing. This is not as good a score as some masters have made here, but Fischer does not play chess as others do. He is not content to sit back and wait for his less experienced opponents to make a mistake, but tries to beat them by his own play. He lost to Eric Bone, former state champion from Baytown, to Bill Jones and to Ross Carbonell, both from the Houston Chess Club. Those who drew were Robert McGregor and Tommy Richardson of Houston and Alan K. Hale of Austin.

His loss to Bone was caused by an outright blunder in a winning position, when he overlooked a liquidating continuation which allowed Eric to emerge with a piece plus. Bill Jones obtained an early advantage in his game, then completely outplayed the champion the rest of the way. The game with Carbonell also was well played.

The exhibition was sponsored by the Houston Chess Club and arranged by Rhodes Cook, club secretary.

Source: *Houston Chronicle*, 1964

---

[55] *Evans Gambit   C52*
RJF–Ross Carbonell
Houston (simul) March 28, 1964

1.e4 e5 2.♘f3 ♘c6 3.♗c4 ♗c5 4.b4 ♗xb4 5.c3 ♗a5 6.d4 exd4 7.O-O ♘ge7 8.♘g5

ECO gives 8.cxd4 d5 9.exd5 ♘xd5 10.♗a3 ♗e6 11.♗b5 ♗b4 12.♗xc6+

bxc6 13.♗xb4 ♘xb4 14.♕a4 ♕d6 15.♘c3 O-O 16.♘e4 ♕f4 17.♘eg5, equal (Sokolsky).
8...d5

8...♘e5 9.♘xf7 ♘xf7 10.♗xf7+ ♔xf7 11.♕h5+ g6 12.♕xa5 was unclear in Sax–Honfi, Hungary 1971.
9.exd5 ♘e5 10.♗b3

Much more common is 10.♕xd4. One wild possibility is 10.d6.
10...O-O 11.♘xh7

Breaking new ground. 11.cxd4 ♘g4 12.♕f3 (12.♗a3 is Andersson–Mieses, Breslau 1867) 12...♕d6 13.♗f4 ♕f6 14.♘c3 Draw, Bronstein–A. Ivanov, Menchik Memorial 1994.
11...♔xh7 12.♕h5+ ♔g8 13.♕xe5 dxc3 14.♘xc3 ♗xc3 15.♕xc3 ♘xd5 16.♕g3

Bobby shows he's in a fighting mood. He could have bailed out with 16.♗xd5 ♕xd5 17.♗b2 f6 18.♕xc7 with a very even game.
16...♗e6 17.♗b2 ♘f6 18.♗c2 ♘h5 19.♕f3 ♕d5

The immediate 19...♕g5 was to be considered.
20.♗e4 ♕g5 21.♗xb7 ♖ab8 22.♖ae1 ♕g4

Black misses the opportunity to keep his disadvantage to a bare minimum with 22...♗c4 23.♖e5 ♕f4 24. ♖fe1 ♕xf3 25.♗xf3 ♖xb2 26.♖c5 ♗xa2 27.♗xh5.
23.♗e5 ♘f6 24.♗xc7??

Bobby makes a rare blunder. He'd have kept an advantage with 24.♖c1.
24...♖xb7 25.♕xb7 ♗d5   0-1

White must give up his Queen to avoid immediate checkmate.

Source: *Oklahoma Chess Bulletin*, November 1996, pg.25

Hollywood - April 12
+47=2-1

Bobby's first exhibition in California was held on Sunday afternoon, April 12, at the Knickerbocker Hotel (1714 Ivar). Sponsored by the Herman Steiner Chess Club, with a fee of $3.50 a board and $1 for spectators, the exhibition started at 1:00 p.m. The three players who scored were junior members of the Herman Steiner Chess Club, sponsor of the event. Donn Rogosin was the sole winner with Andy Sacks and Nicholas Enequist drawing.

[56] *Sicilian Sozin   B87*
RJF–Andy Sacks
Hollywood (simul) April 12, 1964

1.e4 c5 2.♘f3 d6 3.d4 cxd4 4.♘xd4 ♘f6 5.♘c3 a6 6.♗c4 e6 7.O-O ♗e7 8.♗e3 ♕c7 9.♗b3 O-O 10.f4 b5 11. f5 e5

The position reached after 11.f5 is relatively uncommon, as Black normally plays ...♗b7 before ...♕c7. The two GMs who have played this position as Black, Igor Novikov and Roman Dzindzichashvili, both went in for 11...b4. This drives the Knight to a4, but allows White to open up the position with c2-c3.

12.♘de2 ♗b7 13.♘g3 ♘bd7

One of the advantages for Black in this position is that the positionally desirable 14.♗g5 costs a tempo (♗c1-e3-g5) compared to some lines in the Sozin.

14.♘h5 ♘xh5 15.♕xh5 ♘f6 16.♕f3 ♖fd8 17.♗g5

White tries to increase his control over the d5-square. His ideal plan is to trade off two pairs of minor pieces and be left with a Knight on d5 against Black's dark-squared Bishop.

17...b4

This advance puts the question to the Knight and ensures that White won't have time to play ♗g5xf6, ♗b3-d5xb7 and ♘c3-d5.

18.♗xf6 ♗xf6 19.♘d5 ♗xd5 20. ♗xd5

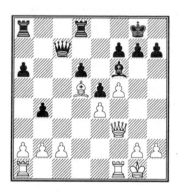

White has achieved some of the goals of the Sozin (6.♗c4) variation — control of d5 and the better minor piece — but Black has compensation in his queenside pressure.

20...♖ac8 21.♖f2 ♕a7 22.♔h1 ♕d4 23.♖b1 ♖c7 24.♖e2 ♖dc8 25.♕b3 a5 26.g3 ♖a7 27.a3 ♖b8 28.a4 ♖c8 29.♕f3 ♖ac7 30.♗b3 ♖c6 31.♔g2 ♖8c7 32.h4 ♖c8 33.♔h3 ♖8c7 34. ♖g2 h6 35.g4?

Correct is 35.♖d1 with complete equality. Then not 35...♕xb2 36.c4.

Now, just when it appears that White is ready to crash through with g4-g5, Black has a strong answer . . .

35...♖c3!

Winning.

36.bxc3 ♖xc3 37.♕xc3 ♕xc3+ 38. ♖g3 ♕d2 39.♖bg1

An interesting alternative is 39.c3 with ideas like 39...bxc3 40.♗d5 c2 41.♖b8+ ♔h7 42.♗xf7.

39...♕e2 40.♗d5

40...♔f8?

Young Sacks misses a chance to finish with glory. The winning move was 40...♕xh4! 41.♖3g2 ♗f2 or 41. ♖1g2 ♕f1 42.♔xh4 ♕h1+. If White plays 41.♔xh4, then Black has 41... ♕h2+.

41.♖3g2

Offering to repeat moves, as 41.g5 is met by 41...hxg5 42.hxg5 ♕h5+ 43.♔g2 ♗xg5.

41...♕f3+ 42.♖g3 ♕e2 Draw

Black could have kept playing with 42...♕f2 43.♖1g2 ♕f1 44.g5 hxg5 45.hxg5 ♗d8.

Donn Rogosin is the son of Hy Rogosin, who lost the famous "pawn game" against Marshall wherein the latter didn't move a piece until move 15 (New York 1940)!

[57] *Sicilian Sozin B88*
RJF–Donn Rogosin
Hollywood (simul) April 12, 1964

1.e4 c5 2.♘f3 d6 3.d4 cxd4 4.♘xd4 ♘f6 5.♘c3 a6 6.♗c4 e6 7.O-O ♗e7 8.♗b3 O-O

Fischer–Blackstone, Davis (clock simul) 1964, continued 8...♕c7 9.f4 b5 10.f5 b4 11.fxe6 (11.♘ce2 e5 12. ♘f3 ♗b7 is bad for White, according to Fischer) 11...bxc3 12.exf7+ ♔f8 13.♗g5 ♘g4! and Black should win. Incidentally, California Junior Champion John Blackstone was the most active player in the United States in 1964, playing 117 games. Right behind him was New York expert Sam Sloan with 107.

9.f4 ♕c7 10.♕f3 ♘c6 11.♗e3 ♘xd4 12.♗xd4 b5 13.e5 dxe5 14.fxe5 ♗b7 15.exf6 ♗xf3 16.fxe7 ♕xe7 17.♖xf3

♖ad8 18.♗e3 ♕b7 19.♖af1 ♖fe8 20. ♘e2 a5 21.c3 ♕e4 22.♘g3 ♕g6 23. ♖xf7?

Bobby plans 23...♕xf7 24.♖xf7 ♔xf7 with the unbalanced position of three minor pieces for two Rooks. However, Rogosin has a simple reply which wins immediately.

23...a4 24.♗c2?

White's best chance was 24.♗d4, but 24...♖xd4 25.♗xe6 ♕xe6 26. cxd4 ♕xf7 27.♖xf7 ♔xf7 is a fairly straightforward win for Black.

24...♕xc2 25.♘h5 ♖f8 26.♖xg7+ ♔h8 0-1

San Francisco - April 13
+38=8-4

U.S. Chess King Rooked in S.F.

The chess champion of the United States came to San Francisco Monday night — and promptly got rooked.

Bobby Fischer, 21, who has won the national title six times, played 50 opponents simultaneously at the Mechanics Institute Chess Club.

He lost four, drew eight and won the rest.

"That would be about par for the average master," explained Kurt Bendit, who arranged the matches, "but not for Fischer. In Los Angeles, he was beaten only once and held to a draw twice."

Arthur Bisguier, who beat Bobby in the first game they played and then scored only one draw in the next fourteen games!

But there were reasons why Fischer, the nation's hope for its first world chess title, had a "fairly rough evening in San Francisco."

"At some tables," Bendit chuckled, "he was playing not one, but several, opponents. They would hold little strategy conferences behind the board while Fischer moved down the line."

Also, it was the champion's 20th exhibition of this type in the past two months, putting him halfway through a nationwide tour.

His conquerors here included Robert L. Henry, 19, of 3940 Casanova Drive, San Mateo, who took 22 moves to win; Max Wilkerson, 31 of 1927 Hayes Street, an artist, who did it in 30, and Robert Burger, an advertising man from Lafayette, who won in 13.

Henry said Fisher "wasted his time in pawn-grabbing" and failed to consolidate his position. Wilkerson said the champ "blundered in an even situation."

Michael Quinlan, 18, of 1634 18th Ave., the fourth winner, attributed his victory to Fischer's sportsmanship.

The champion made a careless, fatal move. He recognized it instantly, and within in a fraction of a second corrected it.

But, in the strict spirit of the game, he resigned at once, because he had left his King untouched on a losing square.

Source: presumably the *San Francisco Chronicle*, April 14, 1964

An amusing reconstruction of the night of April 13, 1964 can be found in the May-June, 1974, issue of *The California Chess Reporter*, in which Jude Acers relates how Robert Burger came to play in the exhibition.

[58] *Two Knights   C57*
RJF–Robert Burger
San Francisco (simul) April 13, 1964

1.e4 e5 2.♘f3 ♘c6 3.♗c4 ♘f6 4. ♘g5 d5 5.exd5 ♘d4 6.c3 b5 7.♗f1 ♘xd5

It is interesting that in answer to 7...h6, Fischer had played his own 8. ♘h7 in a clock simul in Canada, winning easily.

Note: This was J.D.'s comment in *A Legend on the Road*, but no examples of Bobby playing 8.♘h7 have ever surfaced.

8.cxd4 ♛xg5 9.♗xb5+ ♔d8 10.♛f3 ♗b7 11.0-0 exd4

Here, theory considers the natural 11...♖b8, but White has an easy time after the simple 12.dxe5 (if 12...♘f4, then 13.♗c6 or if 12...♘e3 13.♛h3, simplifying).

12.♛xf7??

12.d3 was necessary, but, after 12... ♛f6, Black has a satisfactory game. White threatens mate twice, but . . .

12...♘f6 0-1

The Queen is lost as well as the Bishop. This was Fischer's quickest loss on the tour. Master Robert Burger is a noted problemist and the author of the well-received *The Chess of Bobby Fischer*.

---

[59] *Vienna* C29
RJF–Henry Gross
San Francisco (simul) April 13, 1964

1.e4

The last time these two players faced each other (U.S. Open 1957), Bobby opened with 1.♘f3 and the game ended in a draw.

1...e5 2.♘c3 ♘f6 3.f4 d5 4.d3

This odd-looking line in the Vienna is attributed to Wilhelm Steinitz. John Collins writes in *My Seven Chess Prodigies* about Bobby's admiration for the Austrian World Champion. Fischer often took opening ideas from the games of great players of the past, including Steinitz's 9.♘h3 (1.e4 e5 2.♘f3 ♘c6 3.♗c4 ♘f6 4.♘g5 d5 5.exd5 ♘a5 6.♗b5+ c6 7.dxc6 bxc6 8.♗e2 h6).

4...dxe4

Keith Carson, in game 47, played the sharper 4...♗b4. Also possible are: **4... exf4** 5.exd5 ♘xd5 6.♘xd5 ♕xd5 7. ♗f4 ♗d6, equal, Bronstein–Matanovic, Vienna 1957; **4...♘c6** 5.fxe5 ♘xe5 6.d4 ♘g6, equal, Steinitz–Lasker, London 1899; **4...d4** 5.♘b1 ♘c6 6.♘f3 ♗g4 7.♗e2 ♗xf3 8.♗xf3 ♗d6 9. fxe5, equal, Charousek–Pillsbury, Budapest 1896.

5.fxe5 ♘d5

ECO gives 5...♘g4 6.♘xe4 ♘xe5 7.d4 ♘ec6 (7...♘g6 8.♘f3 with a slight advantage for White, Steinitz–Neumann, Baden-Baden 1870) 8.♘f3 ♘d7 9.♗c4 ♗e7 10.♘fg5 O-O 11.

O-O ♘f6 12.♘xf7 ♕xd4+ 13.♕xd4 ♘xd4, equal, Bronstein–Gorenstein, USSR 1940.

6.♘xe4 ♘c6

Experience with 5...♘d5 is greatly limited. One of the few examples is Steinitz–Den Hertog, Haarlem (simul) 1896, which saw 6.♘xe4 ♗f5 7.♘g3 ♗e6 8.♘f3 ♗e7 9.d4 c6 10.♗d3 ♕c7 11.O-O with a clear advantage for White.

7.♘f3 ♗g4 8.♗e2 ♗xf3 9.♗xf3 ♘xe5 10.O-O ♗e7 11.d4 ♘xf3+ 12. ♕xf3 O-O 13.c3 c6 14.♘g3 ♗g5

Black had a solid alternative in 14... ♕d7 to connect his Rooks.

15.♘f5 ♗xc1 16.♖axc1 ♘e7 17.♖ce1 ♘xf5 18.♕xf5

18...♕c7 19.♖e3 ♖ae8 20.♖h3 g6 21. ♕f6 ♖e6 22.♕h4 f5 23.♖hf3 ♖fe8 24.♕f4 ♕e7 25.♖3f2 ♖e4 26.♕d2 ♕e6 27.a3 ♕c4

Fischer's advantage has been declining for the last 10 moves and now he is at a disadvantage. Perhaps even stronger than the text is 27...♖e3 with a complete bind on White's position. Now Fischer had a chance to escape from his troubles.

28.h3

White could have drawn after 28.♖xf5 ♖e2 29.♕g5 ♖xb2 30.♕h6 ♖xg2+ 31. ♔xg2 gxf5 32.♕g5+ ♔h8 33.♕f6+ with perpetual check.

28...♕b5?

Once again, Black misses the opportunity to play 28... ♖e3, cutting off White's Queen from the queenside.

29.♕g5?

After 28...♕b5?

Fischer misses 29. ♖xf5, which would win a pawn, as 29... gxf5? is met by 30. ♕g5+ ♔h8 (30... ♔f8 31.♖xf5+ ♕xf5 32.♕xf5+) 31.♕f6+ ♔g8 32. ♖xf5, hitting the Queen and threatening 33.♖g5+.

29...♖e1 30.♖xe1 ♖xe1+ 31.♔h2 ♕d5 32.♕f6 ♖e6 33.♕h4 Draw

Source: original scoresheet

Sacramento - April 15
+47=2-1

The following article and game score come from a column by Richard Fauber and Frank Garosi in the *Sacramento Bee*, June 15, 1980.

In January 1964, the legendary Bobby Fischer won another U.S. Championship by going 11-0. The invincible Fischer squashed his leading American rivals like so many bugs. He then went on to demonstrate his prowess to crowds of admiring amateurs.

Reader George W. Flynn has sent us some interesting observations on Fischer's 50-board simultaneous exhibition at McClellan Air Force Base, April 15, 1964.

"First of all, Bobby requested that absolutely no flash pictures be taken during the exhibition, although such pictures were permitted before play. To me this is early evidence that Fischer's light sensitivity is entirely genuine and not a temperamental pose.

"Second, his memory is indeed photographic. In response to an audience question, Fischer played over on a demonstration board his game, originally played months earlier with Bill Addison. His comments were in depth and without notes."

Even more revealing is the awe Fischer inspired in his opponents, Flynn continues: "About moves 25 to 30, I offered to draw! I was a pawn-grabber's pawn ahead and yet reasonably certain the axe was going to drop on me sooner or later. I expected a display of Fischer temperament, since I doubted the etiquette of my own action. Fischer showed no irritation whatever. He even took the offer seriously . . . His eyes moved rapidly back and forth over the board, obviously calculating the endgame. Satisfied, he smiled and said, 'Let's play a little longer.' "

[60] *Sicilian Hyper-Accelerated Dragon B27*
RJF–George Flynn
  Sacramento (simul) April 15, 1964

1.e4 g6 2.d4 ♗g7 3.♘c3 c5

This move order is a favorite of Canadian IM Lawrence Day.

4.dxc5

This move is the only real try to attempt to refute Black's setup. 4.♘f3 cxd4 5.♘xd4 ♘c6 transposes into the Accelerated Dragon and 4.d5 is a Schmidt Benoni.

4...♕a5 5.♘f3

Natural, but there is also something to be said for 5.♗d2 ♕xc5 6.♘d5 b6 7.♗e3 ♕c6 8.♗b5 ♕b7 9.♗d4 f6 10.♘f3 with a big advantage for White, Mestel–Day, Lucerne Olympiad 1982.

5...♘c6 6.♗d3 ♗xc3+

This move might look risky, but Black didn't have a lot of choice, as 6...♕xc5 was strongly met by 7.♘d5.

7.bxc3 ♕xc3+

Going whole hog. Black wins a pawn, but White has excellent compensation.

8.♗d2 ♕xc5 9.0-0 ♘f6 10.♖e1 d6 11.♖b1 a6 12.♗e3 ♕h5 13.h3 ♘d7

Here 13...0-0 was safer.

14.♕d2 ♘de5 15.♘xe5 ♕xe5

If 15...♘xe5, 16.♗e2 is awkward for Black's Queen.

16.f4 ♕a5 17.c3 b5

Flynn fearlessly leaves his King in the center. 17...0-0 was better.

18.e5 d5 19.a4 d4

20.♗e4 dxe3 21.♗xc6+ ♔f8 22.♕xe3 ♖b8 23.axb5 axb5 24.c4 b4 25.c5 ♗f5 26.♖a1 ♕c7 27.♗e4?

Bobby would have retained his advantage with 27.♗d5 ♔g7 28.c6. The text blunders a pawn and leaves Fischer fighting for the half point.

27...♗xe4 28.♕xe4 ♕xc5+ 29.♔h2 e6 30.♖ec1 ♕b5 31.♖c7 ♔g7 32.♖aa7 ♖hf8 33.♖cb7 ♖xb7 34.♖xb7 ♕d5 35.♕xd5 exd5 36.♖xb4 ♖d8 37.♖d4 f6 38.♔g3 f5 Draw

Flynn adds: "Fischer was very friendly to me. After the exhibition he hurried out into the hallway, put his hands on the wall above his head and seemed to be panting from exhaustion. He recovered quickly and started signing scoresheets. I was the second player to reach him and he commented that I had played 'a nice game.' The first player to have his scoresheet signed spoke up and said, 'Say, you signed it *R. Fischer* — can't you sign it *Bobby Fischer*?'

"Bobby never replied, but his expression changed to complete disgust and he stared at the man for a long 30 seconds, then turned away and began a brief but pleasant conversation with me.

"It was the *only* sign of The Fischer Temper and I thought it not entirely without justification."

Davis Clock Simul - April 16
+10=0–0

The following game is number 50 in Fischer's *My 60 Memorable Games*.

---

[61] *Evans Gambit C51*
RJF–Oyvind Celle
Davis (clock simul) April 16, 1964

1.e4 e5 2.♘f3 ♘c6 3.♗c4 ♗c5 4.b4 ♗xb4 5.c3 ♗e7 6.d4 d6?

This is a serious mistake according to theory, which argues that 6...♘a5 was essential, meeting 7.♘xe5 with 7...♘xc4 8.♘xc4 d5 to restore the balance in the center.

7.dxe5 ♘xe5

If Black has any chance to rehabilitate this line his chances lie in 7...♗g4, returning some booty to get his pieces developed.

8.♘xe5 dxe5 9.♕h5!

Fischer remarks that in earlier exhibitions he played 9.♕b3, but got nothing after 9...♗e6 10.♗xe6 fxe6 11.♗a3!? (11.♕xe6 ♕d6 is equal) 11...♕d3!

9...g6 10.♕xe5 ♘f6 11.♗a3!

Tying up Black completely.

11...♖f8

Celle moves his Rook to unpin his Knight and Fischer suggests that this is the only move to offer Black relief.

GM Igor Zaitsev, writing in the unauthorized Russian language version of *My 60 Memorable Games*, suggests that *11...♗e6 12.♗xe6 O-O* deserves consideration. Black sacrifices a piece to trap White's King in the center.

Zaitsev continues *13.♗b3 ♗xa3 14.♘xa3 ♖e8* and "White has no convenient square for his Queen." He then gives 15.♕g5 ♕d3 or 15.♕b5 c6 and goes no further.

The position after 15.♕g5 ♕d3 is certainly unappetizing. More critical is *15.♕b5.* Zaitsev's suggestion of *15...c6*, trying to weaken White's control of d3, works well enough after *16.♗xf7+ ♔g7!* (16...♔xf7 17.♕b3+ followed by 18.O-O is better for White) *17.♕b3 ♕d3!* (17...♖xe4+ 18.♔f1 ♕d3+ 19.♔g1 and White's

King is safe) *18.♗xe8 ♖xe8 19.f3 ♘xe4*, winning for Black. However, *16.♕xb7* seems like a simple refutation, e.g., *16...♖xe4+* 17.♔f1 ♕d3+ 18.♔g1 ♕xc3 19.♕xf7+ ♔h8 20. ♖f1 consolidates (Kozlovskaya and Donaldson) and *16...♖e7* 17.♕xc6 ♖c8 18.♕a6 ♖xe4+ 19.♔f1 leaves Black without a satisfactory followup.

Black has much better in *15...a6*. After *16.♕g5* ♖xe4+ 17.♔f1 ♕d3+ 18.♔g1 ♕xc3 19.♕c1 ♕d4, he has compensation for the piece, as White has serious problems coordinating his pieces. Black also fares well after *16. ♕xb7* ♕d3 17.♗xf7+ ♔xf7 18. ♕xc7+ ♔f8 19.♕c5+ ♔g7.

If this is confusing, also consider that *15...♖xe4+* is not out of the question. After 16.♔f1, Black has 16... ♘g4 meeting 17.h3 with 17...♘xf2 18.♔xf2 ♕d2+ 19.♔g1 ♕e3+ 20. ♔h2 ♕f4+ 21.♔g1 ♕e3+ and a draw by perpetual check. If 17.♔g1, then 17...♕d2 18.♕f1 ♖ae8 looks strong.

These last two lines are very confusing, as theory has always assumed that Black's opening play was very weak. Could it be that Zaitsev's 11...♗e6 makes the line playable for Black?

12.0-0 ♘g4

Fischer suggests that 12...♘d7, intending ...♘b6, is worth a look.

13.♕g3 ♗xa3 14.♘xa3 ♕e7!

Latvian-American expert Oyvind Celle continues to find his best chances to resist.

Apparently Black has freed his game. If now 15.♘c2, 15...♕e5 virtually forces the trade of Queens. 15.♘b5 is rendered harmless by 15...♘e5. How's White to sustain the initiative? –Fischer, *My 60 Memorable Games*

15.♗b5+!

Forcing Black to weaken the d6-square.

15...c6 16.♘c4! ♕e6!

Clearing e7 for the King. It's doubtful that Black saw all the way to the end of Fischer's main line (16... cxb5 17.♘d6+ ♔d8 18.♖fd1 ♗d7 19. ♘xb7+ ♔c8 20.♘d6+ ♔d8 21. ♖d4! ♘e5 22.♖ad1 ♔c7 23.f4 ♘g4 24.h3 ♘f6 25.f5 ♔b6 26.♕e3 ♔c7 27.♖c4+ bxc4 28.♕c5+ ♗c6 29. ♘b5+, winning), but his intuition served him well.

17.♖ad1!

Piling on the pressure. White mustn't amateurishly rush in with 17.♕c7, 17...♕d7!; and he is forced to simplify by 18.♘d6+ ♔e7 19.♘xc8+ ♖axc8 20.♕xd7+ ♔xd7, and his advantage has evaporated. Chess is matter of timing. It's not enough to play the right move, you've got to play it at the right moment. Restraint is one of the most difficult things for the average chess player to learn. —Fischer

Sage advice from the greatest chessplayer of all time!

17...cxb5 18.♕c7 ♗d7 19.♘d6+ ♔e7 20.♘f5+!

Adding fuel to the fire. Now 20...♔e8 is met by 21.♘g7+ and 20...♔f6 loses to 21.♖d6 gxf5 22.♕xd7.

20...gxf5

20...♕xf5 21.♕d6+ ♔d8 (21...♔e8 22.♖fe1+ ♗e6 23.♕d7 mate) 22.♕xf8+ ♔c7 23.♕xa8 ends the game.

21.exf5 ♖ac8 22. ♖xd7+! ♕xd7

23.f6+!

Originally I intended 23.♖e1+ ♘e5 24.♖xe5+ ♔f6 25.♕xd7 ♔xe5 26.♕xb5+ with a won ending. But then I remembered Emanuel Lasker's maxim: "When you see a good move — wait — don't play it — you might find a better one. —Fischer

In the *American Chess Quarterly*, Spring 1964, Bobby points out that 26.♕xb5+ ♔f6 "leads to an ending that I feel certain White can win, but it would still be a long haul, and in a simultaneous exhibition it would be the easiest thing in the world to get swindled out of."

23...♘xf6

As 23...♔e8 24.♖e1+ ♕e6 25.♕xc8 is mate.

24.♖e1+

Note the amusing piece configuration. All the Black pieces are blocking each other in a helpless position. Black has only one legal move — otherwise it's mate! (Fischer in *American Chess Quarterly*).

24...♘e4 25.♖xe4+ ♔f6 26.♕xd7 ♖fd8 27.♕g4 1-0

Ventura - April 22?

A Legend on the Road suggested that Bobby gave an exhibition in Ventura on April 22nd, but that doesn't seem to be the case. The *Ventura County Star Free-Press* of April 24th, mentions that local master George W. Soules gave a simul two days before, defeating 28 opponents, losing three games, and conceding one draw at the Ventura Civic Recreation Center.

Southern California chess historian Frank Berry theorizes that the high turnout suggests that Bobby's appearance was canceled with little notice. Otherwise why would so many players have shown up? Since the players were expecting a simul, the strongest player available stepped forward so as not to disappoint them.

Boston - May 10
+50=2-1

After stopping in Las Vegas and Denver, Fischer returned to the Northeast, giving a simul on May 10 at the Harvard Club. The following game, kindly forwarded by *Boston Globe* columnist Harold Dondis, shows Bobby's skill in fighting the Classical French. Gale, in his letter to the *Globe*, mentions that the first simul he ever played in was against Frank Marshall at the City Club in Boston in October of 1930 and the last, versus Arthur Bisguier in Billerica in June of 1982. He won both of these games, but none in the 52 years between them, despite playing in many exhibitions!

[62] *French Alekhine-Chatard C13*
RJF–W. Gale
        Boston (simul) May 10, 1964

1.e4 e6 2.d4 d5 3.♘c3 ♘f6 4.♗g5 ♗e7 5.e5 ♘fd7 6.h4

The Alekhine-Chatard Attack. Everyone knows Alexander Alekhine, but Chatard is another matter. *The Oxford*

Companion to Chess by Hooper and Whyld mentions that Frenchman Eugene Chatard (1850-1924) looked at 6.h4 around the turn of the century, and that his analysis may have inspired Alekhine to give it a try (Alekhine–Fahrni, Mannheim 1914), but that Romanian-born Adolf Albin was the real originator.

6...f6 7.♕h5+ g6?!

Theory prefers the less weakening 7...♔f8.

8.exf6 ♘xf6 9.♕e2 ♘c6

ECO gives only 9...c5 10.dxc5 ♘c6 11.O-O-O O-O 12.♘h3 with a clear advantage for White, Sanguineti–F. Benko, Buenos Aires 1954.

10.O-O-O O-O 11.♘f3 a6 12.♔b1 b5 13.♗h6 ♖e8 14.♘g5 ♗f8 15. ♗xf8 ♔xf8 16.h5 h6 17.♘f3 ♘xh5

Better is 17...g5 18.♕d2 ♘e7 19. ♘e5 c5 20.dxc5 ♔g7 with advantage to White. After the text, White is winning.

18.♕e3 ♘g7 19.♕xh6 ♕f6 20.♗d3
♔e7 21.♗xg6 ♖f8 22.♖he1 ♔d8
23.♘e5 ♘e7

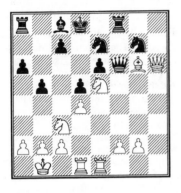

24.♖e3?

An uncharacteristic bit of careless-
ness on Bobby's part. The text costs
White the Exchange, but not the game.
Correct was 24.g4 ♘e8 25.g5 ♕xf2
26.♕h3 with a winning advantage.

**24...♘gf5 25.♕h7 ♘xe3 26.fxe3
♘xg6?!**

Gale considers this too hasty, preferring 26...♗d7 or 26...c6. For example, after 26...c6 27.♖h1 ♘xg6 28.
♘xg6 ♖f7 29.♕h2 ♗b7, the position is about equal. After the text,
White is winning again.

**27.♘xg6 ♕f7?! 28.♘xf8 ♕xf8 29.
g4 c5 30.dxc5 ♕xc5 31.g5 ♖a7 32.
♕h8+ 1-0**

Source: original scoresheet.

Milwaukee - May 14
+48=5–4

Chess in Milwaukee

Walter J. Boeyer
Milwaukee, Wisconsin, June 24, 1964

I just watched Fischer play at
the Pfister Hotel here. He preceded
his exhibition with a talk on his game
with Tal.

He played 55 games, losing 4 . . .
It cost $1.00 to watch the exhibition.
$5 to play. Our local newspaper, the
Milwaukee Journal, co-sponsored the
event so it only cost $2.00 to play:
this newspaper is very generous to
chess and backs an annual chess
event for all the local children on the
city play grounds — a big event.

Source: *Chess*, August 20th 1964

B. H. Wood, the editor and founder
of *Chess* notes, "Milwaukee has for decades been one of the world's leading

chess centers; in fact we understand
that FOUR THOUSAND youngsters
took part in the latest congress."

---

[63] *French Winawer   C19*
RJF–John Dedinsky
Milwaukee (simul) May 14, 1964

Notes by John Dedinsky
**1.e4 e6 2.d4 d5 3.♘c3 ♗b4 4.e5 c5
5.a3 ♗xc3+ 6.bxc3 ♘e7 7.a4 ♕a5
8.♗d2 c4 9.♘f3**

I expected ♕g4.

9...♘d7

I was trying to copy a plan of
Botvinnik's who used the N to
capture the QRP.

10.♘g5 h6 11.♕h5

W's 14th makes this move clear.

11...g6

If 11...♘g6, then 12.♘xe6!

12.♕h3 ♘b6 13.♘f3 ♗d7 14.♕h4

Now it's hard for Black to castle.

Authors' note: White should have played 14.♗e2 with some compensation for the pawn after 14...♘xa4 15.O-O. The text, at best, loses several tempi.

14...♗xa4

I changed plans. I intended ♘xa4, but decided the N could be useful at d7.

15.♕f6 ♖h7 16.h4?

Authors' note: Bobby completely overlooks Black's threat. He had to play 16.♕h4 though Black stands much better.

16..♘f5 17.h5

The Queen has no escape.

17...♘d7 0-1

The White Queen is trapped. On seeing Black's last move Fischer immediately, and with a smile, tipped his Queen.

Report by David Luban:

Alas! The score of my May 14, 1964 game against Fischer vanished mysteriously some time after the game, and my memory -- usually good for chess games of yesteryear -- isn't up to task. At the time, the affectation of our high school chess crowd was to notate our games using Cyrillic (Russian) characters, and I suspect that when I went off to college in 1966 my mother decided to do a general clean-up of my room, came across a page of gibberish, and threw it away. But perhaps this might be useful for your book:

Fischer played an Evans Gambit against me, and after 18 moves had an overwhelming position. With nothing to lose, and hoping to stay at the table for a few more minutes at least, I sacked a bishop at f2 and drew his king into the fray. In the ensuing complications, Fischer allowed his queen to be trapped at g4 and resigned. My combination was no means a forced win of his queen, and a subsequent group analysis showed that it was doubtful even as a forced draw. Players were arranged at the table in order of Elo ratings, and, as your diagram places me, I was on the left side, not the bottom end. In any event, Fischer was spending mere seconds per move at my end, reserving his longer thought for the strong end. I don't take much credit for the win, though my combination wasn't simply silly.

Fischer was completely impassive as he turned over his King. He said only "I could have drawn if I'd done this," and showed me the drawing maneuver. He autographed my score without further comment.

Flint - May 16
+53=5–0

The 1999 June-August issue of *Chess Horizons* featured three major articles on Bobby. The first, written by former Michigan Junior Champion Thomas Richardson, recalls Bobby's visit to Flint. Here are a few excerpts:

My father was president of the Flint Chess Club in Michigan, and he arranged for Fischer to stay with us and give a simultaneous exhbition in Flint in May of 1964. I was in the tenth grade at the time and rushed home from school on the Friday that Fischer arrived. It was a surprise to see him in our backyard dressed in a grey suit and tie, which was his standard attire for the two days he stayed with us. He and my father were seated at a chess board, and my father, who was Director of the Flint Public Library System, had brought home a newly released chess book that Bobby hadn't seen before. Bobby was playing through the games as fast as he could move the pieces, often knocking them over in the process. He would make offhand comments like, "Of course, you know this variation." Or "That's not a good move."

Before long my father proposed that Fischer and I play a game and Bobby suggested pawn and move odds. So I played white and Bobby removed his king bishop pawn. Although I had managed to win the Michigan Junior Chess Championship at age twelve in my first-ever tournament, I had only been playing seriously for about three years and expected to be soundly trounced. Much to my surprise I didn't make any huge blunders, and although I lost my pawn advantage, I was able to hold a draw in the resulting endgame. I was walking on air, but unfortunately didn't think to write down the moves, so that game is only a memory. Maybe it is partially as a result of this experience that I encourage younger players always to record their games."

[64] *Sicilian Paulsen   B42*
RJF–Thomas Richardson
Flint (simul) May 16, 1964

1.e4 c5 2.♘f3 e6 3.d4 cxd4 4.♘xd4 a6 5.♗d3 ♘c6 6.♘xc6 bxc6 7.O-O ♘f6?

7...d5 or 7...e5 is a more solid way to play. Now Black's Knight gets kicked around.

8.e5 ♘d5 9.c4 ♘b6 10.♘c3 ♕c7 11.♗f4 ♗b7

The cramp in Black's position is felt. Attempting to battle for space by 11...d6? fails to 12.exd6 ♗xd6 13. ♗xd6 ♕xd6 14.♘e4 followed by 15. c5 and 16.♘d6+ with a big advantage for White.

12.♘e4

White heads straight for the weakness on d6, but there was something to be said for straightforward development with 12.♕g4 followed by ♖ad1.

12...c5 13.♘d6+

Having said A (12.♘e4), White follows with B (13.♘d6+), but 13.♕g4, maintaining the pressure, was still a good alternative.

13...♗xd6 14.exd6 ♕c6 15.f3 f6?!

Black tries to go after the pawn on d6 (...e6-e5). A reasonable alternative was 15...O-O.

16.♕b3 f5

Now it becomes apparent that 16... e5 isn't possible, as 17.♗e4 wins the Knight.

17.♗e5?!

This is not a bad move, but considerably more to the point is 17.♗xf5! Obviously, 17...exf5 18.♕e3+ ♔f8 19.♕e7+ ♔g8 20.♗e5 mates. Black also has no good defense after 18... ♔d8 19.♕e7+ ♔c8 20.♕xg7 ♖d8 (20...♖e8 21.♖ae1) 21.♕xh7: Black is completely paralyzed and 22.♖ad1 with 23.♗g5 to follow are in the air.

17...O-O 18.♖ad1 ♘c8

Beginning a long maneuver to get the Knight into play on c6. White is clearly better, the challenge is how to open up the position to his advantage.

19.♕c3 ♖f7 20.♗c2 ♘a7 21.♕e3 ♕b6?

Black faithfully follows the above-mentioned plan, but overlooks a tactic. He had to play 21...a5 and only then ...♕b6 and ...♘c6.

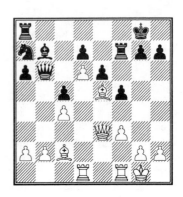

22.b4! ♘c6

Nothing works for Black: after 22... ♕xb4??, 23.♖b1 wins a piece, and on 22...♖c8 23.bxc5, Black can't capture the pawn, as 23...♕xc5 24.♗d4 picks up a Knight and 23...♖xc5 24.♗d4, a Rook!

23.bxc5

White wins not only a pawn, but a highway for his Rooks to enter the Black position. The rest is very easy, as Black has no counterplay.

23...♕a7 24.♗c3 ♖c8 25.♖b1 ♖a8 26.♖b6 ♖c8 27.♖fb1 ♘d8 28.a4 ♕a8 29.h4 ♖c6 30.h5 h6

Black couldn't allow 31.h6, opening the a1-h8 diagonal.

31.♗a5 ♕c8 32.♖xc6 ♘xc6 33.♗c3 ♘d8 34.♖b6 ♗a8 35.f4 ♗b7 36. ♗d4 ♘c6 37.♗d1 ♘xd4 38.♕xd4 ♖f8 39.a5 ♗c6 40.♕e5 ♕a8 41. ♖b3!

White indirectly covers g2 (41... ♗xg2? 42.♖g3!) and prepares to swing his Rook over to the kingside for the attack.

41...♕e8 42.♖g3 ♕f7

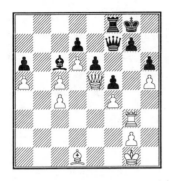

43.♖b3!

More space equals more mobility. Now that Black's pieces are bunched around his King, Fischer decides to go the other way.

43...♗a4

Black gets to trade a pair of pieces, but loses his best-placed piece.

44.♖b1 ♗xd1 45.♖xd1 ♖b8

White was threatening 46.♖b1 followed by ♖b6 or ♖b7; so the text is understandable, but it walks into a nice tactic. If 45...♕xh5, Bobby had 46.♖b1 ♖c8 47.♖b7 ♕e8 48.♖b6 ♖a8 49.c6! dxc6 50.♕c5 with a winning position.

46.c6! dxc6 47.d7 ♖d8 48.♕c7 ♕e7 49.♕xc6 ♔f7 50.c5 ♔f8 51.♕c7 ♔f7 52.♕c6 ♔f8

Since Black is helpless, Bobby takes time to safeguard his King so that after a future c5-c6 there are no complications with ...♕c5+.

53.g3 ♔f7 54.♔h2 ♖b8 55.♕c7 ♖d8 56.c6 ♕f6 57.♕xd8 ♕xd8 58.c7 1-0

Source: *Chess Horizons*, June-August 1999, pages 6-7.

Chess archeologist Jack O'Keefe of Ann Arbor has kindly passed on the following three games from Bobby's exhibition in Flint, Michigan.

[65] *French McCutcheon   C12*
RJF–N. Burns
Flint (simul) May 16, 1964

1.e4 e6 2.d4 d5 3.♘c3 ♘f6 4.♗g5 ♗b4 5.e5

Russian Grandmaster Igor Glek, who is a specialist on the Black side of the MacCutcheon French, had an interesting story to tell about the opening in the French magazine *Europa Echecs* (we found the story, as related by Dutch GM Hans Ree, on Hanon Russell's *Chess Cafe* website). In 1988, when he was doing his military service in the Soviet Union, Glek was approached by Anatoly Karpov. The former World Champion was playing for the Red Army team at the time and asked Glek for advice about what to do against the MacCutcheon. Glek compiled a small file on the line that starts with 5.exd5, which, of course, is not a refutation of the MacCutcheon, but very safe and, according to Glek, gives White good prospects for a minimal positional advantage. "Just what I needed," Karpov said. Glek was rewarded with two weeks extra leave from military service. (In the Soviet Union power and influence — **blat**, in Russian — counted for everything. The world has changed since then and nowadays Karpov has to pay his helpers.)

5...h6 6.♗e3

Fischer faced the MacCutcheon twice in tournament play. Each time he answered 6.♗d2 and after 6...♗xc3, he played the experimental 7.♗xc3 against Petrosian (Curaco 1962) and the main line 7.bxc3 ♘e4 8.♕g4 g6 9.♗d3 vs. Rossolimo (U.S. Championship 1965). The latter is game number 52 in *My 60 Memorable Games*.

6...♘e4 7.♘e2

Here White normally plays 7.♕g4.

7...c5 8.a3 ♘xc3

8...cxd4 9.♗xd4 ♘xc3 10.♘xc3 ♗e7 11.♕g4 O-O 12.♗e3 f5 13.♕g6 ♕c7 14.f4 favored White in Nunn–Beaton, Walsall 1992.

9.♘xc3 cxd4

This move, in conjunction with Black's next, loses time. Normally, Black plays 9...♗xc3+ 10.bxc3 ♕a5 with play reminiscent of the Winawer.

10.♗xd4 ♗e7 11.f4 ♘c6 12.♗b5

Fischer could have aimed for a more complicated game with 12.♗f2.

12...♗d7 13.♗xc6 bxc6

Making the bad Bishop even worse, but Black wants to get in ...c5. White wants to put his Knight there, which explains the following complications.

14.♘a4 ♕a5+ 15.c3 c5

15...♕b5 16.b4 ♗c8 17.♗c5, meeting 17...♗a6 with 18.♗xf8 ♔xf8 19.♘c5, gives White the advantage.

16.♘xc5 ♗xc5 17.b4 ♗xb4 18.axb4

White can try to profit from the opening of the c-file with 18.cxb4, but this allows 18...♕a4.

18...♕c7 19.O-O ♗b5 20.♖f3 g6 21.♗c5

This allows Black to further blockade the game. More accurate was 21.♖a5 a6 22.♗c5, though the closed nature of the game makes a draw quite likely.

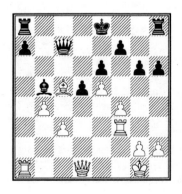

21...a5! 22.♕d4 a4 23.♖a3 h5 24. ♖h3 ♔d7 25.♖e3 ♕c6 26.♖e1 ♖hc8 27.♖d1 ♔c7 28.♕f2 ♔b7

Black's King is safe and the potential breaks to open the game are few.

29.♕h4 ♖h8 30.♕f6 ♖h7 31.h4 ♖g8 32.♔h2 ♖a8 33.♕e7+ ♔c7 34. ♕g5 ♖e8 35.♕g3 ♖a8 36.♕e3 ♖hh8 37.♖da1 ♕c6 **Draw**

Source: original scoresheet

Jack O'Keefe of Ann Arbor, Michigan, is one of America's great experts on Russian chess.

[66] *Sicilian Accelerated Dragon   B35*
RJF–Jack O'Keefe
Flint (simul) May 16, 1964

1.e4 c5 2.♘f3 ♘c6 3.d4 cxd4 4.♘xd4 g6 5.♘c3 ♗g7 6.♗e3 ♘f6 7.♗c4 ♕a5 8.O-O a6?!

This is a bit early. Black should castle here.

9.♘b3 ♕c7 10.♗e2

White could have obtained a clear positional advantage with 10.♘d5 ♘xd5 11.exd5 ♘a5 (11...♘e5 12. ♗e2) 12.♘xa5 ♕xa5 13.c3 d6 14. ♗d4. The pressure against e7 is unpleasant.

10...b5 11.f4

Once again, the idea of ♘d5 was strong. For example, 11.a4 b4 12. ♘d5 ♘xd5 13.exd5 ♘d8 (13...♘a5 14.d6! or 13...♘e5 14.♗d4 with f4 in the offing) 14.♗d4 ♗xd4 15.♕xd4 O-O 16.♖ac1 a5 17.c3 with a big advantage.

11...d6 12.♘d5 ♘xd5 13.exd5 ♘a5

This is the right square for the Knight now that ...d6 is in. Black

needs to trade a second pair of Knights to relieve some of the pressure on his position.

14.♗d4 ♘xb3

Black wants to make sure the Knights come off the board. Here 15. ♗xg7 is met by 15...♘xa1 16.♗xh8 ♕xc2.

15.axb3 ♗xd4+ 16.♕xd4 O-O 17. ♗d3 ♗b7

Black chooses this over 17...♗d7, because he favors putting pressure on d5.

18.b4

Fischer hopes to stop the trade of Queens, but better was 18.♖ae1. If 18...♖fe8, White has 19.f5 ♖ac8? (Black should play 19...♕c5, as 20. ♕xc5 dxc5 21.c4 is better for White, but not so easy to break through) 20. b4 (to stop ...♕c5 at some point) 20... ♗a8 21.fxg6 hxg6 22.♖f4 ♕b7 23. ♗xg6 leads to a winning attack, e.g., 23...fxg6 24.♖e6 wins. Bobby's play on the queenside allows Black to simplify.

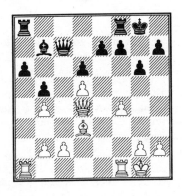

18...a5!

Black alertly seizes the opportunity to grab counterplay on the queenside before White's play on the other wing gets too dangerous.

19.bxa5

Here sharp complications arise after 19.♖fe1 axb4 20.♖xa8 ♖xa8 21.♗xb5 ♕xc2 22.♖xe7 ♖a1+ 23.♗f1 ♕c8, when Black holds. Bobby's method leads to a small pull.

20...♖xa5 20.♖xa5 ♕xa5 21.b4 ♕a2 22.♖e1 ♕xd5 23.♕xd5 ♗xd5 24.♖xe7 ♖c8

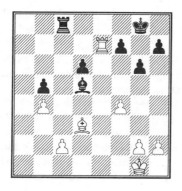

25.♔f2

A sharper try is 25.♖d7 ♖c6 26. ♖b7 ♗c4 27.♔f2 followed by ♔e3 and ♔d4. White still looks better.

25...♖c3 26.♗xb5?!

He should have tried 26.♖d7 with play similar to the previous note. Now the game peters out to a draw.

26...♖xc2+ 27.♔e2 ♖c3 28.♖b2 ♗b7 29.♗e2 ♔f8 30.b5 ♔e7 31.♗f3 ♗xf3 32.gxf3 ♔d7 33.b6 ♔c8 34.b7+ ♔b8 35.♖b6 ♖c7 36.♖xd6 ♔xb7 Draw

Source: original scoresheet.

---

[67] *Sicilian Accelerated Dragon* B35
RJF–D. Thackrey
Flint (simul) May 16, 1964

1.e4 c5 2.♘f3 ♘c6 3.d4 cxd4 4.♘xd4 g6 5.♘c3 ♗g7 6.♗e3 ♘f6 7.♗c4 O-O 8.♗b3

Bobby played 8.f3?! against Panno at the Portoroz Interzonal in 1958. Black instantly equalized with 8...♕b6 (8...e6!? is also interesting), threatening b2 and d4.

8...♕a5 9.f3 d5

This variation has a reputation of leading to a difficult ending for Black.

10.exd5 ♘b4 11.♕d2 ♘bxd5 12. ♘xd5 ♕xd2+ 13.♔xd2

ECO (Kortchnoi) gives 13.♗xd2 as the main line with the following continuation: 13...♘xd5 14.♗xd5 ♗xd4 15.O-O-O ♖d8 16.♗b3 ♗f6 17.♗f4 ♗f5 18.g4 g5 (so far Suetin–Stein, USSR Championship 1963) 19.♖xd8+ ♖xd8 20.♗e3 ♗e6 21.♗xe6 fxe6 22. c3 a6 23.♔c2 with a clear advantage in the ending.

13...♘xd5 14.♗xd5 ♖d8 15.♗b3

Tal–Kortchnoi, Moscow (m-7) 1968, saw 15.c4 e6 16.♗e4 ♗xd4 17.♗xd4 ♖xd4+ 18.♔c3 ♖d7 19.♖hd1 ♖b8 20.♖xd7 ♗xd7 21.♖d1 ♗e8 22.c5 with a big plus for White. Kortchnoi suggests 16...f5 17.♔c3 fxe4 18.fxe4 b6 as a way of keeping White's advantage to a minimum. Bobby's move gives White a small, but clear, advantage.

15...♗xd4 16.♗xd4 ♖xd4+ 17.♔e3 ♖d8 18.♖hd1 ♗d7 19.♖d4 ♗c6 20. ♖ad1 ♖xd4 21.♖xd4 ♔f8

22.♗d5
Fischer steers for the Rook endgame where he is favored by his more active

King and Rook plus the queenside pawn majority.

22...♗xd5 23.♖xd5 ♔e8 24.c4 ♖c8 25.♔d4 e6 26.♖d6 ♔e7 27.c5 b6 28.b4 ♖b8 29.♖c6 ♔d7 30.b5 bxc5+ 31.♔xc5 e5?

This leads to Black's immediate demise. The position is pretty bad, but Black could have put up more resistance with 31...h5, intending ...h5-h4-h3.

32.a4 f5 33.♖a6 ♖b7 34.♔d5 e4 35.fxe4 f4 36.e5 1-0

Source: original scoresheet.

Columbus, Ohio - May 18
+48=2–0

[68] *French Alekhine-Chatard   C13*
RJF–W. Kaufer + two consultants
Columbus (simul) May 18, 1964

1.e4 e6 2.d4 d5 3.♘c3 ♘f6 4.♗g5 ♗e7 5.e5 ♘fd7 6.h4 c5 7.♗xe7 ♕xe7
Theory prefers 7...♔xe7. The text obliges Black to sacrifice material.
8.♘b5 ♘a6??

This move fails to meet the requirements of the position. Necessary was 8...O-O. White wins the Rook after 9.♘c7, but the complications that arise after 9...cxd4 10.♘xa8 f6 11.♕xd4 ♘c6 12.♕d2 fxe5 13.O-O-O ♘f6 14.f3 ♕d6 [Bronstein–Ståhlberg, Budapest (ct) 1950] are anything but clear.

9.♘d6+ ♔d8 10.♗xa6 bxa6 11.f4 ♖b8 12.b3 a5 13.♕d2 cxd4 14.♘f3 ♘b6 15.♘xd4 ♕d7 16.♕xa5 a6 17.♕c5 ♖b7 18.♘c6+ ♔c7 19.♘a5+ ♔d8 20.♘axb7+ ♗xb7 21.♕xb6+ ♔e7 22.♘xb7 ♖c8 23.O-O-O 1-0

Source: *San Francisco Chronicle,*
December 31, 1975.

Venue Unknown

This game against well-known Bridge Master Jeff Reubens appears to have been played during the 1964 tour.

[69] *French Winawer   C15*
RJF–Jeff Reubens
(simul) 1964?

1.e4 e6 2.d4 d5 3.♘c3 ♗b4 4.a3

Fischer normally played 4.e5, but he did play the text from time to time. His record in tournament games with it was two wins, one loss and one draw.

4...♗xc3+ 5.bxc3 c5

This move is uncommon, but not that bad. Petrosian, Vaganian and Furman have all played it.

6.♕g4

Kholmov–Furman, Tbilisi 1959, continued 6.exd5 exd5 7.dxc5, trying to open the position for the Bishops.

6...♘e7

Here 6...♘f6, along the lines of Semenova–Khugashvili, USSR 1969, is more aggressive, but the text leads to a good position.

7.♕xg7 ♖g8 8.♕xh7 ♕c7 9.♘f3 cxd4 10.♗b5+ ♗d7 11.♗xd7+ ♘xd7 12.O-O ♘f6 13.♕h4 ♘xe4 14.♗f4 ♕xc3 15.♘e5 ♘f5 16.♕h7 O-O-O

Taking time out to defend f7 with 16...♖f8 makes sense, especially as it threatens 17...♘f6, which would force the Queens off.

17.♕xf7 ♖xg2+??

Hallucinating. Better was 17...♖ge8 with a reasonable game.

18.♔xg2 ♘h4+ 19.♔g1 ♕h3 20.♕g7 ♘f6

Black threatens 21...♖g8 and hopes to drive White's Queen away from the defense of g2. However, in trying to generate threats against Fischer's King, Black has been negligent in watching out for the safety of his own.

21.♘c6!

Threatening 22.♘xa7 mate and 22.♕c7 mate.

21...♘f3+

Black can try the tricky 21...e5, but White has an adequate defense in 22.♘xd8 exf4 23.f3.

22.♔h1 e5 23.♘e7+ 1-0

Bobby's completely in control: 23...♔b8 24.♕xf6 exf4 25.♘c6+ ♔c7 26.♕xd8+ ♔xc6 27.♕f6+ ♔d7 28.♕xf4 wins.

Source: *New York Times*, October 11, 1971.

Articles, 70s Simuls, Blitz and Last Game

Boys Life Articles

Bobby had a column in *Boys Life*, the official magazine of the Boy Scouts of America, from Dec. 1966 to Dec. 1969. The following annotations show the skillful way Bobby was able to comment on games for a wide audience.

Notes based on Fischer's annotations in *Boys Life*.
Direct quotes appear thus.

---

[70] *King's Indian Attack   A08*
RJF–IM Lhamsuren Miagmasuren
Sousse Interzonal 1967

1.e4 e6 2.d3 d5 3.♘d2 ♘f6 4.g3 c5 5. ♗g2 ♘c6 6.♘gf3 ♗e7 7.0-0 0-0 8.e5!

The key strategical thrust. My plan is first to drive his defensively well-placed Knight to an inferior

square, then slowly ring his cramped King's position with my pieces — to mate him. Of course, Black gets counterplay on the opposite wing. The question is: Who comes first?

8...♘d7 9.♖e1 b5 10.♘f1 b4 11.h4 a5 12.♗f4 a4 13.a3

Believe it or not, I actually spent more time on this innocuous push (15 minutes) than on any other move in the game! I didn't want to allow Black to get in ...a3, which would practically force me to reply with b3, thereby creating "holes" (weak squares) on c3 and d4. On the other hand, by stopping to meet his positional threat, I am forced to postpone my own schemes for at least one move. Chess is a matter of delicate judgement, knowing when to punch and how to duck.

13...bxa3 14.bxa3 ♘a5

Placing the Knight on the rim is dubious. Better is 15...♗a6.

15.♘e3 ♗a6 16.♗h3

Preventing Black from playing ...f6 or ...f5.

16...d4

Gaining the d5-square, but giving up the e4-square, which will later play a decisive role in White's attack.

17.♘f1

This Knight retreats temporarily, but will later maneuver to the hole at e4.

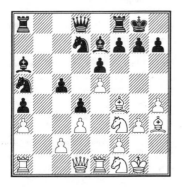

17...♘b6 18.♘g5 ♘d5?

Better is 18...h6 19.♘e4 c4.

19.♗d2 ♗xg5

Now 19...h6 is impossible due to 20. ♘xe6 fxe6 21.♗xe6+ ♔h8 22.♗xa5 ♕xa5 23.♗xd5. Black's best try is 19...c4.

20.♗xg5 ♕d7 21.♕h5 ♖fc8 22.♘d2

More pieces are coming to the kingside for the decisive attack.

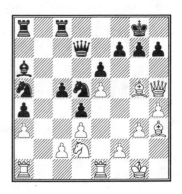

22...♘c3

22...c4 was still the best move.

23.♗f6!

Threatening 24.♕g5 g6 25.♕h6. The Bishop is immune because of 23... gxf6 24.exf6 ♔h8 25.♘f3 ♘d5 (25... ♖g8 26.♘e5) 26.♘g5 ♘xf6 27.♕h6 ♕e7 28.♗f5 ♖g8 29.♘xh7, winning.

23...♕e8 24.♘e4

White will exchange the Knight on c3 in order to bring the Rook to the kingside via e4. 25.♘d6 is threatened.

24...g6 25.♕g5 ♘xe4 26.♖xe4 c4

Black's queenside counterplay is too slow.

27.h5 cxd3 28.&h4! &a7

If 28...dxc2, then 29.hxg6 fxg6 30. &xh7 c1=&+ 31.&xc1 &xc1+ 32. &xc1 &xh7 33.&c7+, mating, or 30... &xh7 31.&h4+ &g8 32.&h8+ &f7 33.&g7 mate. The text move counters this threat by guarding h7. According to Fischer, 28...&c7 would have been better, although White would still be winning.

29.&g2!

The Bishop enters the attack by repositioning on the e4-square.

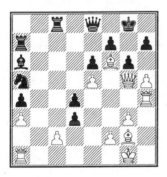

29...dxc2

Black started to get excited, thinking I had miscalculated by allowing him this dangerous passed pawn. But he has no better defense. On 29...&b7 30.hxg6 fxg6, 31. &xh7! as in the previous note. The point is: Had Black played 28...&c7 (instead of ...&a7), this line would not have worked, because 31.&xh7 would have been met simply by ...&xh7. White's best, therefore, would have been 30.cxd3 followed by an eventual doubling of Rooks on

the h-file, with a finish similar to the actual game.

30.&h6 &f8

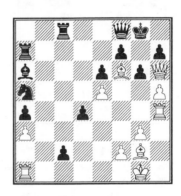

31.&xh7+! 1-0

A spectacular finish! If 31...&xh7, then 32.hxg6+ &xg6 33.&e4 mate or 32...&g8 33.&h8 mate.

---

[71] *King's Indian* E60
E. Nikolic–RJF
Vinkovci 1968

1.c4 g6 2.&c3 &g7 3.g3 e5 4.&g2 d6 5.e3 &f6 6.&ge2 O-O 7.O-O

It is not good to commit the King so early if White intends to play d4.

7...c6 8.d4

Both Kings are now safe behind their fianchettoed Bishops. You should try this setup, too. It will prevent a quick checkmate even against a very strong player! Things look pretty even, but do you notice that White's Knight has no place to go? Also, that Bishop at c1 isn't very active, is it? Poor planning on White's part.

8...♖e8 9.♖b1 e4

Advancing the pawn to e4 and strongpointing it. Fischer and others have won many games with this pattern. With the center blocked, White can't coordinate his pieces to reach the kingside quickly enough to defend against a sudden, sacrificial attack.

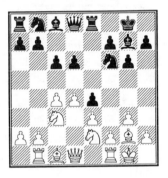

10.b4 ♗f5 11.h3 h5 12.♘f4 ♘bd7 13.a4 ♘f8 14.c5

This blocks the position, making Black's attack even stronger. According to Fischer, 14.b5 was better. White's position was already difficult.

14...d5 15.b5 ♘8h7 16.♗d2 ♘g5 17. ♖b2 ♕d7 18.♔h2 ♗h6

A very important move. The Bishop indirectly attacks the Knight on f4 and creates a square for the King on g7.

19.a5

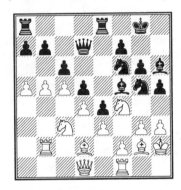

Now Black has built up maximum force with five pieces zeroed in — with more to come. The question is, how to break through? Should I now move 19...h4 or 19... ♗g4 or *19...♘f3+?*

I thought a long time about this. 19...h4 didn't pose an immediate threat — but it's not a bad move. 19...♘f3+ was also a possibility with 20.♗xf3 exf3 21.♕xf3 ♗xf4 22.gxf4 cxb5 and Black gets his pawn back with a very good game, because if White takes on b5, then ...♗d3! wins the Exchange. But 19...♗g4! leads to a series of forced moves and now my Rooks come to the attack along the h-file.

19...♗g4!

The decisive breakthrough is made by placing the light-squared Bishop *en prise*. Black's idea is to strongpoint the f3-square.

20.hxg4

White will not survive long after 20. ♕b3 ♘f3+ 21.♗xf3 (21.♔h1 ♗xf4)

21...♗xf3 22.bxc6 bxc6 23.♕b7 ♕f5 24.♕xc6 ♗xf4 followed by ...♘g4+.
20...hxg4

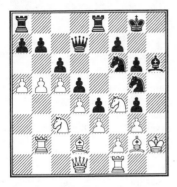

21.♖h1

If 21.♗h1, then 21...♘f3+ 22.♔g2 ♗xf4 23.exf4 ♕f5 24.♖g1 ♕h5 25.♔f1 ♕h2 26.♗xf3 exf3 26.♗e3 ♖xe3 28. fxe3 ♕xb2, winning.

21...♘f3+ 22.♗xf3 gxf3 23.♔g1 ♗xf4 24.exf4 ♔g7

White has no defense to Black's occupation of the h-file.

25.f5

25...♖h8

Black must still be careful. Not 25... ♕xf5, as 26.♗h6+ shuts down the h-file.

26.♗h6+ ♖xh6 37.♖xh6 ♔xh6 28. ♕d2+

If 28.a6, then Fischer gives the following finish: 28...♕xf5! 29.axb7 ♖h8 30.bxc6 ♔g7 31.b8=♕ ♖h1+! 32. ♔xh1 ♕h3+ 33.♔g1 ♕g2 mate.

28...g5 29.bxc6 ♕xf5 30.♘d1 ♕h3 31.♘e3 ♔g6 0-1

Fischer's annotations to the following game are very instructive. They are in the form of a novice asking Fischer questions as he plays through the game.

[72] *Pirc Austrian*   *B09*
RJF–Jovanovac

Vinkovci 1968

1.e4 d6 2.d4

Why this move, Bob?

I want to get control of the center.

2...♘f6

What was Black's idea here?

This is the Pirc defense. He has to get the Knight out so that he can later "fianchetto" his Bishop and castle his King into safety. The only other Knight move is ...♘h6. That's a terrible square for his Knight. It would be exposed to attack. For example, I could play h3 followed by g4 and storm that position. If Black castled later I'd win his Knight with g4-g5!

3.♘c3

Why a Knight move here?

It's a developing move, giving me a further grip on the center and defending my e-pawn.

3...g6 4.f4

Why this pawn move?

I now have three pawns in the center with a threat of a breakthrough on e5 later on.

4...♗g7 5.♘f3

This is to get a further grip on the center, isn't it?

Right.

5...O-O 6.♗d3

This is easy to see, Bob. You want to be free to castle your King into safety. But wouldn't your Bishop be just as effective on, say, c4 as it is on d3?

No, Black could drive it back by 6...c6, followed by 7...b5 etc. I'd be exposing the Bishop to harassment.

6...♘fd7?

This notation means that the Black Knight at f6 hops to square d7, right?

That's right. But it's a poor move. It breaks a couple of rules. The Knight is blocking his own Bishop on c8. Also, it's usually good to avoid moving the same minor piece (Knight or Bishop) twice before moving other pieces out. A better move would have been 6...♘c6, or 6...♘a6 followed by 7...c5.

7.O-O e5

Black needs to fight back in the center, but, according to Fischer, this is not the right way to do it. He gives 7...c5 as better, as it doesn't block the Bishop's diagonal.

8.dxe5

Why not fxe5, Bob?

I'd be taking a little guard away from my King. More important, after I took 8.dxe5 and he took back ...dxe5, I wanted to attack with my f-pawn at f5. You'll see what I mean in a minute.

8...dxe5 9.f5

Fischer considers Black to be positionally lost here because of the wedge White has on the kingside.

9...c6

What's the point of this move, Bob?

To keep me out of d5, for one thing.

10.♘g5!

I notice you marked this move with an exclamation point, meaning you considered it a very good move. Why so? Looks to me as though you're just moving your Knight into a spot where it can be attacked by pawns or a Bishop and Queen.

I wanted him to play 10...h6. Then I'd have a winning combo, because I'd play 11.fxg6! he'd take my Knight with ...hxg5 (or 11...fxg6 12.♗c4+ ♔h8 13.♘f7+ wins) and I'd play 12.♕h5, threatening mate at h7. Now he has two moves. First, if he plays 12...fxg6, then I play 13.♗c4+. That's practically the game right away, because he has to put his Rook on f7 to block mate. Second, if he moves 11...♘f6 to protect against mate, I simply capture his Knight at f6 with my Rook.

10...♘b6 11.a4!

I see, Bob, that you've marked this move as very good. Why?

I want to drive his Knight away from its defensive position with a5.

11...a5 12.♗e3 ♗h6 13.♕d2 f6 14. ♕f2

I see this, Bob. Your Bishop and Queen are now threatening his hanging Knight.

Right. I wanted to break through into his position. So I'm ready to get rid of his Knight at b6. This will hurt him, because he hasn't many pieces developed.

14...♗xg5

Why not the ...fxg5 move?

Because after 14...fxg5 15.♗b6 ♕f6 16.♗c5 ♖d8 17.♗e3!, threatening 18.h4 followed by 19.♕d2 or, vice versa, 18.♕d2 and 19.h4, and White will win at least a pawn.

15.♗xb6 ♕d7 16.♗c5 ♖e8 17.h4

Now you're after his Bishop and heading for the breakthrough of his King's protecting pawns, right Bob?

Right.

17...♗f4

If 17...♗h6, then Fischer gives 18. fxg6 hxg6 19.♕xf6.

18.g3 gxf5 19.gxf4 fxe4 20.♘xe4 ♔h8 21.f5

Not 21.♘xf6?? ♕g7+.

21...♘a6 22.♗xa6 bxa6 23.♔h2 1-0

Wait a second, Bob. I don't see an immediate checkmate. Can't he get out of this bind?

Nope. If he moves 23...♕f7, I move 24.♘d6 and fork his Queen and Rook . . . If he moves 23...♕g7, then 24.♖g1 ♕h6 25.♘d6 and he must move 25...♖f8 (If he goes ...♖e7, I can simply take his Bishop with my Knight, threatening his Rook at e7 with my Bishop.) 26. ♗e3 ♕h5 27.♕g3, threatening ♕g7 mate.

Summing up this game Bob, what seemed the most critical mistake he made, besides playing you?

His downfall started on his sixth move. And he doubled his trouble on his seventh move, as we've mentioned. The moral is: Learn at least seven or eight sound moves for any defense you choose to play. That way, you won't lose almost before you've started.

Fischer Simuls in the 1970s

Munster 1970

Shortly after the Siegen Olympiad in 1970, Fischer gave a 20-board exhibition in Munster, Germany, against some of the best players from the region. His result was 15 wins, 4 losses, and one draw.

[73] *Sicilian Sozin   B87*
RJF–F. Middendorf
                    Munster (simul) 1970

1.e4 c5 2.♘f3 d6 3.d4 cxd4 4.♘xd4 ♘f6 5.♘c3 a6 6.♗c4 e6 7.♗b3 b5 8.0-0 ♗b7 9.♖e1 ♘bd7 10.♗g5 **♕a5?!**

Black's innovation is supposed to lead to a lost game, to our knowledge 10...♕a5?! has never been repeated, but it might not be that bad. Theory is 10...h6 11.♗h4 (11.♗xf6 is also popular) 11...g5 (11...♘c5? 12.♗d5! gave White a terrific attack in Fischer–Rubinetti, Palma de Mallorca Interzonal 1970) 12.♗g3 ♘e5. Russian GM Semyon Dvoirys has had good success on the Black side of this variation.

11.♗xf6 ♘xf6 12.e5! dxe5

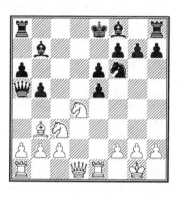

13.♘xe6! b4?

On 13...fxe6, one cute variation is 14.♖xe5 ♗c8 15.♗xe6 ♕c7 16.♗d7+ ♔f7 17.♗e8+ ♘xe8 18.♕d5+ ♔g6 19.♖g5+ ♔h6 20.♕d2, winning. The key question is what happens after the natural sequence 14...♖d8 (instead of 14...♗c8) 15.♖xe6+ ♗e7 16.♕e2 ♕c7 17.♖e1 ♖d7. White has two pawns for the piece and a strong position, but no obvious way to increase the pressure.

14.♘xg7+ ♗xg7 15.♕d6

With the twin threats of ♖xe5+ and ♗a4+.

15...♘d7 16.♗xf7+ ♔xf7 17.♕xd7+ ♔f6 18.♖ad1 ♖hg8 19.♖d6+ ♔g5 20.h4+ ♔xh4 21.♕f5

This does the job in workmanlike fashion, but even faster was 21.♖e4+ ♗xe4 (21...♔g5 or 21...♔h5 is met 22.♕g4 mate) 22.♕h3+ ♔g5 23.♘xe4+ ♔f4 24.♕f3 mate.

21...♗xg2 22.♔xg2 ♗h6+ 23.♔f3 1-0

The source for this game appears to be the *Stuttgarter Zeitung* of March 19, 1971.

Fischer Simuls in Spain

The 1970 Palma de Mallorca Interzonal in Spain was one of Bobby Fischer's greatest victories and set the stage for his triumphant run for the World Championship. A short time after his crushing victory at Palma (18.5-4.5, 3.5 points ahead of the field) Bobby gave two simultaneous exhibitions in Spain.

Bobby faced 20 opponents in Madrid and didn't lose a single game. His encounter with Garcia Bachiller

from the exhibition is a wonderful game. It was first published in Pablo Moran's *Bobby Fischer, su vida y partidas* (1971, pages 221-222) and later reprinted in *Inside Chess*, 5:4:3.

Now Carlos Almarza-Mato of Leon, Spain, adds to the picture of Bobby in Spain by forwarding the following game from a December 23, 1970, simul in Seville. This was Fischer's only loss in 20 games.

[74] *Kings Indian Fianchetto   E68*
RJF–Eugenio Gomez
Seville (simul) 1970

1.d4

This is a real rarity for Bobby. He almost never played 1.d4 in his tournament career and there is not a single documented case from his 1964 simul tour around the United States. He had two Queen's Gambits in his 1972 World Championship match with Boris Spassky, but both arose via 1.c4.

1...♘f6 2.c4 g6 3.♘c3 d6 4.g3 ♗g7 5.♗g2 0-0 6.♘f3 ♘bd7 7.0-0 e5 8.e4 ♘e8?!

This move, which makes ...f7-f5 possible, doesn't make a lot of sense when the center is still fluid.

9.♖e1 c6 10.♗e3 ♕e7 11.♕d2 ♘b6?!

Yes, this does allow Black to develop his Bishop on c8, but the Knight is completely out of play on b6.

12.b3 ♗g4

13.h3?

An inexplicable blunder by Bobby. With 13.♖ad1 or 13.d5, White would have a clear advantage (8...♘e8?! and 11...♘b6?! don't make a good impression).

13...♗xf3 14.♗xf3 ♕f6

Oops! Bobby must lose both of his center pawns to avoid losing a piece. The rest of the game is pretty straightforward.

15.♕d1 exd4 16.e5 dxe5 17.♘e4 ♕e7 18.♗g5 f6 19.♗c1 ♘c7 20.a4 ♘e6 21.a5 ♘d7 22.a6 b6 23.♗a3 c5 24.♘d2 ♖ad8 25.♗d5 ♔h8 26.♖b1 ♘c7 27.♗b7 ♘b8 28.b4 ♘cxa6 29.♗xa6 ♘xa6 30.bxc5 ♘xc5 31.♖b5 ♕c7 32.♗xc5 bxc5 33.♘e4 ♕f7 34.♖xc5 f5 35.♘d2 e4 36.♕a4 ♖fe8 37.♖a5 ♖e7 38.c5 e3 39.♘f3 f4 40. g4 d3 41.♕d1 ♗c3 0-1

Source: *Jaque,* May 1996, pp. 8-9.

[75] *Sicilian Paulsen   B43*
RJF–Garcia Bachiller
Madrid (simul) 1970

1.e4 c5 2.♘f3 e6 3.d4 cxd4 4.♘xd4 a6 5.♘c3 ♕c7 6.♗d3 ♘f6 7.0-0 b5 8.♖e1 ♗b7

This is an uncommon move in an uncommon position (Black normally doesn't develop his King Knight to f6 early when he plays a quick ...b5). The main try has been 8...♗c5 (Larsen once tried 8...♗d6) 9.♗e3 (9.♘b3 ♗d6 10.g3 ♗b7 11.♗xb5 h5 12.♗f1 h4 13.♗g2 hxg3 14.hxg3 ♘c6 with murky compensation for the pawn, Ligterink–Piasetski, Karlovac 1977) 9... d6 10.♗xb5+ axb5 11.♘dxb5 ♕c6 12.♗xc5 dxc5 13.e5 ♘g8 14.♕d6 ♕xd6 15.♘xd6+ ♔d7 16.♘xf7 ♔e7 17.♘xh8 ♘h6 18.♖e4 ♗d7 19.♖c4 ♘a6 20.♖d1 ♖xh8 and White has a slight advantage, Sibarevic–Miladinovic, Banja Vrucica 1991.

9.e5 ♘d5 10.♘xd5 ♗xd5 11.a4 b4 12.♗e4 ♗xe4

Black gets Rook, Bishop and pawn after 12...♕xe5 13.♘f3 ♕xe4 14. ♖xe4 ♗xe4, but must be careful after 15.♕e2 and play 15...♗b7, for 15... d5? loses to 16.♘g5 ♗f5 17.g4 ♗g6 18.♘xe6 fxe6 19.♕xe6+.

13.♖xe4 ♘c6 14.♗f4 ♖c8 15.♖c1

The darkside of an early ...b4 is that White often has the opportunity to open the position with c2-c3.

15...♕a7?

Black gets out of the way of c2-c3, but loses precious time. Much better was 15...♗e7, meeting 16.c3 with 16... bxc3 17.♖xc3 O-O.

16.c3 bxc3 17.♖xc3 ♗c5 18.♗e3 O-O??

Black had to play 18...♗b6, but after 19.a5 ♗xd4 20.♗xd4 White has a big advantage.

19.♖xc5 ♕xc5 20.♘xe6 ♕a5

Black can drag things out with 20... ♕xe3 21.♖xe3 dxe6 but the end result will still be the same.

21.b4 ♘xb4 22.♘xf8 ♘d5 23.♘xd7 ♘c3 24.♕g4 ♖c6 25.♘f6+ ♔h8 26. ♕xg7!+ 1-0

Source: pp. 221-2 of *Bobby Fischer —su vida y partidas* by Pablo Moran (Barcelona, 1971)

Fischer in Argentina

In 1999, Bobby Fischer gave an interview on Phillipine radio. He had this to say about his simuls in Argentina.

When I played in Argentina [in 1971], I played Tigran Petrosian a Candidates Match and beat him to qualify to play Spassky in Iceland the next year, you know. After I played, I gave an exhibition tour down there, a simul exhibition tour. I don't remember exactly how many I played. I have to check the record, twenty-five, thirty simul exhibitions.

And before every simultaneous exhibition it was announced that all the players had to give me their copy of the score. So I had a complete record. They didn't give me the carbon copy, I insisted on the original copy. I've got hundreds and hundreds . . . I don't know, maybe about between six hundred and a thousand scores. None of these games have ever been published anywhere. And I, only I had the original scores. What the hell are they worth? Thousands, millions of dollars.

I'll tell you something else. I don't like to brag, but those were great, great

Bobby and a gaucho

simultaneous games. I was in great form. And they played the openings badly down there, 'cause you know, they're pretty far from Europe, nowadays, of course, it doesn't matter. Everybody can get any literature superfast.

But then they didn't get the latest theoretical journals and books on chess. So they didn't know the openings well at all. But if you didn't smash them down in the openings, watch out, 'cause later on they got stronger and stronger. So I knew this. I learned this real fast. So I made a real attempt to make sure I completely got an overwhelming game before they got into the middlegame, so I could be sure to win. These games were so instructive.

---

[76] *Caro-Kann Two Knights   B10*
RJF–R. Padula
Buenos Aires (simul) 1970

1.e4 c6 2.♘c3 d5 3.♘f3 dxe4 4.♘xe4 ♗f5?

Black confuses the position with 1.e4 c6 2.d4 d5 3.♘c3 dxe4 4.♘xe4. The text is a known opening mistake.

5.♘g3 ♗g6 6.h4 h6 7.♘e5 ♗h7 8.♕h5

This is quite good for White, but 8. ♕f3 (8...♘f6 9.♕b3, hitting f7) may be even stronger.

8...g6 9.♗c4

The extra tempo (2.♘c3 instead of 2.d4) really helps White. Once again, the text is quite natural, though 9. ♕f3, forcing 9...f6, is interesting.

9...e6 10.♕e2 ♕e7 11.d4 ♗g7 12.c3 ♘d7 13.♗f4 ♘gf6 14.0-0-0 0-0 15.f3

White starts to drift and eventually loses his advantage. More convincing is 15.♕d2.

15...♘d5 16.♗xd5 cxd5 17.♘xd7 ♕xd7 18.♕d2 h5 19.♗h6 ♖fc8 20. ♗xg7 ♔xg7

The position looks really terrific for White (the Black Bishop on h7 is especially bad.), but it's not easy to prove an advantage.

21.♔b1 ♖c6 22.♕g5 ♔f8 23.♖he1 ♖ac8 24.♖e5?

This move, in conjunction with White's next, is a mistaken strategy. The correct plan was to bring the Knight to the queenside by ♘g3-e2-c1. The Knight on c1 would be an excellent defender for the King.

24...♖b6 25.♕f6? ♖xc3

Black has another good move in 25...♕b5.

26.♕h8+ ♗g8 27.♕h6+ ♔e8 28. ♕g7

28...♕a4!

The threat of 29...♕c2+ is a winner.

29.♕xg8+ ♔e7 30.♘f5+ gxf5 31. ♕g5+ ♔d7 32.♕d2

32..♖a3!

This should win instantly.
33.♕c2 ♕xc2+?!

Missing an easy win with 33...
♖xb2+ (34.♕xb2 ♕xd1+; 34.♔xb2
♖xa2+). Even so, Black is still easily
winning after the text.
**34.♔xc2 ♖xa2 35.♖b1 ♖a4 36.g4
fxg4 37.fxg4 ♖xd4**

Black could have taken on g4 and
then brought his King over to g7. How
he wins here is more a question of
taste.
**38.♖f1 ♖xg4 39.♖xf7+ ♔d6 40.
♖xh5 ♖g2+ 41.♔c3 ♖bxb2 42.♖hh7
♖gc2+ 43.♔d3 ♖d2+ 44.♔e3 d4+?**

This hasty check drives White's
King to where it could only dream of
going. The correct plan was 44...
♖e2+, which either forces White to
exchange Rooks (45.♔f3 ♖f2+) or to
allow his King to be driven to the
queenside.
45.♔e4 e5?

Compounding his error, Black starts
to go on tilt. Instead, 45...b5 46.♖xa7
♔c5 47.♖hc7+ ♔b4 48.h5 ♖e2+ 49.
♔f4 e5+ 50.♔g4 d3 51.♖d7 e4 was
still winning, but after the text the
game is equal.
**46.♖h6+ ♔c5 47.♖c7+ ♔b4 48.
♖xb7+ ♔c5 49.♖xa7?**

Bobby blunders, perhaps feeling fa-
tigued. The correct move was 49.
♖c7+, forcing a draw after 49...♔b5
50.♖b7+. Black will get mated if he
tries for more, i.e., 50...♔c5 51.
♖c7+ ♔b4 52.♖b7+ ♔c3?? 53.♖c6
mate.
49...♔b5?

Black blunders back and misses his
chance to drive away the White King.
He could have obtained a big advan-

tage after 49...♖e2+ 50.♔f5 ♖f2+ 51.
♔g4 ♖f4+ 52.♔g3 ♖b3+ 53.♔g2
d3.
50.♔d5

Bobby plays for the win. He could
have drawn with 50.♖b7+ ♔c5 51.
♖c7+.
50...♖bc2??

This should be the losing move.
Black could still have held the balance
with the far-from-obvious 50...♖e2.
For example, 51.♖c6 ♔b4 52.♖b7+
♔a5 53.♖a7+ ♔b4 yields a draw by
perpetual check. Black must keep his
Rook on the b-line to avoid mating
threats.
51.♖b7+ ♔a5 52.♖h8 ♔a6 53.♖b4?

This wasn't Bobby's night. White
could have played 53.♖hh7, forcing
mate or the win of a Rook (53...♔a5
54.♖a7+ ♔b4 55.♖hb7+ ♔c3 56.
♖a3 mate).
53...♔a5??

The final error. Black was only
slightly worse after 53...♔a7 54.♖h7+
♔a8 (forced, as 54...♔a6 allows 55.
♖bb7 as in the previous note) 55.
♔xe5 ♖c5+ 56.♔e4 ♖c8 57.♖d7
(57.♖xd4? ♖e8+ picks up a Rook)
57...♖e8+ 58.♔d5 d3, though after
59.♔d4 White can still play on.
54.♖b3 ♔a4 55.♖b7 1-0

There is no defense against 56.♖a8
mate.

Bobby stayed in Argentina after defeating Petrosian and gave simuls on
November eleventh and fourteenth.
We are not sure which exhibition this
game is from. IM Jorge Smetan
writes:

Fischer's in Buenos Aires was a curious simultaneous. It took place in an event hall of the San Martin Theatre in downtown Buenos Aires, the same place where the Najdorf Tournament is held every year. In principle, Fischer was to compete with 12 to 15 players, with clocks. On arriving, Fischer changed his mind and said he wanted to play without clocks. So then it was a simultaneous, on very few boards, with the big disadvantage that Fischer came back rapidly and never allowed the players to slow down. If the player did not have a move ready, Fischer became slightly impatient and lightly tapped the table as a warning. The team was strong enough, with various IMs and first class players.

---

[77] *King's Gambit Falkbeer   C31*
RJF–IM Jorge Szmetan
Buenos Aires (simul) 1970

1.e4 e5 2.f4 d5 3.♘f3

Lutikov–Lisitsin, USSR 1955, arrived at this position by the funny and highly transpositional move-order 1.f4 (Bird's Opening) 1...e5 (From's Gambit) 2.e4 (King's Gambit) 2...d5 (Falkbeer Countergambit) 3.♘f3 (obscure sideline).

3... dxe4 4.♘xe5 ♘d7 5.♘c3

Bobby plays a sideline in a sideline. Most games with 3.♘f3 have seen 5.d4 here.

5...♘gf6 6.♗c4

We couldn't find another game with this move.

6...♘xe5 7.fxe5 ♕d4 8.♗xf7+ ♔xf7 9.exf6 ♗c5 10.♕e2 gxf6 11.♖f1 h5?

Black stops the threat of 12.♕h5+, while threatening 12...♗g4. However, the move allows the forced win of a piece. It would have been more prudent to play 11...♗d7, although Fischer still would have had a significant advantage.

12.b3?

Bobby misses the chance to put his opponent away with 12.♘b5! ♕e5 13. d4! ♗xd4 14.♕c4+, winning a piece. Now Jorge Szmetan, a future IM, gains the upper hand.

12...e3! 13.♕c4+ ♕xc4 14.bxc4 exd2+ 15.♗xd2 ♖e8+ 16.♔d1 ♗g4+ 17. ♔c1 ♗a3+ 18.♔b1 ♖ad8 19.♘d5 ♖e6 20.♗c1 ♗e2 21.♖e1 ♗c5 22.a4 ♗xc4?!

Black should have driven the White Rook out of play before capturing the pawn on c4, i.e., 22...♗f2! 23.♖h1 ♗xc4.

23.♖xe6 ♔xe6 24.♘xc7+ ♔f5 25.a5 ♖d7 26.♖a4 ♗f7 27.♘b5 ♖d1 28. ♔b2 ♗e8 29.♖c4 ♗c4 30.♘c3 ♖d4 31.♖c7

It's not immediately obvious, but White would have been better off

playing 31.♖c8 and only after 31...
♗d7 32.♖c7. Then 32...♖b4+, as in
the next note, would not work.

31...♗c6?!

The correct move was 31...♖b4+
32.♔a3 ♖g4 33.g3 ♗xh2 34.♖xb7
♖xg3+.

32.♘e2 ♖b4+ 33.♔c3 ♖b1?

Correct is 33...♗c5 with equal
chances. If 34.a6, then 34...♗d6.
Now Fischer gains the upper hand.

**34.♘xg1 ♖xc1 35.♘e2 ♖b1 36.
♘d4+ ♔e5 37.♘xc6+ ♔d6 38.♖f7
♔xc6 39.♖xf6+ ♔c7 40.♖f5 h4 41.
h3 ♖a1 42.♖g5 ♔c6 43.♔c4 ♖a2
44.♔b3 ♖a1 45.♖g6+ ♔b5 46.♖g5+
♔a6 47.♖g4 ♖b1+ 48.♔c4 ♔xa5
49.♔c3 ♖g1 50.♖g7 ♔b6 51.♔c4
♖c1 52.♖g6+ ♔a5 53.♔d3 ♔b5
54.♖g4 a5**

Better was 54...♖g1 with approximate equality.

**55.♖xh4 a4 56.♔c3 a3 57.♖b4+
♔c5 58.♖a4 ♖g1 59.♖xa3 ♖xg2 60.
♔b2 ♖h2 61.♖c3+ ♔b5 62.♔b3
♖h1 63.♖g3 b6 64.♖g5+ ♔a6 65.
♖h5 ♖b1+ 66.♔c3 ♖h1 67.♖h8
♔b5 68.h4 ♖h3+ 69.♔d4 ♔b4 70.**

h5 ♖h4+ 71.♔e5 ♔c3 72.h6 ♔xc2
73.♔f6 b5 74.♔g5 ♖h1 75.♖b8
♖g1+ 76.♔f5 ♖h1 77.♔g6 ♖g1+
78.♔f7 ♖h1 79.♔g7 ♖g1+ 80.♔h8
♖g5 81.h7 ♔c3 82.♖c8+ ♔d4 83.
♖g8 ♖h5 84.♖g4+ ♔c3 Draw

In *Inside Chess* 8:22:18, we ran
"Fischer in Argentina." Now, with
the help of NM Steven Gordon of Salt
Lake City, we are able to shed more
light on the mysterious Mr. Weberg
who played Bobby in Buenos Aires
back in 1971. Readers might recall
that Argentine chess historian Eduardo
Bauza Mercere had no knowledge of
anyone named Weberg playing in
South America at the time, especially
someone of master strength. Gordon
has the answer.

> Several weeks after the Fis-
> cher–Petrosian match a strong
> player showed up at the Anchor-
> age, Alaska, Chess Club. During
> his visit, Weberg mentioned that
> he worked for Scandinavian Air-
> lines and that he had attended
> part of the F–P match and shortly
> after drew Bobby in a simul. He
> never showed up at the club
> again.

[78] *Ruy Lopez Marshall* C89
RJF–O. Weberg
Buenos Aires (simul) November 1971

**1.e4 e5 2.♘f3 ♘c6 3.♗b5 a6 4.♗a4
♘f6 5.O-O ♗e7 6.♖e1 b5 7.♗b3
O-O 8.c3 d5 9.exd5 ♘xd5 10.♘xe5
♘xe5 11.♖xe5 c6 12.d4 ♗d6 13.
♖e1 ♕c7?!**

Everyone plays 13...♕h4 here, but
the text isn't actually a novelty.

14.g3

Ader–Stekel, Santiago 1959, went 14.h3 ♗f5 15.♘d2 ♖ae8 with some compensation for the pawn.

14...♗h3 15.♘d2 ♖ae8 16.♘f1 ♖e7

Black missed an opportunity. He could have played 16...♗g4!, forcing the awkward 17.♕d2. Black would have definite compensation, e.g., 17...♘f6 18.♘e3 ♗f3.

17.♗e3 ♖fe8 18.♕d3 ♖e4 19.♘d2 ♖4e7 20.♘f1 f5?!

Weberg could have offered to repeat moves with 20...♖e4, but Bobby would have varied, maybe with 21.f3. Instead of the text, Weberg might have considered 20...♕d7 with play on the light squares.

21.♗xd5+ cxd5 22.a4 g5?

Weberg continues his aggressive play and Bobby happily grabs another pawn. Black should have played 22...♕c4 with the idea of answering 23.♕xc4 with 23...bxc4, pressuring b2.

23.axb5 axb5 24.♕xb5

24...f4 25.♗d2?

There was nothing wrong with capturing the d-pawn and then playing ♗d2, i.e., 25.♕xd5+ ♔h8 26.♗d2.

25...♗xf1?

This makes White's task easier. Instead 25...♖xe1 26.♗xe1 ♕f7 still gives Black some pressure for his pawns. For example, 27.♖a7? is met by 27...♖xe1 28.♖xf7 ♔xf7.

26.♖xf1?!

Once again, capturing on d5 was indicated.

26...♕b7 27.♕xb7?!

White's still winning after the text, but 27.♖a5! was much simpler.

27...♖xb7 28.gxf4

Here 28.♖a5, meeting 28...♖xb2 with 29.♖xd5 ♖xd2 30.♖xd6, was easily winning.

28...♗xf4 29.♗xf4 gxf4 30.♔g2?!

Simpler was 30.♖a5.

30...♖xb2 31.♔f3 ♖e4 32.♖g1+ ♔f7 33.♖g4 ♖c2 34.♖a3 ♖ee2 35.♖g2?

This must be fatigue, as 35.♖xf4+ would cause Black to resign.

35...♔e6 36.♔xf4 ♖xf2+ 37.♖xf2 ♖xf2+ 38.♔g3 ♖c2 Draw

A surprising decision, as White could play 39.♖a6+ with the idea of 39...♔f5 40.♖c6 and Black still must struggle to draw.

Here is one more game of Bobby's from Argentina. It was published in the Argentine magazine *Ajedrez Revista Mensual*, issue 12 of 1971 (p. 490). Thanks to Nick Pope of Ann Arbor for unearthing it.

This is one of Bobby's worst defeats in the many simuls he gave. Note that his opponent, Carlos Garcia Palermo, later went on to become a GM and beat Karpov at Mar del Plata in 1982, while only an IM. The only other IM we know who beat Karpov during his reign as World Champion was Igor Ivanov.

---

[79] *King's Gambit Falkbeer   C31*
RJF–GM Carlos Garcia Palermo
Cordoba (simul) 1971

1.e4 e5 2.f4

Bobby invariably played 2.♘f3 in tournament games, but he did essay the King's Gambit three times in his career. His record was 3-0, with wins over GM's Evans and Minic and IM Wade. The sole time he defended the King's Gambit, he lost a memorable game to Boris Spassky.

2...d5 3.exd5 e4 4.♗b5+

Bobby met the Falkbeer (2...d5, 3...e4) a few times in simuls, but played the main line 4.d3.

4...c6 5.dxc6 ♘xc6

ECO prefers 5...bxc6, giving the line 6.♗c4 ♗c5 7.♘e2 ♘f6 8.d4 exd3 9.♕xd3 ♕e7 10.♘c3 O-O 11.h3 ♖d8 12.♕f3 ♗f5 with a better position for Black (Kortchnoi). GM Robert Byrne varied with 11.♗d2 in two little-known games from the 1946 US Open in Pittsburgh. Weaver Adams, of "White to Play and Win" fame, chose 11...♖d8 and after 12.♕f3 ♗g4 13.♕g3 ♗xe2 14.♗xe2 ♘e4 15.♘xe4 ♕xe4 16.♗c3 ♗f8 17.♖d1 ♘d7 18.♕f3 ♕xc2 19.O-O White had a small advantage. Gordon tried 11...♘g4 12. ♖f1 ♖d8 13.♕e4 ♕f6 14.♗d3 ♗g6 15.♕c4 ♗e3, but after 16.O-O-O White still had some advantage.

6.d3

If 4.♗b5+ is uncommon, then the text is a real rarity. We could find only a single game out of a million-game database. Typically, the one example

was played by the great Mikhail Chigorin, a player Bobby respected for his creativity.

6...♘f6 7.dxe4

A novelty. Chigorin–Marco, Vienna 1898 saw 7.♕e2.

7...♕a5+?!

Black should play 7...♕xd1+ 8. ♔xd1 ♘xe4 9.♗xc6+ bxc6 10.♗e3 ♗g4+ 11.♘f3 O-O-O+ with good compensation for the pawn.

8.♘c3 ♗g4 9.♕d4

Here 9.♘f3 was safer, but Fischer still has a significant advantage.

9...♗e7 10.♕a4 ♕b6 11.h3?!

This loses valuable time. 11.e5 is much better.

11...O-O-O?!

The text is tricky, but ultimately unsound. Black should have played 11... ♗d7.

12.♗xc6??

Fischer walks right into an uppercut. He should have played 12.hxg4, when Black has insufficient compensation for the piece.

12...♘xe4!

A real bolt from the blue by a future Grandmaster. Now Bobby has to give up his Queen to stop mate. The threats of 13...♗h4+ and 13...♕f2+ are impossible to meet.

13.♗d7+

13.♘xe4 is met by 13...♖d1 mate.

13...♖xd7 14.♕xd7+ ♗xd7 15.♘xe4 ♗e6 0-1

Blitz

The question of who is the greatest player of all time always produces lively debate, but perhaps an even greater riddle is posed by asking who the strongest blitz player in the history of the game is. Both Karpov and Kasparov are contenders for the throne, but it was the late Mikhail Tal who won the title of World Blitz Champion, and $C 50,000, in Saint John, New Brunswick, Canada, in 1988.

Bobby's credentials, too, are quite impressive. He won the Blitz Tournament of the Century at Herceg Novi in 1970 with a score of 19-3. Among the participants in the all-GM field were Tal, Kortchnoi, and Petrosian—all noted blitz aficionados. A year later, in between his Candidates matches with Larsen and Petrosian, Bobby steamrolled an all-Master field 21.5-0.5 at the Manhattan Chess Club, drawing only SM Walter Shipman. Here are two of his victories from Herceg Novi and one from New York.

Fischer's comments are from *Chess Meets of the Century* by Bobby Fischer and Dmitije Bjelica.

[80] *King's Indian Classical   E97*
GM Viktor Kortchnoi–RJF
Herceg Novi (blitz) 1970

1.d4 ♘f6 2.c4 g6 3.♘c3 ♗g7 4.e4 d6 5.♗e2 O-O 6.♘f3 e5 7.O-O ♘c6 8.d5 ♘e7 9.♘d2 c5

I think this is a logical move. Black takes a tempo from his kingside play to slow down White's queenside initiative. White usually comes quickly with b4. c5 etc.

10.a3 ♘e8 11.b4 b6 12.♖b1 f5!

Having taken all the necessary precautions on the other flank, Black is ready to start his kingside attack.

13.f3 f4 14.a4 g5 15.a5 ♖f6! 16. bxc5?

This is, as Kortchnoi pointed out afterwards, a "terrible mistake," because now White is unable to generate any initiative on the queenside.

16...bxc5 17.♘b3 ♖g6 18.♗d2 ♘f6

18...h5! may have been more exact.

19.♔h1 g4

Again 19...h5 was probably best.

20.fxg4

Forced due to the threat of 20...g3 21.h3 ♗xh3!

20...♘xg4 21.♖f3?

21.♗f3! offered much better chances to resist.

21...♖h6 22.h3 ♘g6 23.♔g1 ♘f6 24.♗e1

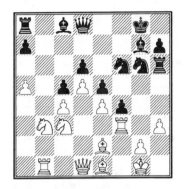

24...♘h8!!

A great recycling maneuver by Bobby, who has in mind ...♘h8-f7-g5.

25.♖d3 ♘f7 26.♗f3 ♘g5 27.♕e2 ♖g6 28.♔f1

If 28.♔h2, then 28...♕d7 with the unstoppable threat of 28...♘xh3.

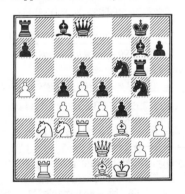

28...♘xh3! 29.gxh3 ♗xh3+ 30.♔f2

At this moment my hand hovered over White's pawn on e4 — but at the last second I realized that 30...♘xe4?? is answered by 31. ♕xe4 and White wins.

30...♘g4+ 31.♗xg4 ♗xg4 0-1

Kortchnoi thought for a minute and a half before resigning. White has no answer to the double threat of 31... ♗xe2 and 32...♕b4+.

---

[81] *Ruy Lopez Schliemann   C63*
RJF–GM Milan Matulovic
Herceg Novi (blitz) 1970

1.e4 e5 2.♘f3 ♘c6 3.♗b5 f5

This is Matulovic's specialty, the same as his gambit in the Sicilian.* In blitz games, there is no problem for White because of the weakness of the Black King. I know this variation very well, and because of that I was surprised at Matulovic's choice.

* In parts of Europe 1.e4 c5 2.d4 dxc3 3.c3 is identified with Matulovic.

4.♘c3 fxe4 5.♘xe4 d5 6.♘xe5 dxe4 7.♘xc6 ♕g5

7...♕d5 probably gives White more problems.

8.♕e2 ♘f6 9.f4 ♕xf4 10.d4 ♕h4+ 11.g3 ♕h3

So far the same as Gheorghiu–Maric, Skopje 1968. Gheorghiu played 12.♘xa7+, but did not obtain any advantage. I analysed this position all night with Gheorghiu and Robatsch in Vinkovci. Gheorghiu showed me his game with Maric, which I found very interesting. The move 12.♗g5 is our idea.

12.♗g5 a6 13.♗a4 ♗d7 14.♗xf6 gxf6 15.♕xe4+ ♔f7

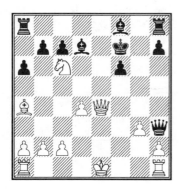

16.②e5+ fxe5 17.罝f1+ ⾦e7

Black has many problems. If *17...
⾦g8*, then 18.罝f6! 罝e8 (18...罝xa4
19.豐d5+ with 豐f7 mate) 19.⾦b3+
⾦g7 20.罝f7+ ⾦h6 21.dxe5. If *17...
豐xf1+ 18.⾦xf1 ⾦xa4 19.豐f5+ wins.*

18.⾦xd7 ⾦xd7

18...豐xd7 19.0-0-0

19.罝f7+ ⾦e8??

19...⾦e7!! gave chances for a successful defense.

**20.罝xc7 ⾦d6 21.罝xb7 罝c8 22.
0-0-0 豐xh2 23.dxe5 ⾦e7**

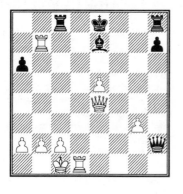

**24.罝xe7+ ⾦xe7 25.豐b7+ ⾦e6 26.
豐d7+ ⾦xe5 27.豐d5+ ⾦f6 28.罝f1+
⾦g6 29.豐f5+ ⾦h6 30.豐e6+ ⾦h5
31.罝f5+ ⾦g4 32.罝f4+ ⾦xg3 33.
豐g4+ 1-0**

I don't know what Petrosyan,
Kortchnoi, Bronstein, and Smyslov
counted on before the start of the
tournament, but I expected them
to be the most probable rivals for
the top prizes. Fischer had until recently played fast chess none too
strongly. Now much has changed:
he is fine at fast chess. His playing is of the same kind as in tournament games: everything is
simple, follows a single pattern,
logical, and without any spectacular effects. He makes his moves
quickly and practically without errors. Throughout the tournament
I think he did not leave a single
pawn *en prise*, whereas all the
others managed to lose a whole
set of pieces in this way. Fischer's result is very, very impressive . . .

Mikhail Tal in *Russians vs. Fischer*, p. 172

[82] *Sicilian Alapin   B22*
NM Louis Levy–RJF
New York (blitz) August 8, 1971

1.e4 c5 2.c3 ②f6 3.e5 ②d5 4.d4 cxd4
5.cxd4 d6 6.②f3 ②c6 7.豐b3 e6 8.
⾦b5 ⾦e7 9.②c3 ②xc3 10.bxc3 0-0
11.0-0 ⾦d7 12.⾦f4 ②a5 13.豐b2
⾦xb5 14.豐xb5 d5 15.②d2 a6 16.
豐b2 罝c8 17.豐c2 豐d7 18.⾦e3 罝c6
19.f4 罝fc8 20.罝ac1 豐c7 21.②b1
②c4 22.豐e2 ②xe3 23.豐xe3 b5 24.
f5 exf5 25.罝xf5 b4 26.罝f3 h6 27.
罝c2 豐b6 28.豐f4 罝f8 29.罝g3 ⾦g5
30.豐f3 bxc3 31.②xc3 豐xd4+ 32.
豐f2 豐xf2+ 33.⾦xf2 d4 0-1

Source: *New York Times*, August 9, 1971.

The Last Recorded Game

The following game was played under rather unusual circumstances. The book *No Regrets* by Yasser Seirawan and George Stefanovic, the definitive account of the 1992 match between Fischer and Spassky, paints the picture under the title:

Lady's Dream Comes True

At the press conference, WIM Cathy Forbes asked Bobby if he would play a game of chess with her, noting that it was a lifelong dream. Bobby asked how strong she was, and she said 2100. Bobby said maybe.

At the closing ceremony the next night, over two hundred people had shown up for a night of drinks and music. Bobby was sharing a table with Boris and a few top muckymucks of the Yugoskandic organization. With the band blaring and people dancing a folk dance all over the room, Cathy approached Bobby — about that chess game. It was a sight to behold. With all the revelry, music, chatter, smoke going on, there was Bobby playing a game of chess, oblivious to everything around him. It was also funny when measured against the fact that Bobby throughout the match in Sveti Stefan had demanded perfect playing conditions. Now, in a party setting, Bobby had tuned out all the distractions, making a young lady's dream come true.

[83] *Pirc*   B08
Cathy Forbes–RJF
Sveti Stefan (offhand) 1992

1.d4 ♘f6 2.♘f3 g6 3.♗f4 ♗g7 4.♘c3 d6 5.e4 O-O 6.h3 c5 7.dxc5 ♕a5 8.♗d2 ♕xc5 9.♗d3 a6 10.a4 b6 11.O-O ♗b7 12.♖e1 ♘bd7 13.♗e3 ♕c7 14.♕e2 e6 15.♗f4 e5 16.♗g3 ♘c5 17.♘d2 ♘h5 18.♗h2 ♘f4 19.♗xf4 exf4 20.♘b3 ♘d7 21.♕d2 f3 22.g3 ♘e5 23.♗f1 h5 24.♖ad1 ♖ad8 25.♘d5 ♗xd5 26.exd5 ♘c4 27.♕d3?

As Bobby pointed out, 27.♕f4 was a better chance to resist, as both sides have vulnerable pawns.

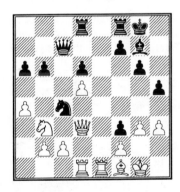

27...♘xb2

And Cathy chose the right moment to resign against Bobby Fischer.

0-1

Source: *No Regrets*, pp.306-7.

Fischer's Originality, Analysis, Suggestions, and Interviews

Fischer's Originality

Fischer was always ahead of his time. Vladimir Kramnik observed, "Fischer played twenty-five years ago like we do today." The following game, featuring modern ideas such as ...♗g4 and ...♖b8-b6-a6, is but one example of his fertile mind at work.

---

[84] *Sicilian Closed B26*
GM Vassily Smyslov–RJF
Rovinj/Zagreb 1970

1.e4 c5 2.♘c3 d6 3.g3 g6 4.♗g2 ♗g7 5.d3 ♘c6 6.♗e3 ♖b8 7.♕d2 b5 8. ♘f3 b4 9.♘d1

Black's early advance of his b-pawn has left Smyslov no choice but to put his Knight on d1.

9...♗g4!?

Fischer played this same maneuver against Hort at the Palma de Mallorca Interzonal later in the year. In that game, he followed up with ...e6 and ...♘ge7.

10.h3 ♗xf3 11.♗xf3 ♘f6 12.♗g2 O-O 13.O-O ♖e8 14.♗h6 ♗h8 15. ♘e3 ♘d7?!

Putting the question to the b-pawn, but allowing White a nice trick.

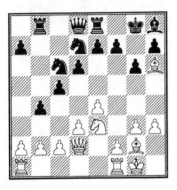

16.♖ab1?!

This is the normal way to guard the b-pawn, especially since 16...♕a5 is answered by 17.♘c4. However, Smyslov has overlooked a strong shot. Can you find it?

Pat yourself on the back if you found 16.e5! The point is that the pawn isn't edible, i.e., 16...♘cxe5 17. f4 or 16...♘dxe5 17.f4. In both instances, Black loses a piece. White doesn't win material with 16.e5, but he does open the position for his Bishops.

This same theme was seen in the game Vaganian–Lautier, Manila Interzonal 1990, after 1.♘f3 ♘f6 2.g3 g6 3.♗g2 ♗g7 4.c4 O-O 5.♘c3 d6 6. O-O e5 7.d3 ♘c6 8.♖b1 a5 9.a3 ♖e8 10.♗g5 (Bobby's patent) 10...h6 11. ♗xf6 ♗xf6 12.b4 axb4 13.axb4 ♗g7 14.b5 ♘e7 15.♘d2? e4! 16...♖b6!?

The idea of deploying a Rook on a closed file may have been seen before, but never against a former World Champion. Bobby plans to bring his Rook to a6 to attack the weakness on a2.

17.♘c4 ♖a6 18.a3 ♘b6 19.axb4 cxb4 20.♗e3 ♘xc4 21.dxc4 ♖a2

22.f4!

Smyslov, one of the world's leading experts on the Closed Sicilian from the 1940s to the 1970s, shows his great feel for the position. Sensing that 22.b3 is too passive, he sacrifices a pawn to open the board for his Bishop. He's not called "the Hand" for nothing.

22...♗xb2 23.e5 ♗c3 24.♕d5 ♖a6 25. e6 fxe6 26.♕xe6+ ♔h8 27.f5 ♘d4 28.♗xd4+ ♗xd4+ 29.♔h1 g5 30. ♖xb4 ♗f6 31.♖fb1 ♖b6 32.♖xb6 axb6 33.♗d5 ♖f8 34.♕e3 ♕c8 35. g4 ♕c5

White owns the White squares and Black, the Black!

Draw

Analyzing with Bobby

In his book *No Regrets*, Yasser Seirawan describes analyzing a position with Bobby Fischer that shows that Fischer can still take apart a position like no other.

Fischer–Spassky,
Sveti Stefan (m-11) 1992

Black played **17...f6** in this position which may not be the best move.

Right after the game Bobby and Boris held a postmortem and considered that the position after 17.♘xh6 was critical. Boris was sure that 17... f6 was a mistake. The players immersed themselves in the forcing sequence **17...♗xa1** (probably the best practical try) **18.♛xa1 ♛xd6 19. ♛xh8+ ♚e7**.

The next day Bobby, Eugenio Torre, Svetozar Gligoric, Yvette Nagel and I spent a late afternoon analyzing this position. It is an excellent position for practical work. I suggest you take a few minutes to look at the lines following 20.♛xh7 and 20.♛g7.

Initially, Bobby was strongly for 20.♛xh7, munching a pawn. He got bogged down over the line 20...♖f8 21. h4 (to clear the back rank and pound home h4-h5) 21...♛d2 22.♖e3. White seems to be on a joyful attacking crunch, but his pieces are misplaced: 22...♛xc2 23.♛g7 (since 23.h5 runs into ...♛d1+h5+) 23...♛c1+ 24.♚h2 ♛c5, again restraining h4-h5. Now Black has two passers on the queenside and his King can trot to safety.

Fischer spent a lot of time trying to make 25.e5 ♗d5 26.h5 work, but came away dissatisfied. At length, he was talked into declining the h7-cutie. "Man, I really want that guy!" he exclaimed. We began looking at 20.e5 ♖xh8 (20...♛xd2!?) 21.exd6+ ♚f6 22.♖e7 ♗d5 before Fischer's "Nah" ended things there. Finally, 20.♕g7 ♖f8 21.♘g8+ ♖xg8 22.♕xg8 a5!? (White's Queen is trapped) 23.♕g7 a4, when, despite being an Exchange down, Black is still kicking. Indeed, the whole line isn't forced, as Black doesn't have to sac the Exchange. Bobby was vexed. "You guys are busted. Give me a sec to find the killer." Finally, Bobby said, "First, give me my pawn" and produced *20.♕xh7 ♖f8 21.♕g7 ♕d2*.

Bobby now uncorked his killer: 22. ♕a1! What a shot! Suddenly, White has a crushing coordinated attack. He threatens 23.♘f5+ gxf5 24.exf5+ ♔d7 25.♖d1, picking up Black's Queen. If 22...♕xh6, then 23.♕xa7 regains the piece with an easy win. A line like 22...♖c8 23.♘f5+ ♔e6 (23...gxf5 24. exf5+ ♔f8 25.♕h8 mate) 24.♘d4+ ♔e7 (White has gotten his Knight back into the game, all with tempo.) 25.♖d1 ♕c3 26.♕xa7 nets two pawns and the attack. We were forced into the ending 22...♕c3 23.♕xc3 bxc3 24. f3 a5 25.♖a1 ♖a8 26.♘g4 a4 27.♔f2 a3 28.♔e3 a2 29.♔d4 ♖a3 30.♘e3– this is hopeless for Black!—(Fischer). We all had to concede that Bobby is as sharp an analyst as ever.

No Regrets, pp. 109-110

Bobby Refutes the Russians

[85]   *Sicilian Maroczy Bind   B36*
GM Paul Keres
GM Tigran Petrosian
                    Curacao (ct) 1962

1.e4 c5 2.♘f3 ♘c6 3.d4 cxd4 4.♘xd4 g6 5.c4 ♘f6 6.♘c3 ♘xd4 7.♕xd4 d6 8.c5 ♗g7 9.♗b5+ ♗d7 10.♗xd7+ ♕xd7 11.cxd6 O-O 12.♗g5 ♘e8 13. ♕b4 ♘xd6 14.f3 a5 Draw

Bobby points out that after 14...a5! Black is winning by force: 15.♕b3 (15.♕a3 b5; 15.♕b6 ♖a6; 15.♕c5 ♖fc8) 15...a4 16.♕a3 (16.♕b4 a3!) 16...♘c4 17.♕b4 ♕d3! (17...a3 was also good) 18.♖d1 ♘xb2!

(**Author's note:** Although this does seem to be overwhelming, White has some resources. Instead of 16.♕a3, 16.♕b4 offers better chances. After 16...a3 17.bxa3, Black has a couple of choices. He gets the initiative with 17...♖ac8 18.♖c1 ♖c4 19.♕b3 ♖fc8 20. ♘e2, but White seems to be holding. Black can win the Exchange by 17...♘b5, but White gets a measure of compensation after 18. ♘xb5 ♗xa1 19.♗xe7 ♖fc8 20.O-O ♗g7 21.♗c5. Nevertheless, we agree with Bobby that Black should not agree to a draw in such a position.)

                    Source: *Bobi Fisier: ante portas*,
                    pp. 43 and 125.

Bobby points out that Petrosian and Keres drew their first three games in 17, 21 and 22 moves.

Fischer Letters to Larry Evans

American chess was booming after the 1972 Fischer–Spassky match, with the United States Chess Federation experiencing a massive membership gain, but trouble was soon in store. Many of the new members faded away in the next few years as Bobby went into what was to prove to be a twenty-year hibernation. Fischer went underground after beating Spassky, but he surfaced in 1974-75 with two letters to his old friend Larry Evans at *Chess Life and Review*.

Letter to "Larry Evans on Chess," *Chess Life and Review*, November 1974.

Dear Larry,

I have a question or two for you. In June/74, p. 398, you state in answer to Larry Jadczak, "It certainly does (draw). A very neat resource too."

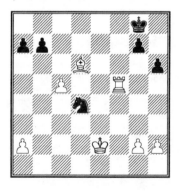

This is typical of your disappointing tendency to give superficial and incorrect answers. After 29.♔d3 ♘xf5 30.♗e5! Black has a very long way to go before a draw. As a matter of fact, to me, Black's game looks hopeless: i.e., 30...♔f7 31.♔e4 ♘e7 (or

31...g6 32.♗f4 h5 33.♔e5 etc. wins) 32.♗c3! followed by ♔e5 wins. Maybe you'll still try and demonstrate some rinky-dink draw to your readers in this endgame, but remember you're not fooling me one bit — Black is dead lost.

I'm also enclosing a copy of Mr. Cramer's compilation of the Rules of the World Championship matches, and a copy of my telegram to the FIDE delegates for your information and enlightenment.

In April/74, p. 271, you state my rules are not fair. What nonsense! As if I had some great advantage because of the nine to nine tie clause. Alex Binder wrote, "In Jan/74, p. 30, a cablegram from Bobby Fischer to FIDE stated: 'Urge adoption of ten wins to decide 1975 match, draws not counting, champion to retain title in nine wins to nine.' This means that the champion needs only nine to win and the challenger must win by at least two. Do you feel this fair and why?" Your answer: "No, it isn't fair. The whole idea of not counting draws is to eliminate a draw match. Historically the first player to win six games was good enough for Lasker, Capablanca, and Alekhine. Why isn't it good enough for Bobby Fischer?"

Okay. Here's my answer to Mr. Binder and then to you, Larry. Mr. Binder should have read more carefully, because he seems under the illusion that if 9 wins to 9, I win the match. But I said 9 wins to 9 retains title. That's a big difference. If my match with Spassky would have been 12 to 12, he would have retained the title — not won the match (and not even having to win a single game at that, if it so turned out every game was a draw). The money would be split equally and the match declared a draw — but Spassky would have kept the title. Okay? Nothing unfair there! Then Mr. Binder says, "the challenger must win by at least two." When the champion gets 9 points, the match isn't automatically over, although at that stage his title is secure. It continues until he wins 10 games, unless the challenger wins 9 first to tie him. This is much the same as the first Petrosian–Spassky match, when Petrosian got the needed 12 points before 24 games were played: his title was secure, but the match continued until he got at least 12 1/2 or Spassky tied him 12 to 12.

Now to your answer: "No, it isn't fair. The whole idea of not counting draws is to eliminate a draw match." Nonsense! The whole idea is to make sure the players draw blood by winning games, and the spectators get their money's worth. And most importantly as an accurate test of who is the world's best player.

Then you say: "Historically the first player to win six games was good enough for Lasker, Capa-

blanca and Alekhine. Why isn't it good enough for Bobby Fischer?"

What was good enough for them is not necessarily always good enough for me and I'm sure if they were alive today the feeling would be mutual. The real question is: which is the best title system?

But if you go back why isn't what was good enough for Steinitz, Tchigorin, Lasker (too), Gunsberg, Zukertort, etc., good enough for Larry Evans? Because they all played under the ten win system I proposed (and some matches with the 9-9 tie clause). Incidentally, Larry, the Capa–Alekhine match did have a draw clause at 5-5. Yes, Alekhine had to win by 6-4 to take the title just the same as my match proposal. So you don't know what you're talking about altogether on the subject.

The Russians are also making a big to-do about this tie clause, even though they are well aware from their own books of these facts. Yet they pretend that I'm asking for an unprecedented advantage! (See page 18 *Ten Champions of the World*, Moscow 1972, in Russian for Capa–Alekhine regulations — fotocopy enclosed.)

In conclusion I would like to answer on a last wild rumor that the Russians are busily spreading — namely that in 1971 when FIDE changed the match system to the first player to win six games (no tie clause, effective 1975) that this was my proposal and at my behest. This is completely untrue. I also proposed ten wins at that time and, as a matter of fact, I proposed that the ten win system go into effect for the 1972 title match! I am responsible for what I told Mr. Edmondson (the U.S.

representative to FIDE) not for the compromise he and FIDE worked out without my approval or even knowledge. These are the facts—if anyone is interested in those.

Letter to "Larry Evans on Chess," *Chess Life and Review*, January 1975.

I have another question. I'm sure I'm wrong, but in Karpov–Pritchett, Nice Olympiad 1974, this position was reached.

Pritchett played 22...exf4? and eventually lost. Doesn't 22... ♘e2 +! bust White? For example 23.♖xe2 ♗xe2 24.♕xe2 ♕xc4 and if 25.♗f1? ♕d4 +. Or if 24. ♘xe5 ♖d1 + (or 24...♗d3! [less effective is 24...♗xc4 25.♗e3] 25.♘xd3 ♖xd3 and Black's initiative is decisive. Better in this line is 25.♗e3 ♗xe4, though hopeless for White in the long run) 25. ♔f2 ♗xc4 26.♕c2 (best) ♕b6 +! 27.♗e3 (or 27.♔f3? ♖xe5 28. ♗e3 ♖xa1! etc.) 27...♖xa1! 28. ♗xb6 ♖a2 29.♕xa2 ♗xa2 with a won endgame for Black.

By the time this is published my analysis may have appeared elsewhere under a different name, because I've shown it to a few people. Please show me what I've overlooked.

Regards,
Bobby

A: Thanks again for writing. Good to know you're alive and well!

Authors' Note: This is how Pritchett commented on the move 22...exf4??:

Well, I was short on time, but this is hardly an excuse for missing 22...♘e2+ 23.♖xe2 ♗xe2 24.♕xe2 ♕xc4 25. ♗f1 — what else? 25...♕d4+ and wins. 24.♘xe5 ♗xc4 is better, but hardly good enough.

The 1974 World Chess Olympiad
by Keene and Levy

Fischer's Winning Chess Tips

According to Fischer, in an article in *Boys Life*, these four ingredients are essential.

(1) CONCENTRATE Just one slip can cost the game. Many players use only a fraction of their energy. Chess requires total concentration. Keep your mind completely on the game. Play to win. Nobody's interested in excuses when you lose.

(2) THINK AHEAD Distrust your first instinct in selecting a move. Sit on your hands. Look ahead to picture your opponent's best reply and how you will answer that. Remember, it's essential for your development as a chessplayer to adhere to touch move — once you touch a piece you must move it. Give no quarter and ask for none!

(3) **LEARN FROM YOUR LOSSES** The Cuban World Champion Jose Capablanca admitted that he only learned from his losses. Record all your offhand games and go over them later to try to find where you made your mistakes — if you don't already know. You aren't likely to lose the same way twice and you also retain a permanent record of your own progress.

(4) **STUDY** Play over recent games of masters in books and magazines. Combine this study with actual play against strong opponents. And, of course, spend as much spare time at the game as you can.

Botvinnik on Fischer's Style (1971)

In the opening:

» Prior to each tournament Fischer prepares a new variation (sometimes several). He has variations (for example in the Sicilian Defense) that he has analysed through and through, and plays with ease and confidence.

» Playing White in the Sicilian, he frequently uses the ♘c3, ♘b3, ♗d3, ♗e3 and ♕f3 setup.

» In several openings his preference is for ...♗g7, ...d6 and ...♘e5.

» In unexpected situations in the opening (especially in theoretical positions), his choices are almost always unhappy.

» Fischer does not like pawn chains. He needs room for his pieces.

In the middlegame:

» Against opponents known to be weak, he likes to advance forcefully with his kingside pawns.

» He likes clearcut positions. When he enjoys a positional advantage, he welcomes any simplifications.

» In the face of sudden changes in the character of play (e.g., from attack to defense) his responses lack confidence.

» When he loses, he does so mainly in sharp positions. Technical defeats are few in his case.

» He protects his pawn formations.

» He likes to spoil his opponent's pawns.

» He likes to sacrifice the Exchange for central pawns.

» He likes to transfer his Rooks via the third rank (♖f1-e1-e3).

» He likes long moves with his Queen.

» He likes to advance the a-pawn against a Knight on b3 or b6.

» He parts with Bishops easily (frequently both ♗f8-b4xc3 and ♗c8-g4xf3).

In the endgame:

» He likes a Knight against a Bishop.

» He likes to send his King on long raids.

» He likes Bishops of different colors when there are Rooks on the board.

General observations:

» In the past, he's willingly sacrificed pawns in exchange for mobility and action. Over the years, he has become greedier toward material.

» He likes to gobble up pawns. In doing so, he sometimes sells himself short.

» He has a keen positional sense, enabling him to evaluate the negative and positive features of piece interaction.

» He does not like his opponents to have strong pieces and seeks to exchange them as soon as possible.

» He is an excellent tactician and sees a lot.

» When a piece of his is attacked, he often replies by attacking a piece of his opponent's (*Zwischenzug*).

Some additional observations:

» No material should be sacrificed to Fischer on general grounds alone. If there exists a specific refutation, he'll find it.

» Aggressive action by Fischer must be countered!

Russians versus Fischer, pp. 202-203

Interviews with Bobby and about Bobby

Interview at the Havana Olympiad of 1966

At the Stockholm Interzonal of 1962 I played for six whole weeks. That's hard work. I quite convincingly took first place and got $750 in prize money. I usually get that kind of fee for a couple of simultaneous exhibitions lasting a few hours each. I suggested that the winner of such a large tournament should get $5000.

He showed me his own book *Fischer Teaches Chess*. He even dedicated and gave one copy to Fidel Castro.

I must also point out that I haven't put forward these proposals in order to win big money, but to safeguard the interests of all the professionals in the world.

What else is wrong in the world of chess?

The system of matches is no good either. The player to win the first game has a great advantage. Besides that there are also many draws in the match for the Championship title. I think it would be better for the player who first wins six games to become champion.

What does the future hold for Bobby? Having spent the past four years in Budapest, Fischer seems to have developed a liking for the Hungarian capital. Informed sources report that he is considering buying a home there and that he has no intention of returning to the United States in the near future. Before such a return would be possible Bobby would have to pay the United States government roughly one million dollars in back taxes for the three-million-dollar purse he won in Sveti Stefan, as well as address the warrant out for his arrest for violating the Trading with the Enemies Acts.

Opinions about Bobby's play in Sveti Stefan, where his revolutionary clock got its first practical test, have ranged the gamut from high praise to being written off as that of a hack. Canadian GM Duncan Suttles, in the March 1994 issue of the British Columbia Chess Federation publication *Counterplay*, had this to say about Bobby's play in an interview with Suleman Jamal.

Suttles on Fischer

What is your opinion on the Fischer comeback?

Well, I was very, very happy to see him play again. I think he did very well.

What would you rate his strength at?

Well, he's only played the one match. I believe from what I have seen that on a strategical level, he is unmatched. He may be . . . there were some technical lapses which are to be expected after a prolonged absence. I believe that were he able to recover some of his technique, that he would be the strongest player. In fact, I believe that his play from a strategic point of view is stronger than it was when he left. It showed a lot of thought. He wasn't sitting on his hands during that long absence.

There have been mixed reviews on that one.

There was a stylistic change . . . When . . . he was much younger it was

his personality that carried him through. What you're looking at here is somebody who probably has a greater understanding of the game than he ever has had and he knows that he cannot just, by force alone, push through certain things and it shows up as a refinement of his strategical thinking in the game. Unfortunately, maybe people misinterpreted a few lapses in technique as weakness, when, in fact, you see progress in the strategic side.

Did you go over all of the games?

I did analyses of several games in depth. Some of the comments made on them were quite superficial. The games he lost were very finely balanced. They weren't anywhere near as one-sided as the media made them out to be. Comments that he was crushed simply weren't true. In fact, the games were consistently of a much higher caliber than the Candidates Matches being held concurrently.

A Bookstore in Argentina

Notes in { } are from Jonathan Berry
Notes in [ ] are from the original article.

by FM Pedro F. Hegoburu

Originally published in the magazine Jaque. *Translated from the Spanish by Jonathan Berry.*

I came to know Bobby Fischer through the hand of Destiny. The afternoon of Wednesday, June 26th, I dropped over to Juan Morgado's bookstore at about 6:30. As usual, I had nothing in particular in mind. Upon arrival, I saw a very tall man leaning over some books; he supported himself with his left arm to inspect the books closest to the floor. I did not see his face. Nearby was another person, with Asiatic features, much shorter, and also leafing through chess literature. Before I can take a step, Morgado tells me: "Have you seen who is looking at books? It's Bobby Fischer!"

I could not believe it. The American genius had arrived just a few moments before, accompanied by Philippino Eugene Torre (that would explain his Asiatic features) and Armando de Hiebra, well known in this part of the world as director of Argentine chess.

Bobby went on looking at books. He was scanning the Yugoslav *Informant* opening monographs. At some point, he said to Torre: "You know, chess players are all hungry for this kind of material, for opening theory. Larry Evans told me that years ago, people want these books." Torre grunted in assent.

After this verbal rapture, Bobby continued looking at books. He noted that he felt at ease among chess players (I do not feign to call us *peers*). It is an atmosphere that agrees with him, as opposed to press conferences, where he is sure to *waste time* with people who know nothing of chess. On a higher bookshelf he found *Bled 1931* and *Moscow 1936*. He enjoys the books for a moment, then remarks that he knows them and that they are two of his favorites. He finished with those and took the two volumes of *Fifteen Pretenders to the World Crown*, by Najdorf. "These are two good books." He showed them to Torre and after leafing through them, returned them to their place.

BF: Morgado, don't you have the tournament book of Curacao 1962? And the one with the two matches between Reshevsky and Najdorf?

It is now late. Bobby looked at the books he had chosen and took out an envelope full of dollars. He put on his short chestnut-colored leather coat, and a black leather cap to protect his grey matter from the cold Buenos Aires winter.

My attention was drawn to the fact that he did not much resemble the Fischer whose image sells periodicals. He is not so old, nor so bald, and he is very accessible. To see Fischer is to behold a most human image: he is no unapproachable deity. Bobby Fischer is a child who scatters books, who will argue any strange point, who is convinced of what he says. His love for chess remains, although he promotes Fischerandom. Beneath his arm were three volumes of games by Tal, an endgame book by Kasparian, the book *Chess Kaleidoscope* by Karpov and Cik; *Karpov/Korchnoi* by Roman Toran; a recent *New in Chess*; and the two most recent bulletins of the Argentine Postal Chess Circle (CAPA).

Bobby promised to return another day; he would like to examine more books. For me, there was still much to learn. One doesn't often meet an idol face to face, even rarer might that idol be so generous with his time. As he left, we asked him to autograph a copy of the CAPA bulletin. Before signing, he honored us by leafing through it.

BF: This is a postal chess magazine?

PH: Yes, we publish it four times a year for the members of our circle.

BF: This is serious material: all the games are annotated . . .

Fischer went over to the chess board and showed us from memory the games that Spassky played with Tal and with Karpov from the Montreal 1979 tournament. His fingers dance with agility around the board. He grasps each piece with confidence and moves it at once to the correct square. From time to time he pauses for a few seconds, remembering the precise move order. Nonetheless, he did not make a single mistake.

BF: Remember that Karpov, for many years starting in 1975, never lost to Russian or ex-Russian players outside the Soviet Union. Inside the Soviet Union he lost games, but when he played international tournaments abroad he was never de-

feated by Russians or by former Russians. Really, it's very strange.

{Divinsky shows no Karpov losses against the top Soviet (or ex-) players abroad between 1975 and 1986, aside from Kortchnoi. Then he lost to Andrei Sokolov at Bugojno 1986 and Belfort 1988, to Beliavsky at Tilburg 1986 and Brussels 1988, to Salov at Rotterdam 1989, to Ivanchuk at Linares 1991, to Kamsky at Tilburg 1991, and many times to Kasparov. A database search turned up a loss to Spassky in Hamburg 1982, but that was a TV game.}

Bobby selected a pile of books to buy. In Buenos Aires he didn't have a lot to do. He probably spent the free time reading all he could about chess.

From a top shelf he took *The Even More Complete Chess Addict* and asked if it was the same book as *The Chess Addict*. Even though it is different, he refused it, saying that it was full of foolishness, it wasn't a serious chess book.

PH: But Bobby, you can't spend 24 hours a day studying serious chess! I think that would be a good book to read in the bathroom. You don't know how much I read in the bathroom!

Fischer laughed and put the book in the buy pile. It was another interesting stack: *Kasparov* by Angel Martin; *Capablanca/Alekhine* from Editorial Sopena; *Grossmeisterskie Kompozitsii* by Archakov, in Russian; *The Inner Game* by Dominic Lawson; *The Even More Complete Chess Addict*; *Timman's Selected Games* by Timman; *Chess Scandals*; *Kasparov New World Cham-*

pion by Kasparov; *Steinitz Complete Games*.

Bobby put on his coat and hat, and got ready to leave. Morgado found a camera, but Bobby firmly refused to be photographed. Torre, one foot on the street, called back to tell us that there would be no problem with photographs at the next press conference, at La Plata city.

Source: *Inside Chess* 9:25-26:4-9

The Political Bobby
Bobby and Kirsan?

This Fischer story concerns a letter published in bulletin number 10 of the Yerevan Olympiad supporting Kirsan Iljumzhinov in his bid for reelection. There are considerable doubts about the authenticity of the letter. Yes, Bobby is said to have received $100,000 from Iljumzhinov for past Russian royalties on a pirated edition of *My Sixty Memorable Games*, an issue that has bothered him for a long time. It's also true that 85-year-old Andre Lilienthal, who is a good friend of Fischer's, receives a pension from FIDE. That said, it's hard see Bobby having anything to do with FIDE under any circumstances, considering his long-term grudge. Certainly, the letter wasn't written by Fischer, as its stilted style suggests it was penned by someone whose native tongue wasn't English. Here is the text.

To the delegates of the General Assembly of FIDE

Ladies and Gentlemen,

Our long stay in the chess world, a great life experience and finally our modest contribution to the development of the chess art, let us hope that the representative of World Chess Federation, being present at the FIDE Congress in Yerevan, will be kind enough to follow us for a while. We witnessed all the chess history, beginning from the thirties, as well as the whole history of FIDE. Like in real life there were periods of ebbs and tides, rises and falls.

Alongside with a bunch of wonderful chess players and remarkable organizers being among the FIDE leaders, there were some people, grudging, vain and random.

The trouble of the latest years of this organization was not only that certain players have had some disagreements (it used to happen before) but rather it was caused by the fact that FIDE did not manage to become an unbiased judge that would treat everyone with respect and strongly defend its own decisions, rules and regulations.

Life changes rapidly and that, of course, is reflected in chess. Staying behind the realities FIDE has changed too slowly, and alas, those were right who have recently criticized it.

But a year ago at the very critical moment when our organisation was at the edge of collapse, a young leader of one of the Russian republics and also a well-known businessman came to be President. His first steps made could be assumed quite extraordinary and some of them, even disputable. However, the main point came into view: FIDE survived, it came to be outspoken, new real sponsors offered their support. What the most important is that its President Kirsan Iljumzhinov has appeared to be a Man of his word: step by step he fulfilled his promises given no matter how unreal they seemed to most of us. We would like to remind you of the World Championship match Karpov--Kamsky, which was delayed nearly for a year by the former administration, as well as of the support given to the chess veterans, a complete program for the support of children's movement in the world, also the project for the holding a new World Championship.

We admit that Iljumzhinov's ideas are not clear enough and contain some debatable points. However, innovative and practical financial approaches, business and communication abilities with the people with any rank are unquestionable.

Not everybody comprehend and accept it. But for the sake of chess and it's future we appeal to your sober estimation of the present situation in FIDE. And according to it the President duties can be carried out only by Kirsan Iljumzhinov. The man who not only cares for chess but also understands its problem, as well as the ones of the chess organizations and individual players; a broad-minded person who is able to support them financially and improve its reputation.

This is the reason we appeal to the delegates to elect Kirsan Iljumzhinov, the man of the 21st century, as FIDE president, by making amendments in the FIDE regulations that will satisfy modern life conditions.

R.Fischer,
World Champion
Andre Lilienthal,
International Grandmaster

The U.S. Congress

While Bobby was in hibernation, others were active in working on his behalf. Chess-playing Congressman Charles Pashayan, a friend of GM Lev Alburt, introduced the following resolution in the House of Representatives. It passed by a voice vote on March 13, 1986.

Recognizing Bobby Fischer as
the official World Chess Champion

Resolved by the Senate and House of Representatives of the United States of America in Congress assembled, That the United States Government recognizes Bobby Fischer as the official World Chess Champion.

The State Department

The following U.S. Government action was not pro-Bobby.

Dear Mr.Fischer:

It has come to our attention that you are planning to play a chess match for a cash prize in the Federal Republic of Yugoslavia (Serbia and Montenegro) (hereinafter "Yugoslavia") against Boris Spassky on or about September 1, 1992. As a U.S. citizen, you are subject to the prohibitions under Executive Order 12810, dated June 5, 1992, imposing sanctions against Serbia and Montenegro. The United States Department of the Treasury, Office of Foreign Assets Control ("FAC"), is charged with enforcement of the Executive Order.

The Executive Order prohibits U.S. persons from performing any contract in support of a commercial project in Yugoslavia, as well as from exporting services to Yugoslavia. The purpose of this letter is to inform you that the performance of your agreement with a corporate sponsor in Yugoslavia to play chess is deemed to be in support of that sponsor's commercial activity. Any transactions engaged in for this purpose are outside the scope of General License No.6, which authorizes only transactions to travel, not to business or commercial activities. In addition, we consider your presence in Yugoslavia for this purpose to be an exportation of services to Yugoslavia in the sense that the Yugoslav sponsor is benefiting from the use of your name and reputation.

Violations of the Executive Order are punishable by civil penalties not to exceed $10,000 per violation, and by criminal penalties not to exceed $250,000 per individual, 10 years in prison, or both. You are hereby directed to refrain from engaging in any of the activities described above. You are further requested to file a report with this office with 10 business days of your receipt of this letter, outlining the facts and circumstances surrounding any and all transactions relating to your scheduled chess match in Yugoslavia against Boris Spassky. The report should be addressed to: The U.S. Department of the Treasury, Office of Foreign Assets Control, Enforcement Division, 1500 Pennsylvania Avenue, N.W., Annex - 2nd floor, Washington D.C. 20220. If you have any questions regarding this matter, please contact Merete M. Evans at (202) 622-2430.

Sincerely,

Richard Newcomb

Director, Office of Foreign Assets Control

The Fischer Generation

The following American titleholders all started playing around the time of Bobby's run for the World Championship title. The generation of 1972 is one of the best in American chess history (9 GMs and 16 IMs).

Grandmasters

Joel Benjamin
Larry Christiansen
Nick deFirmian
John Fedorowicz
Ronald Henley
Michael Rohde
Yasser Seirawan
Jonathan Tisdall
Michael Wilder

International Masters

Calvin Blocker
Jay Bonin
Michael Brooks
Richard Costigan
Mark Diesen
John Donaldson
Mark Ginsberg
Vince McCambridge
Walter Morris
Steve Odendahl
Ken Regan
Bruce Rind
James Rizzitano
Doug Root
Jonathan Schroer
Eric Tangborn

Works by and about Bobby

Bobby Fischer has had more books written about him than about any other player in the history of chess. The match with Spassky in 1972 alone resulted in a couple dozen Fischer-related books hitting the market. More than twenty-five years later there is still a steady stream of new books appearing, from Petra Dautov's relation of her personal experiences with Fischer, to Taimanov's reminiscences of his 0-6 drubbing, to Alex Avshalumov's analysis of Fischer's endings.

Fischer was not the most prolific writer among World Champions, but what he did produce was of the highest quality. His book *My 60 Memorable Games* is justly regarded as one of the classic pieces of chess literature. His annotations for various American magazines in the 1960s were exceptional. What follows is a comprehensive examination of Fischer's writings and a selective look at various authors' treatment of Bobby.

Works by Bobby Fischer

Books:

1. *My 60 Memorable Games*

Published by Simon and Schuster in 1969, this ranks among the greatest chess books ever written. GM Peter Biyiasas became an IM by studying — devouring might be a better word! — only two books: Fischer's *My 60 Memorable Games* and Smyslov and Levenfish's *Rook Endings*. Peter went through Bobby's book several times from cover to cover.

My 60 Memorable Games has been translated into many languages. Though essentially Fischer's book, the Russian edition, which appeared in 1972, does include some editorial changes (read editing out what the authorities felt to be anti-Soviet statements) and an assessment of Fischer's style by GM Igor Zaitsev.

The 1995 Batsford edition, edited by GM John Nunn and Graham Burgess, produced a minor furor when the original plan of transcribing the moves from descriptive to algebraic notation was expanded to correcting minor errors and typos and adding more diagrams. Some gaffes from the editors understandably raised Bobby's ire.

Russian Revelations

1972 was marked by an interesting departure from tradition in Soviet chess publishing. For the first time since *Alekhine's 300 Games* came out in 1954, it was decided to issue translations of game collections by foreign players: Fischer's *My 60 Memorable Games* and Larsen's *Selected Games*.

These books were published in accordance with Soviet practice, i.e., without the author's permission, but non-transferable rubles might be available if the authors were to visit the U.S.S.R.

The Fischer book came out first and was translated by someone who did not have a complete grasp of American colloquialisms, and has taken the liberty of omitting or paraphrasing a few sentences which he clearly thought were anti-Soviet. The quality of the Larsen translation is better.

Both books have supplementary articles bringing the story of their heroes up to date, and assessing their playing styles. For Fischer this was done by Suetin, for Larsen by Polugaevsky, who as early as 1966 was warning that the Dane has some unpleasant surprises in store for Soviet players.

Chess, April 16, 1973, pg.190

Bobby wasn't the only one to suffer from this *borrowing* without permission. The organizers of the 1979 Tournament of Stars in Montreal produced an outstanding daily bulletin and sold the rights to reproduce annotations to various magazines. The Soviets, who by this time had agreed to honor international copyright laws, produced a tournament book drawn heavily from the official bulletins, but did not provide compensation. The translator of the Pergammon edition of *Montreal 1979*, Ken Neat, notes, "A few changes have been made from the original Russian edition, where several of the annotations were taken more or less directly from the tournament bulletin."

2. *Bobby Fischer's Games of Chess*

This 97-page book, written with the assistance of John W. Collins, was finished in August of 1958, on the eve of Bobby's departure for the Interzonal in Portoroz. It offers a unique glimpse of Fischer as his star was about to go into supernova — he was soon to join the world's elite.

Fischer's Games starts with a seven-page biography that chronicles Bobby's early career, emphasizing the period May 1955 to May 1958. It's thorough and makes a point of noting the scores in many of the simuls that he gave. It was a primary source for Frank Brady's *Profile of a Prodigy*.

Bobby annotates all the games from his victorious 1957/58 U.S. Championship and his famous victory over Donald Byrne in the 1956 Rosenwald tournament. His unannotated games from the Portoroz Interzonal are given at the end.

Respected chess historian Ken Whyld, reviewing the book in the English magazine *Chess* when it first came out, mentioned the maturity shown by the young Fischer: ". . . [H]e gives no trimmings to his victories and losses. No boasting is attached to accounts of his triumphs, nor excuses to his defeats . . ."

3. *Bobby Fischer Teaches Chess*

This instructional work for beginning players, written by Bobby in collaboration with Stuart Margulies and Donn Mosenfelder with assistance from NM Leslie Ault, appears to be the best-selling chess book of all time (Milton Hanauer's *Chess Made Simple*, Irving Chernev's *Logical Chess Move-by-Move* and Chernev and Harkness' *An Invitation to Chess* are three other big sellers). It's been translated into many languages and over one million copies have been sold.

It was first published by Xerox as a hardback in 1966, but later sold to Bantam. Its paperback edition, released in 1967, had sold only 10,000 copies as of early 1972. The Fischer–Spassky match changed all that. The book was reprinted eight times alone in 1972 and was number two on the *New York Times* non-fiction best seller list for many months.

Though the book was first published in 1966, work for *Bobby Teaches Chess* started around 1961/62. According to Margulies, Bobby made it clear from the start that he wanted to produce a first-rate book that was free of chess errors. To achieve that goal, the proofreading team of Michael Valvo and Raymond Weinstein was brought on board. Valvo, who was later to gain the IM title, was already a strong master, and Weinstein had already played in the U.S. Championship and was a member (with Fischer) of the silver-medal-winning American team at the Leipzig Olympiad.

4. *Chess Meets of the Century*
Written in collaboration with Dimitrije Bjelica and published in Sarajevo in 1971, this 154-page, English-language paperback contains a personal look at the 1970 USSR-vs.-the-World match, the ultra-strong blitz tournament in Herceg-Novi, Yugoslavia, the same year, and the 1971 Fischer–Taimanov and Fischer–Larsen matches. Most of the book is written in Bjelica's somewhat broken English, but Fischer's brief comments to his own games are more than worth the price of admission.

5. *I was tortured in a Pasadena Jailhouse*
This self-published work appears to have been published in 1981, though it is undated. It recounts Bobby's misfortune of being mistaken for a man wanted by the police and Bobby's subsequent arrest and detention. The booklet covers what happened to him between 2:00 p.m., May 26, 1981, and 1:30 p.m., May 28, 1981.

6. *Beginners Chess*
It's hard to know where to list this combination novice-oriented work and inexpensive chess set. It was published by Milton-Bradley in 1966(?).

Articles:

1. *Chess Life*
The official publication of the United States Chess Federation, *Chess Life* was published as a newspaper when Bobby first started out. When it switched over to a monthly magazine in the early 1960s under Frank Brady and later J. F. Reinhardt, Bobby became a frequent contributor. He was especially active in 1963 and 1964, annotating many of the games he played in American Swisses and U.S. Championships. During 1964, he covered the Steinitz–Dubois match in fantastic style in his new column "Fischer Talks Chess." His notes were interesting and instructive, filled with information that couldn't, and can't, be found anywhere else.

Fischer refuted plenty of Russian analysts in his column in *Chess Life*. One example comes from the following line of the Meran:

1.d4 d5 2.c4 c6 3.♘c3 e6 4.♘f3 ♘f6 5.e3 ♘bd7 6.♗d3 dxc4 7.♗xc4 b5 8.♗d3 a6 9.e4 c5 10.e5 cxd4 11. ♘xb5 ♘xe5 12.♘xe5 axb5 13.O-O ♕d5 14.♕e2 ♖b8 15.♗g5 ♗e7 16. f4 O-O 17.♖f3 ♗b7 18.♗xf6? ♗xf6 19.♘d7? ♕xd7 20.♗xh7+ ♔xh7 21. ♖h3+ ♔g8 22.♕h5

And Black cannot stop the twin threats of 23.♕h7 and 23.♕h8 mate — B. Weinstein (note this may be B. Vainstein).

Chess Life, page 172, 1963.

22...♗h4! 23.♕xh4 f6 24.♕h7+ ♔f7 25.♖g3 ♖g8 and Black wins. (Fischer).

2. *American Chess Quarterly*

Bobby was a frequent contributor to GM Larry Evans' magazine which was published from 1961 to 1965 in four volumes (17 issues). Fischer's most famous article was "A Bust To The King's Gambit" where he proposed 1.e4 e5 2.f4 exf4 3.♘f3 d6 as a complete antidote. His main line ran 4.♗c4 h6 5.d4 g5 6.O-O ♗g7 7.c3 ♘c6 8.♕b3 ♕e7 9.h4 ♘f6 10.hxg5 hxg5 11.♘xg5 ♘xe4 12. ♗xf7+ (12.♘xe4 ♕xe4 13.♖xf4 ♕e1+ 14.♖f1 ♕h4 15.♗xf7+ ♔d8 16.♕d5 ♘e5! 17.dxe5 ♗xe5 18.♖d1 ♕g3, winning) 12...♔d8 13.♘xe4 ♕xe4 14.♗xf4 ♘xd4, winning.

3. *Leaves of Chess: A Journal of Scaccography*

Edited by O. Southard issued from January-February 1957 through May 1961 for a total of 96 pages, this little-known, but interesting, gazette published Bobby's notes to the last game of his 1957 match with Cardoso.

4. *1966 Havana Olympiad*

Bobby annotated his game with the Cuban IM Jimenez, an Exchange Ruy Lopez which Bobby won, for the official tournament book, which appeared in several languages.

5. *Second Piatigorsky Cup*

Bobby annotated his win over GM Miguel Najdorf in round 16 for the tournament book. Incidentally, this tournament, which offered a then-record $20,000 prize fund ($5,000 first to $1,000 for last place) attracted large crowds to the Miramar Hotel in Santa Monica. Held in August of 1966, it averaged over 500 paid spectators a day. The attendance for the penultimate round on Sunday, August 14, was over 900. The 1954 USA–USSR match, held in New York City, is probably the only better-attended event in U.S. chess history. The tournament book for the event, with both players annotating almost every game, is a classic.

6. *Boys Life*

Bobby's column ran sporadically between December 1966 and December 1969. The January 1970 issue had the answer to his problem from the 12/69 issue, and so was technically his last contribution. Issues later on had some columns by Evans with the note that "he was filling in for Bobby," but no further Fischer columns appeared.

7. *Chess Digest*

Bobby wrote his only formal book review for NM Ken Smith's magazine in 1969 (2:2:33-34). He examined Soviet author Mikhail Yudovich's book *King's Indian Defense* (Moscow, 1967). The review showed clearly that Fischer knew much more about the King's Indian than the author did, and that his suspicions of Soviet shenanigans were not idle paranoia. Fischer called the book a great disappointment, pointing out that most of the references were from the late 1950s and early 1960s.

None from the Havana Olympiad, practically none from *Shakmatny Bulletin* or minor Soviet tournaments. There was very little I didn't already know. 229 pages of nothing.

Yudovich undertook too much in trying to cover the King's Indian in such a small book. The Saemish Attack alone or the Benoni Defense could rate a study this size. The finished product is nothing more than a potboiler written for first category or "A" players."

Bobby then goes on to point out that the author can't even get his sources right. After **1.d4 ♘f6 2.c4 g6 3.♘f3 ♗g7 4.g3 O-O 5.♗g2 d6 6.O-O c5 7.d5 ♘a6 8.♘c3 ♘c7 9.♘d2 ♖b8 10.a4 e5 11.dxe6 ♗xe6 12.♘2e4**, White, with the exception of one super blunder, which Black failed to take advantage of, won brilliantly.

According to Yudovich, the reference is Boleslavsky–Reshevsky, Zurich 1953 (p.141). In fact, it was Reshevsky–Boleslavsky. As Bobby puts it:

Anyone can make such a mistake. It is curious, however that a Russian who lost is inadvertently transposed to the winning side. There is a bias running through Soviet chess literature in general; they dislike giving credit for opening innovations to foreigners. A typical example was the game Lombardy–Sherwin, U.S. Championship 1958/59.

1.e4 e5 2.♘f3 ♘c6 3.♗b5 a6 4.♗a4
f5 5.♘c3!? b5 6.♗b3 b4 7.♘d5 fxe4
8.d4!! exf3 9.♕xf3

This game caused quite a stir and was analysed extensively, but the Soviets never gave Lombardy, who found the sacrifice over the board (!), credit for his discovery.

Having found ample grounds to criticize Yudovich's book, Bobby is classy enough to point out one new idea he got from the book, and recommends it as a good buy at $1.50. As he puts it: "If you win one game with it, it's worth it. Right?"

8. *CHESSWORLD*

One of the best, if shortest-lived, American chess magazines of this century, *CHESSWORLD*, edited by Frank Brady, appeared only three times in 1964 before folding, but it contained many gems. Among them was a piece by 21-year-old Bobby, as told to Neil Hickey, entitled "The Ten Greatest Masters in History." The article created quite a furor, as the list lacked several World Champions, including Lasker and Botvinnik. Bobby's top ten were: 1) Paul Morphy; 2) Howard Stauton; 3) Wilhelm Steinitz; 4) Siegbert Tarrasch; 5) Mikhail Chigorin; 6) Alexander Alekhine; 7) Jose Capablanca; 8) Boris Spassky; 9) Mikhail Tal; and 10) Samuel Reshevsky.

At the beginning of the article Bobby explained his reasoning for putting each man on the list. In his opinion, it was the games of the player rather than performance than counted. When queried on this point, Bobby replied: "Just because a man was a champion for many years does not necessarily mean he was a great player— just as we wouldn't necessarily call a ruler of a country 'great' merely because he was in power for a long time."

Bobby's Capsule Summaries

Morphy:

A popularly held theory about Paul Morphy is that if he returned to the chess world today and played our best contemporary players, he would come out the loser. Nothing is further from the truth. In a set match, Morphy would beat anybody alive today.

I have played over several hundred of Morphy's games, and am continually surprised and entertained by his ingenuity. It has taken me twenty minutes at times to find the proper response to one of his moves. Morphy always fought on in bad positions, and found winning possibilities in situations that looked hopeless. In addition, he had very fine endgame technique. Perhaps his only weakness – and it was most apparent in his match with Anderssen – was in closed games like the Dutch Defense. But even then, he was usually victorious because of his resourcefulness.

Staunton:

Staunton was the most profound opening analyst of all time. He was more theorist than player, but nonetheless he was the strongest player of his day. Playing over his games, I discover that they are completely modern; where Morphy and Steinitz rejected the fianchetto, Staunton embraced it. In addition, he understood all of the positional concepts which modern players hold so dear, and thus—with Steinitz—must be considered the first modern player.

Stauton appears to have been afraid to meet Morphy and I think his fears were well-founded. Morphy would have beaten him, but it wouldn't have been the one-sided encounter that many writers now think it would. It would have been a great struggle."

Steinitz:

Steinitz's book knowledge didn't compare with Morphy's and – where Morphy was usually content to play a book line in the opening – Steinitz was always looking for some completely original line. He was a man of great intellect – an intellect he often used wrongly.

He understood more about the use of squares than did Morphy, and contributed a great deal more to chess theory. It is also possible that Morphy might have had his own theories, but they were never put in writing.

Tarrasch:

Tarrasch's play was razor-sharp, and in spite of his devotion to this supposedly scientific method of play, his game was often witty and bright. He was a great opening theorist, vastly superior in this respect to Emanuel Lasker, for example, who was a coffee-house player: Lasker knew nothing about openings and didn't understand positional chess.

Chigorin:

Chigorin, who was beaten twice by Steinitz, was the finest endgame player of his time, although judging from his notes, he often overestimated his position.

Chigorin had a very aggressive style, and was thus a great attacking player. He was always willing to experiment and as a result was often beaten by weaker players. He was easily discouraged, a fact that held him back from even greater heights. He was not really an objective player; at times, he would continue playing a bad line even after it had been refuted.

Alekhine:

Alekhine is a player I've never really understood; yet, strangely, if you've seen one Alekhine game, you've seen them all. He always wanted a superior center; he maneuvered his pieces toward the King side, and around the twenty-fifth move, began to mate his opponent. He disliked exchanges, preferring to play with many pieces on the board.

His play was fantastically complicated, more so than any player before or since.

Alekhine has never been a hero of mine, and I've never cared for his style of play. There's nothing light or breezy about it; it worked for him, but it could scarcely work for anybody else. He played gigantic conceptions, full of outrageous and unprecedented ideas. It's hard to find mistakes in his game, but in a sense his whole method of play was a mistake.

Capablanca:

Capablanca was among the greatest of chess players, but not because of his endgame. His trick was to keep his openings simple, and then play with such brilliance in the middlegame that the game was de-cided—even though his opponent didn't always know it—before they arrived at the ending.

Reshevsky:

For a period of ten years – between 1946 and 1956 – Reshevsky was probably the best chess player in the world. I feel sure that had he played a match with Botvinnik during that time, he would have won and been world champion.

His chess knowledge is probably less than that of any other leading chess player; many B players have greater opening knowledge than he. Had he really studied instead of settling for knowledge of a few main columns in *Modern Chess Openings*, he would have a lot easier time of it today.

Books on Bobby Fischer

Many books have been written about Bobby Fischer. We estimate the number at well over a hundred. The vast majority are either about the 1972 match or one of a number of unannotated game collections. Some books such as *Searching for Bobby Fischer* or *The Bobby Fischer I Knew and Other Stories* have little or nothing to do with Bobby, but many others can be quite interesting for the Fischer fan.

What follows here is a two-part look at Fischer literature. The first is a personalized top ten list of books about Bobby in English. Thereafter we give a fairly comprehensive, but hardly complete, listing of other books with brief annotations when appropriate.

A Fischer Top Ten List of Books Published in English:

1. *Bobby Fischer : A Study of His Approach to Chess* by Ellie Agur

This thought-provoking book proves that it doesn't take a strong GM to write something of lasting worth. Agur takes a fresh look at many classic Bobby games and finds much that is new.

2. ***Bobby Fischer: Profile of a Prodigy*** by Frank Brady
This is the definitive story of Fischer's life. There are a few small
faults (see Walter Goldwater's review in *Chess Life and Review*
January 1974, page 28), but this book is a balanced and well-written look at the greatest player of all time by someone who knew
him well.

3. ***The Chess of Bobby Fischer*** by Robert E. Burger
The games of Fischer serve as the examples in a textbook on
chess improvement by the Northern California master and
problemist.

4. ***Both Sides of the Chessboard*** by Robert Byrne and Ivo Nei
This book, by an American GM and Estonian IM, is probably the
best book on the 1972 match.

5. ***My Seven Chess Prodigies*** by John Collins
The noted chess teacher and master offers a warm look at
Bobby's career — particularly in the 1950s. William Lombardy, the
Byrne brothers and Raymond Weinstein are some of the other
prodigies who are covered.

6. ***A Legend on the Road*** by John Donaldson
Bobby's 1964 transcontinental chess tour is the subject of this
book, which combines accounts of the time, reminiscences and
lots of games.

7. ***Bobby Fischer: Complete Games of the American
World Champion*** by Lou Hays
This is the largest and most complete of all the Fischer game col-
lections.

8. ***How to Beat Bobby Fischer*** by Edmar Mednis
Clear annotations make this book by the Queens grandmaster a
very instructive read. Mednis starts with Bobby's loss to Matulovic
in 1958 and goes through all of Fischer's subsequent defeats.
There are few examples from the 1970s — Bobby stopped losing!

9. ***Russians versus Fischer*** by D. Plisetsky and S. Voronkov
This English-language, but Russian-produced, book is one of the
most fascinating ever written on Fischer. Recently released docu-
ments from Russian sources reveal that Bobby's anti-Soviet feelings were well founded.

10. ***No Regrets*** by Yasser Seirawan and George Stefanovic
The definitive account of the Fischer–Spassky rematch. Seirawan's notes are first-rate.

A selection of other books on Bobby

Endgames

Best Endings of Capablanca and Fischer edited by Alexander Matanovic (*Chess Informant, 1978)*
Informant-style notes to some of Bobby's best endings.

Game Collections

White Fischer (Riga, 1991) by Bagirov and Kirilovs
In this game collection, instead of a chronological arrangment, the games appear by opening variation. This 208-page hardback gives all the games Fischer played with White and features interesting opening overviews by GM Bagirov. Mikhail Tal's introduction must be one of the last pieces he wrote. The companion book, *Black Fischer*, has yet to appear.

Gesammelten Partien von Robert J. Fischer (De Variant, Nederhorst den Berg, 1986) by Christian Bijl
Written by one of the former curators of the chess collection at the Royal Dutch Library in the Hague, this is one of the pioneering comprehensive game collections on Bobby. A paperback version was published in Nurnberg in 1989.

Bobby Fischer:The Greatest? by Dr. Max Euwe
Tries to answer the big question.

Bobby Fischer and his predecessors in the world chess championship by Dr. Max Euwe
This book compares Bobby to earlier titleholders in a positive light.

Bobby Fischer by Alex Fishbein
A fresh look at some of Bobby's best games with high quality notes.

Fischer's Chess Games with an introduction by Raymond Keene
Yet another Fischer complete game collection. Strange diagrams with awkward looking pieces make this hard to recommend — especially as it has nothing new to offer vis-a-vis Hays or in previous years Bijl and Wade/O'Connell.

Fischer by T. Krabbe, Alexander Muninghoff and Jan Timman
A Dutch language work where J.T. analyses 5 games in depth (Fischer–Bisguier, U.S. Championship 1957, Tal–Fischer, Curacao Can-

didates1962 (3...♝c5), Fischer–Matanovic, Vinkovci 1968, Gligoric–Fischer, Siegen Olympiad 1970, and Fischer–Petrosian, Buenos Aires 1971.

Schachphanomen Robert Fischer by H. Kramer and S. H. Postma
This was one of the first Fischer books to appear in Western Europe (Holland, 1966).

How Fischer Plays Chess (Collins 1975) by David Levy
This was later published by RHM in the United States, but without the photos. Fischer's game with Casado from Havana 1956 first surfaced here.

Robert Fischer by G. Pawinski and D. Sobiecki
These two booklets offer bare-bones, unannotated Fischer games and little more.

Secretele marilor maestri Fischer, Gheorghiu, Karpov by C. Stefaniu
An odd Rumanian-language work where native son Gheorghiu is compared with two world champions!

Bobi Fiser: ante portas by Trifunovic and D. Bjelica
A mid-1960s work in Serbo-Croatian on Bobby's career that offers very little original. There is next to nothing on Bobby's match with Matulovic.

The Complete Games of Bobby Fischer edited by Robert Wade and Kevin J. O'Connell
This is the original Fischer omnibook. No longer the most complete game collection, it contains several well-written pieces on Bobby and high quality photos which make it a worthy edition to any Fischer library.

Fiction

Auto de Fé by Nobel-prize-winning author and chess player Elias Canetti
The novel features an obsessive chessplayer called Fischerle (which he shortens to Fischer). According to the fascinating *The Complete Chess Addict*: "Like the great Bobby, Canetti's Fischer is a chess phenomenon: like Bobby, he lives, sleeps, breathes the game; like Bobby, he dreams of the day when chess will bring him enough money to buy hundreds of hand-made suits, and to live in

a chess palace modeled on the pieces (a Bobby fantasy); and he imagines making (like Bobby) huge financial demands for his services. The spooky thing is that *Auto da Fé* was published eight years before the real Bobby Fischer was born."

Master Prim by James Whitfield Ellison

Bobby served as the model for Julian Prim, the principal protagonist of this chess novel. Ellison seems to have used the notorious 1961 Fischer interview with Ralph Ginzburg as primary source material, though there is considerable doubt about some of its authenticity. Frank Brady deals with this controversy in *Profile of A Prodigy*. Brady asked Ginzburg, a fellow New Yorker, if he could listen to the interview tapes a few years after the interview, but was told they had been disposed of.

Ellison writes: "I am going to hire the most famous architect in the world to build my house. He will build it in the shape of a rook . . . It will be an ancient castle, . . . medieval. With a moat, spiral staircase, parapets, everything. I see it in my mind. Every detail is clear. I want to live the rest of my life in a house shaped exactly like a rook."

Ginzburg has Bobby saying seven years earlier: "I got strong ideas about my house. I'm going to hire the best architect and have him build it in the shape of a rook. Yeh, that's for me. Class. Spiral staircases, parapets, everything. I want to live the rest of my life in a house built exactly like a rook." Speaking of houses shaped like rooks, FIDE President Kirsan Iljumzhinov, the ruler of a part of southern Russia bordering the Caspian Sea called Kalmykia, offered to build Bobby his dream house gratis in the Kalmyk capital Elista. It doesn't appear that Bobby took him up on his offer.

General

Bobby Fischer Vs the Rest of the World by Brad Darrach

Darrach's book provides a frequently inaccurate and unsympathetic behind-the-scenes account of Bobby's 1972 World Championship match with Boris Spassky.

The Bobby Fischer I Knew & Other Stories
by Arnold Denker and Larry Parr

Denker, an excellent storyteller, paints a bright portrait of many of the luminaries of American chess in the 1930s and 40s. However, this isn't a book for die-hard Fischer fans expecting chapter after chapter on Bobby, for the section on Bobby is very short.

Denker does offer some interesting and original anecdotes about Bobby when he was just starting out as a young boy, and much later when Denker tried to serve as a go-between to get Bobby back into chess after the first match with Spassky. Grandmaster Denker mentions Fischer's high sense of loyalty and relates an incident from 1969 when he asked Bobby to play for the Manhattan Chess Club against the archrival Marshall Chess Club. Asked about what his fee might be for such an event, Bobby never hesitated. "I wouldn't charge you anything," he said, "because you're a friend."

The Riddle of Fischer (Moscow, 1992) by E. A. Mansurov
This 304-page, Russian-language paperback, whose title could also be translated enigma or mystery, is an exhaustive bibliography of articles and books on Bobby. The author draws heavily on Soviet chess periodicals. There isn't a lot of original material here, but Mansurov has done a fantastic job of locating material. All sources are carefully cited. Interesting, but poor quality, photographs of Bobby round out the book. The print run for this book was 25,000 copies.

Bobby Fischer's Outrageous Chess Moves
by Bruce Pandolfini
A selection of one- and two-move combinations to solve.

Match books

Fischer v. Spassky by C. H. O'D. Alexander
One of the best books on the match, the 144-page paperback features well-annotated games and interesting observations by one of England's top players from 1940s through 1960s.

Fischer v. Spassky: Move by Move by Larry Evans and Ken Smith
This paperback offers lots of diagrams to help the reader to play over the game without a board.

Bobby Fischer's Conquest of the World's Championship
by Reuben Fine
The former World Championship contender has produced a book that tells us more about the author than about Bobby. Fine's annotations often reveal an ignorance of theory, for Fine had not played in two decades. One example pointed by IM Anthony Saidy in his excellent review in *Chess Life and Review*, June 1974, is game

four, where a psychological reason is given for Spassky's avoiding 6...g6, after 1.e4 c5 2.♘f3 ♘c6 3.d4 cxd4 4.♘xd4 ♘f6 5.♘c3 ♘c6 6.♗c4. The refutation 7.♘xc6 bxc6 8.e5 is widely known.

Fine also has the curious idea that many of Fischer's errors occur on the "edge." Saidy points out that Fine's definition of the "edge" takes in the two files and two ranks closest to the four sides of the board, i.e., fully 75 percent of the squares!

One area where Fine does shine is as a prognosticator. The July 1972 issue of *Chess Life and Review* had an article by Bill Goichberg wherein various top U.S. players made their predictions for the Fischer–Spassky match. If we take out Fischer's default in game two, then GM Fine (along with former World Correspondence Champion Hans Berliner and NM John Meyer) was right on the money at 12.5-7.5. NMs Herbert Seidman, Joseph Platz and John N. Jacobs gave Bobby the nod 12.5-8.5. *Conquest* is a very odd book by a player who probably wished later in his life that he had taken a shot at the title in 1948.

Fischer Vs. Spassky; World Chess Championship Match
by Svetozar Gligoric

This book is quite good for a commercial product aimed at the average player. It sold hundreds of thousands of copies.

Fischer v Spassky, the World Chess Championship, 1972
by Harry Golombek

An above-average recounting of the 1972 match, which must have set a record, bar none, for the most books written about.

Fischer–Spassky From The Soviet Point Of View
translated by Andrew Karklins

This account of the match doesn't have fancy production values, but it offers some of the best notes on the match.

Fischer–Spassky II : The Return of a Legend
by Raymond Keene

This potboiler offers the reader even less than magazines that came out immediately after the match.

How Fischer won: world chess championship, 1972
by C. J. S. Purdy

Purdy, well known for his instructive style, gives a good account of the match.

In-depth analysis of the Fischer/Spassky chess match
by Samuel Reshevsky
Sammy's account is aimed at the man in the streets with bare-bones notes.

Fields of Force; Fischer and Spassky at Reykjavik
by George Steiner
One of the more scholarly and philosophical books on chess.

tweekamp Spasski–Fischer 1972
by Jan Timman and Max Euwe
This Dutch-language match book contains excellent notes by Timman and a short introduction by Euwe.

Odds and Ends

Championship Chessmate: Fischer–Spassky
by Hoi Polloi, Inc. (New York City, 1972).
A move-by-move sliding device that enables the student to play solitaire chess. The games of the 1972 match are offered in descriptive notation without notes.

The Ballad of Bobby Fischer (record)
sung by Joe Glazer and the Fianchettoed Bishops
This 1972, seven-minute song (Collector Records, Silver Springs, MD) was set to the theme from the television show *The Beverly Hillbillies*. Sung in a twangy, country-music style, it relates Bobby's career from the beginning ("he opened his mouth on the day he was born . . . and said move that pawn") through his school days ("Sittin' in the classroom he could barely think, 'cause chess was his food, chess was his drink") on through the Interzonal and the Candidates Matches ("Despite his attempts to innovate, Larsen was bent right out of shape").

Bobby's Books for Sale

The Brooklyn Public Library consigned Bobby's books and papers, which it had acquired in 1967, to Swann galleriess in 1987. Fischer, who had been indigent in 1967, had sold his books and papers to a bookshop, which had then sold them to the library. According to a *Sports Illustrated* article in the November 30, 1987, issue:

The first lot offered was a 1956 lab notebook containing notes, homework assignments and drawings by Fischer for his ninth-grade science class. Fischer, then 13, had already gained national prominence as a chess prodigy, but he didn't have much luck in science. He got a 65 on one true-false test, and his teacher had commented, "Not satisfactory," on it, to which Fischer had written, "Tough." The composition book also contained a page of grotesque heads drawn by Fischer, and this passage unrelated to either science or chess: "I just can't take it anymore. Baby listen to what I'm puttin' down. Hey everybody, gather round, cmon (sic) and let's dig these Rockin' Sounds, we got the rugs on the floor . . . Come on now I wanna swim with you."

The notebook sold for $660. It was a bargain, not only for the insights it offered into Fischer's adolescent mind, but also in comparison to what the other lots brought. The next offering, a typescript of Fischer's 1968 book *My 60 Memorable Games* with numerous handwritten revisions, was expected to bring $400, and it fetched $6060. A lot of 200 various books, estimated at $76, went for $1100.

All told, the 10 lots, estimated at $3335, realized $13,035.

Appendix

The April 1962 issue of Skakbladet *has about two pages on Bobby's visit to Copenhagen. The following material is based on this article and NM Allan Jensen's recollections.*

by Allan Jensen

On the way home from Bled in 1961, Fischer paid a very short visit to Copenhagen and promised to stay a few days in Copenhagen after the Stockholm Interzonal the following spring. He was a guest of the Copenhagen Chess Federation from March 9-11, 1962. Originally, he was promised $500 for an exhibition with GM Bent Larsen and a simul, but after his great victory in Stockholm, his honoraria increased considerably (no amount mentioned!). He arrived tired in Copenhagen the afternoon of Friday, March 9, and went directly for a visit to the US ambassador. In the evening, he played a game with Larsen and won. This game, which featured the Dane essaying his favorite Bird's Opening is published in all standard Fischer game anthologies. On Saturday, Bent and Bobby worked on a radio/TV program based on the game. Sunday was the day of the simultaneous exhibition.

Fischer played against 41 strong players, and it was said that no one else had ever played against so strong a group. He won 27, lost seven and drew seven. Erik Poulsen, who sat di-rectly to my left, won. Two of the other players who won, Finn Petersen and Peter H. Nørby, later became strong national masters and olympiad players! Jørgen Hvenekilde, who drew, later became champion of Copenhagen. The event took six hours with 200 spectators watching. After two hours, there was a tea break. Bobby was furious and told the organisers that the opposition was too strong. Further, some received help from the people watching. Fischer thought he would lose 12-15 games, which he was definitely not used to. It didn't turn out quite so badly, because, as Fischer later said, the Danish players were not so good in the endgame

---

[86] *Ruy Lopez Steinitz Deferred* C75
RJF-NM Allan Jensen
Copenhagen (simul) March 11, 1962

1.e4 e5 2.♘f3 ♘c6 3.♗b5 a6 4.♗a4 d6 5.c3

Fischer played this line (C75-76) five times (+4-1) in his career against the solid Steinitz Deferred.

5...♗d7 6.d4 ♘ge7 7.♗b3 h6 8. ♘bd2

Fischer varied with 8.♕e2 later in the year at the Varna Olympiad to win a miniature: 8...♘g6 9.♕c4 ♕f6 10. d5 b5 11.♕e2 ♘a5 12.♗d1 ♗e7 13. g3 O-O 14.h4 ♖fc8?? 15.♗g5 and 1-0 shortly (Fischer–Ciocaltea). **8...♘g6 9.♘c4 ♗e7 10.♘e3 O-O**

Black often plays 10...♗g5 to get rid of his bad Bishop.

11.O-O ♖e8 12.♘d5 ♗f8 13.dxe5 ♘cxe5

This position is not very well known to theory. The three examples we were able to track down saw Black answer 13.dxe5 with ...dxe5. Trupan–Steinsapir, USSR 1949, went 13...dxe5 14.a4 ♘ce7? 15.♗xh6 ♘xd5 16.♕xd5 ♗e6 17.♕xd8 ♖axd8 18.♗xe6 gxh6 19.♗c4 and White emerged with an extra pawn.

14.♘xe5 ♘xe5

On 14...dxe5 15.♗e3 gives White a pull.

15.f4

This might be a bit premature. 15.♖e1, maintaining the small central advantage, looks a little better for White.

15...♘g4

Black's plan is to trade off Knights, as he has less space.

16.♕f3

On 16.h3 ♘f6 Black is ready to swap Knights.

16...c6 17.♘e3 ♘xe3 18.♗xe3 ♕e7 19.♗c2?!

This leads to some trouble for White. Instead 19.♕h5, or the sharp 19.e5 dxe5 20.fxe5 ♗e6 21.♗xe6 ♕xe6 22.♗b6 keeps the position unclear.

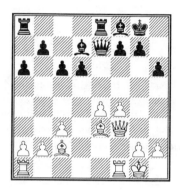

19...♗f5

This isn't a bad move, but much better was 19...f5!, when 20.e5 dxe5 21.fxe5 ♕xe5 22.♗b3+ ♗e6 23.♗xe6+ ♖xe6 24.♗d4 ♗c5 leaves Black on top with a clear pawn ahead.

20.exf5 ♕xe3+ 21.♕xe3 ♖xe3 22.♗d1?!

A better way to hold the position was 22.♖fe1 ♖ae8 23.♖xe3 ♖xe3 24.♔f2 ♖e8 25.♖e1 with the draw in sight.

22...d5 23.♗f3 ♗c5 24.♔h1 ♖ae8 25.♖ad1 a5 26.g3 ♔f8 27.♔g2 ♗b6

Black is slightly better (27...a4), but converting his advantage against Fischer would have been a difficult task.

Draw

From the simul in Columbus, Ohio

The following game is a late addition to the "1964 Tour" chapter. Many thanks to GM Alex Yermolinsky who shared his insights into this game.

[87] *Alekhine B03*
RJF–Arturs Zageris
Columbus (simul) May 18, 1964

1.e4 ♘f6 2.e5 ♘d5 3.d4 d6 4.c4 ♘b6 5.exd6 cxd6

Fischer–Lense, from the same exhibition, saw 5...exd6 6.♘c3 ♘c6 7.♘f3 ♗e7 8.♗d3 ♗g4 with a draw in 32 moves.

6.♘c3 g6 7.♗d3

This sideline was Fischer's favorite against the Alekhine. The main strategical idea is to place the King Knight on e2 to take the sting out of ...♗g4.

7...♘c6 8.♘ge2 ♗g7 9.♗e3 O-O 10. O-O e5 11.d5 ♘b4 12.b3 ♘xd3 13. ♕xd3

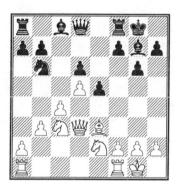

13...f5?

This natural-looking move is, in fact, a serious positional error. Black kills his light-squared Bishop, as Bobby will never allow ...f5-f4-f3! Anything else would be better, including the recommendation 12...♖e8!, unclear, as given in *Nunn's Chess Openings*.

14.f4!

Of course! Bobby fixes the black f-pawn in its tracks.

14...e4?

Now Black's position loses all its vitality. White has a free hand to put his Knight on e3 and play for breaks with c4-c5 or g2-g4. It was absolutely essential for Black to leave his pawn on e5.

15.♕d2 ♘d7 16.♗d4 b6 17.♗xg7 ♔xg7 18.b4

This denies Black c5 for his Knight and prepares an eventual c4-c5. Note that it is not easy to attack the c-pawn, as 18...♗a6 runs into 19.♘d4!

18...a6 19.♖ac1 ♖e8 20.♘d4 ♘f6 21. ♘d1 ♗d7 22.♘e3 ♖ac8 23.a4!?

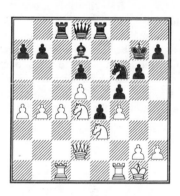

An interesting decision. Bobby realizes that his position is strategically winning, but he wants to win quick! By putting his pawn *en prise*, Fischer hopes to sucker Black into capturing on a4. The immediate 23...♗xa4 is refuted by 24.♘e6+; so Black goes into contortions to prepare ...♗xa4. We should mention that Bobby saw much deeper and knew that ...♗xa4 would always be a bad move.

23...♕c7 24.♕b2 ♖a8 25.♖c3 ♔f7 26.♖fc1 ♗xa4?

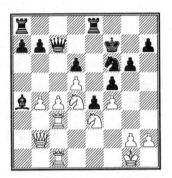

This is a truly horrible move that quickenly ends all resistance. The Bishop may not be lost, but the text loses control of the e6-square and requires the Black pieces to use a lot of energy to keep a4-Bishop alive. Black had to play 26...a5!, trying to clarify the situation on the queenside. Bobby would have probably answered with 27.b5, intending to break through later with g2-g4. In addition, the Knight gets a huge outpost on c6.

27.♘e6 ♕b7 28.b5 ♖ec8 29.h3!

Fischer shows admirable restraint. Instead of trying to hunt down the Bishop he simply creates *Luft*, prepares a future g2-g4, and waits for Black to commit suicide by opening the c-file.

29...axb5

It's hard to suggest better, but the text loses instantly.

30.cxb5 ♖xc3 31.♖xc3 ♘xd5

Equivalent to resignation, but 31...♖c8 32.♖a3 wasn't pretty.

32.♘xd5 ♕xd5 33.♘g5+ ♔g8 34. ♖c7 1-0

Source: original scoresheet.

Player Index for Fischer Games

Numbers refer to games: **bold** indicates that player had White, ( ) indicates imbedded game,
* indicates that player was Fischer's partner.

Player Index for non-Fischer Games

ECO Index

Alexander Alekhine Series

Alekhine In the Americas

Alekhine In Europe & Asia

To honor the 100th anniversary of Alekhine's birthday lesser-known Alekhine efforts are brought here into the public eye.

The purpose of the book is to investigate Alekhine's quite fascinating non-tournaments efforts which took him all over the globe and made him the original frequent traveler.

His efforts include the Franco-Russian Chess Champ's four barnstorming tours of the U.S. and Canada as well as visits to South America.

Over 140 games, 88 diagrams.

Paperback $ 8.95

This super-sequel to *Alekhine in the Americas* features 619 non-tournament chess games.

They come from a variety of formats including simultaneous displays, exhibitions, clock simuls, blindfold play, exhibition games, blitz events, correspondence games, and consultation parties.

A careful review of his games shows that Alekhine used exhibitions as a special training tool to develop his powers.

Over 100 annotated games, many rare photos, history, charts, and statistics, painstakingly compiled.

Paperback $ 15.95

Please add 15% for Shipping and Handling costs
Authors: IM John Donaldson, IM Nikolay Minev, GM Yasser Seirawan.

International Chess Enterprises
P.O. Box 19457
Seattle WA, 98109

Phone: 206-286 9764
Fax: 206-283 4363
Email: orders@insidechess.com

http://www.insidechess.com

Akiba Rubinstein Series

Uncrowned King

Occupying a unique position in chess history, Akiba Rubinstein was one of the strongest players never to win the Chess World Championship.

This exhaustively researched book offers 474 games from the years 1882-1920, many of them deeply annotated with notes translated from the top players of the pre-WWI era. With crosstables, archival photos, indexes, and a thorough bibliography. Algebraic notation, 321+ pages.

"Together with the second volume (...) Uncrowned King is bound to become an indispensable source of information on Rubinstein and his contemporaries" - New In Chess Magazine

"The painstaking detail of the collateral material in this book sets a new standard." - Chess Horizons

"The most complete work on Rubinstein's life and games (...)." - The Washington Post

The Later Years

Chronicles the second half of this great Polish Grandmaster's life. This volume contains 513 chess games and game fragments from the later years of this tragic figure.

Starting in 1921 where the previous volume, Uncrowned King, leaves off *"The Later Years"* contains many hidden treasures that have not seen the light of day for more than 50 years. Algebraic notation, 306+ pages.

"An outstanding work." - Chess Monthly

"It is a must for those who enjoyed the first volume 'Akiba Rubinstein: Uncrowned King'." - The Washington Post

"A superb work of research, an excellent production, well worth every penny and the companion volume to the similarly voluminous Akiba Rubinstein: Uncrowned King." - The British Chess Magazine

By IMs John Donaldson & Nikolay Minev

Paperback Only $ 27.95	**Paperback $ 27.95 or Hardback $ 34.95**

Please add 15% for Shipping and Handling costs

International Chess Enterprises
P.O. Box 19457
Seattle WA, 98109

Phone: 206-286 9764
Fax: 206-283 4363
Email: orders@insidechess.com

http://www.insidechess.com

Five Crowns

Five is the number of world chess championship matches that Garry Kasparov and Anatoly Karpov contested from 1984 to 1990.

Yasser Seirawan deeply analyses all 24 games of the 1990 New York/Lyon World Championship Match. Yasser answers all the big questions: who was brilliant, who was belligerent, who blew it, and why.

Jonathan Tisdall reports all the news from ringside. Also includes every game (unannotated) played between Kasparov and Karpov, as of June 1991, by opening.

Yasser Seirawan, one of the top US grandmasters was a match commentator in New York and Lyon.

Jonathan Tisdall is a chess correspondent for Reuters.

"I highly recommend Five Crowns to all chess players." - Georgia Chess

"Five Crowns" is particularly notable; it was by far the best book on that match." - Chess Perspectives

Paperback, AN, 256 pages, $19.95+$3 S/H.

GM Yasser Seirawan & IM Jonathan Tisdall

International Chess Enterprises — P.O. Box 19457 – Seattle, WA 98109
Tel: 206-2869764 — Fax: 206-2834363 — Email: orders@insidechess.com
Inside Chess Online: http://www.insidechess.com

No Regrets

"Fischer - Spassky 1992."

All 30 games of the historic World Chess Championship rematch between Bobby Fischer and Boris Spassky are deeply and insightfully annotated by GM Yasser Seirawan.

Includes the players' own post-game commentary on every round, all nine press conferences, interviews with leading Grandmasters, and a *"Bobby Revealed"* section based on Seirawan's personal meetings with Fischer.

The definitive book on the match, the only one by a GM who was there, it ranks with Seirawan's *Five Crowns* as one of the best match books ever.

"No Regrets and Five Crowns take their place as two of the finest match books ever written."
- Chess Perspectives

"An absolutely incredible book."
- The Chess Gazette

Paperback, AN, 320 pages, $24.95+$3 S/H.
Hardback, AN, 320 pages, $34.95+$4.50 S/H.

GM Yasser Seirawan & George Stefanovich

International Chess Enterprises — P.O. Box 19457 – Seattle, WA 98109
Tel: 206-2869764 — Fax: 206-2834363 — Email: orders@insidechess.com
Inside Chess Online: http://www.insidechess.com

Bobby Fischer barnstormed the U.S. and Canada from coast to coast. Fischer's entertaining lectures, high level of play and personable manner won many new admirers.

Legend on the Road: Bobby Fischer's 1964 Simul Tour gives a comprehensive look at the tour with lots of newspaper reports, magazine articles, personal reminiscences and lots of games, many of which have never been published before.

128 pages, 151 games, many annotated for the first time in print. A chess treasure trove for every Fischer fan.

"A fascinating book." - Chess Monthly.

"It is a diligently researched bit of American chess history and one of those rare chess books you can just relax with and enjoy." - Michigan Chess.

Legend on the Road

International Chess Enterprises
P.O. Box 19457
Seattle WA, 98109

Phone: 206-286 9764
Fax: 206-283 4363
Email: orders@insidechess.com

http://www.insidechess.com

"An excellent tribute to America's greatest player." - British Chess Magazine.

Paperback $16.95 or Hardback $26.95.
An ICE publication.